K·I·S·S

DK

The Only Guides You'll Ever Need!

THIS SERIES IS YOUR TRUSTED GUIDE through all of life's stages and situations. Want to learn how to surf the Internet or care for your new dog? Or maybe you'd like to become a wine connoisseur or an expert gardener? The solution is simple: Just pick up a K.I.S.S. Guide and turn to the first page.

Expert authors will walk you through the subject from start to finish, using simple blocks of knowledge to build your skills one step at a time. Build upon these learning blocks and by the end of the book, you'll be an expert yourself! Or, if you are familiar with the topic but want to learn more, it's easy to dive in and pick up where you left off.

The K.I.S.S. Guides deliver what they promise: Simple access to all the information you'll need on one subject. Other titles you might want to check out include: Gardening, the Internet, Pregnancy, Astrology, Weight Loss, and many more to come.

K·I·S·S

GUIDE TO

Online
Investing

THERESA W. CAREY

Foreword by EDWARD A. FINN, JR.
(Editor-in-Chief, *Barron's* Magazine)

A Dorling Kindersley Book

LONDON, NEW YORK, SYDNEY, DELHI, PARIS,
MUNICH, AND JOHANNESBURG

DK Publishing, Inc.

Senior Editor Jennifer Williams
Editor Ruth Strother
Category Publisher LaVonne Carlson

Dorling Kindersley Limited

Project Editor Julian Gray
Project Art Editor Justin Clow

Managing Editor Maxine Lewis
Managing Art Editor Heather McCarry

Jacket Designer Neal Cobourne
Production Heather Hughes
Category Publisher Mary Thompson

Produced for Dorling Kindersley by **Cooling Brown**
9–11 High Street, Hampton, Middlesex TW12 2SA

Creative Director Arthur Brown
Art Editor Pauline Clarke
Senior Editor Amanda Lebentz
Editor Fiona Wild

Copyright © 2001
DK Publishing, Inc.
Text copyright © 2001 Theresa W. Carey

2 4 6 8 10 9 7 5 3 1

Published in the United States by
DK Publishing, Inc., 95 Madison Avenue, New York, New York 10016

Carey, Theresa.
    KISS guide to online investing / by Theresa W. Carey.-- – 1st American ed.
        p. cm. -- – (Keep it simple series)
    "A Dorling Kindersley Book."
    Includes index.
        ISBN 0-7894-8013-1
        1. Electronic trading of securities.   I. Title. II. Series.
    HG4515.95 .C36 2001
    332.6'0285'4678--dc21

                                                                    2001001485

DK Publishing, Inc. offers special discounts for bulk purchases for sales promotions or premiums.
Specific, large-quantity needs can be met with special editions, including personalized covers,
excerpts of existing guides, and corporate imprints. For more information, contact Special Markets Department,
DK Publishing, Inc., 95 Madison Avenue, New York, NY 10016 Fax: 800-600-9098.

Color reproduction by ColourScan, Singapore
Printed and bound by Printer Industria Grafica, S.A., Barcelona, Spain

For our complete catalog visit

www.dk.com

Contents at a Glance

CONTENTS

PART ONE The Big Picture

CHAPTER 1 The Online Revolution for Investors   20

CHAPTER 2 Reasons to Invest Online   32

CHAPTER 3 Necessary Equipment   42

APPENDICES

Foreword

WHETHER YOU ARE INVESTING for your retirement or for your children's education, I encourage you to read this book. Online investing should be an important part of almost every family's financial future, for trading stocks, buying mutual funds, or gathering information to make informed choices. There is no one better to guide you on that journey than Theresa Carey.

When Theresa started rating online-brokerage services for Barron's in 1996, the industry was still in its infancy. Back then, a mere 1 per cent of all stock trades by individual investors were done on the Internet. As Theresa has reported, in the ensuing years online trades have come to make as much as 50 per cent of all retail trades, and some finance executives predict that percentage could eventually rise to 70 per cent or more. Clearly, online trading has revolutionized the way Americans invest, and Theresa has been at the forefront of covering that revolution.

When the history of the 20th century is written, the 1980s and 1990s will be remembered as a time when the average American took control of his or her finances. The reason is clear: More companies began handing out a fixed amount of money to employees each week and requiring them to invest it for retirement. This stood in marked contrast to the system that prevailed in earlier decades, when companies themselves took the responsibility of guaranteeing workers a weekly pension payment from retirement until death. Under the new arrangement, retirement money in the '80s flowed first and most heavily into mutual funds. As we entered the '90s, more Americans took the lessons they had learned from mutual-fund investing and began striking out on their own, putting money directly into stocks.

This trend was sharply accelerated in the late '90s by the rise of online trading. But as with most popular trends, online investing featured some excesses. Most notable in the American mind were the murders of several online investors in Atlanta by a desperate individual who had lost all his money while Internet trading. Many other neophytes who mistook online trading for a get-rich-quick scheme lost their nest eggs in the process. Yet, these lost fortunes will not mark the end of online trading – quite the opposite. In the case of online investing, the long-running pattern is likely to be continued growth, even if that growth is at a slower pace than the one that prevailed in the late 1990s, when the bull market was running strong.

Online investing is a tool – a tool that can help investors trade more quickly and at lower costs than they would be able to trade using full-service brokers. Equally important, the Internet offers investors a wide range of research reports, analysis, and data that can give them many of the advantages once enjoyed only by Wall Street professionals. To learn how you can best navigate the fascinating and fast-changing world of online trading, I strongly advise you to read this book.

EDWARD A. FINN, JR
Editor-in-Chief, Barron's Magazine

Introduction

FIRST THINGS FIRST: Thank you for investing in this book. By making the K.I.S.S. Guide to Online Investing part of your investing life, you've taken a huge stride down the road toward becoming a knowledgeable investor.

Investing successfully takes an intense combination of education and information. Benjamin Disraeli, a 19th-century British politician, novelist, and investor, once said, "As a general rule, the most successful man in life is the man who has the best information." Thanks to the Internet, even novice and intermediate-level investors can get their hands on more information than was easily available to professionals just 10 years ago.

What this means to the newly minted investor is confusion! There's so much out there – so many online brokers clamoring for your business, and so many web sites reaching out for your attention. Combine that with the feeling that investing involves more luck and voodoo than skill, and a potential investor can be overwhelmed by the complexity of it all.

I've been covering online financial resources for 10 years now, and I have seen the industry develop to the point where an investor can do it all on the Internet – research, trading, money management, even shopping with the resulting investment gains. But at the same time all this growth and development has taken place, I've also seen the online investing world touted as both a magical place and an extremely dangerous place.

The main problem with online trading is that it's so easy and there's nobody offering reality checks. You can be seduced into guessing rather than making knowledgeable choices, and as the old Chinese proverb says, "To guess is cheap. To guess wrong is expensive." I'm concerned about the message many online brokers have set out in their advertisements, saying you can get rich quick if you just invest online. There's so much more to it – take a long look before you leap!

My goal in creating this guide to online investing is twofold: First, to coach you to a better awareness of your own financial situation and your plan for the future; and second, to introduce you to the incredible wealth of resources that will serve as your electronic assistants. Throughout my tenure as a columnist for Barron's, I've become an advocate for my readers, looking out for them and telling them which sites to visit and which to avoid. Due to space constraints, I can't go into as much depth in the magazine as I'd like, so in this book I bring you the issues I think are important for the novice online investor.

I started covering the online world about the time my personal financial situation evolved from, "Will we make the mortgage payment this month?" to "What are we going to do about college tuition and retirement?" In my decade of writing about – and using – online investing tools, I've found resources that are so valuable to me that I want to share them with you. What I'm hoping to inspire in you, dear reader, is enough savvy to go exploring on your own. This book will show you what it takes to get started, and it will also give you ideas about other resources you can find on your own once you're comfortable.

Again, thanks for inviting me along on your journey. Let's get started.

THERESA W. CAREY

Dedication

This book is for my daughters, Colleen and Kate. I can't imagine life without you. I also have to thank my dog, Hershey, for lying on my feet and keeping me company. And, of course, thanks to my husband, Kent, for his ongoing support and encouragement.

What's Inside?

THE INFORMATION IN *the* K.I.S.S. Guide to Online Investing *is set up so you can start with the big picture and then focus on your particular areas of interest as you learn more.*

PART ONE

In this section, I'll tell you who's investing online, and give you some reasons why you should – or shouldn't – join in the action. I'll also go over the necessary hardware and software you'll need.

PART TWO

I'll show you what it takes to set up your online investing "shop" in this section, starting with your investment account and your analytical tools. Then I'll coach you through setting up your own personalized news agency and ways of monitoring your portfolio.

PART THREE

This section is devoted to choosing the appropriate online broker for your investment style, and examining how much it will cost. I'll also tell you about the downside of online investing and show you how to avoid scams and frauds.

PART FOUR

Now that you've established yourself online and have chosen a broker, I'll bring you additional online resources to add to your investment toolkit. Community investing, technical analysis, and online banking are the focus of this section.

PART FIVE

In Part Five, I'll describe the fast-moving world of day trading, including techniques and strategies, and the specialized tools of the trade.

The Extras

THROUGHOUT THIS BOOK, *you'll find special tidbits and tricks, highlighted with little pictures, to help you along.*

Very Important Point
This symbol indicates some information that you simply must read. You really need to know this information before continuing to read on.

Complete No-No
I use this symbol to specify actions that you should avoid. Just say no!

Getting Technical
The little professor indicates extremely technical information that you should read carefully if you want to understand the subject in greater depth.

Inside Scoop
These are special hints and tips about online investing that I've picked up over my years of covering the industry.

Throughout the book, you'll also find little boxes of information – some are fact-filled, some are just for fun.

Trivia...
These boxes are filled with historical tidbits or amusing personal experiences of mine that are intended to educate and amuse.

DEFINITION
Investing has its own special vocabulary. In these boxes, I'll explain some terms I think you should **understand.** *You'll find a glossary at the back of the book as well.*

INTERNET
www.internet.com
These boxes send you online to discover specific investing resources. All of these web sites are summarized in the appendix.

PART ONE

THE BIG PICTURE

Y OU NEED A MAP of what's out there before you can plan your online investing journey. You also need to know what you'll be taking with you when you start on your investing trek. I'll give you an overview of the *resources* available for online investors, and discuss the reasons why you should – or, perhaps, should not – join the community yourself.

Getting online involves setting up a computer system, so I'll describe the type of *equipment* you'll need, as well as additional software that will help smooth your path. I'll also guide you through understanding your starting point, or your *current financial condition*, so you can choose the right course.

Chapter 1

The Online Revolution for Investors

IF YOU'RE NOT TRADING ONLINE YET, you probably feel like you've got a target painted on your forehead considering the barrage of television and print ads hollering "Trade Now!" at you. Online trading, thanks to extensive advertising, media attention, low brokerage fees, and improvements in Internet-based offerings, has hit the mainstream with a vengeance. Much of the online volume is generated by a small percentage of frequent traders, but now we're seeing a second wave of less experienced online customers who seek more information about investment decisions. This book is dedicated to helping people such as yourself, newcomers to the online investing scene, find your way through the hype and promises

In this chapter...

✓ **The growing market**

✓ **A panoramic snapshot**

✓ **Basic ways to find what you need**

THERE'S NOW A WEALTH OF ONLINE RESOURCES FOR LESS EXPERIENCED INVESTORS

The growing market

DURING THE YEAR 2000, *online investing* hit a major milestone: Over half of all US retail trades were placed online, surpassing most analysts' wildest expectations. At the end of 1999, industry watchers had estimated that nearly one in two retail trades had been placed online, a huge jump from 1998's mark of almost one in three. Not only was there a tremendous leap in the number of trades placed online, but the brokers themselves upgraded their sites considerably, making them easier to use and adding resources for investors to help them make profitable trades.

DEFINITION

Online investing should be easy to define, but it has a couple of guises. One, of course, is trades that are placed by an investor using a computer. Many brokers count trades placed using a Touch-Tone phone as online trading as well.

Phenomenal growth in online trading

Back in 1996, only 8 percent of US *retail trades* were placed online, and there were only 12 online brokers from whom to choose. At the end of 1999, 48 percent of trades took place online, and the number of online brokerages was over 100. The exact number is difficult to pin down on a daily basis, with new players entering the market as older ones get snapped up by their competition or just disappear. There are almost 19 million online brokerage accounts open as of the end of 2000.

DEFINITION

Retail trades are those conducted by individuals. The other main type of trade is called institutional trades and is conducted by large portfolio managers such as mutual fund and pension fund managers.

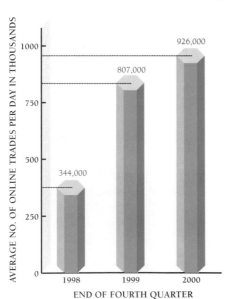

The number of online trades nearly tripled between fall 1998 and fall 2000. Quarter by quarter, those of us who watch the numbers saw significant growth in online trading until mid-2000. The downturn in the market created a slowdown in online trading also, but the percentage of trades conducted online did not drop.

■ **The number of online trades** *soared from over 300,000 in fall 1998 to over 900,000 in fall 2000 in the United States alone. This level of growth, coming on the heels of a slowdown, took many analysts by surprise.*

Online trading is at least as popular outside the United States as it is in the United States. According to financial analysts in Korea, for example, approximately two-thirds of retail trades have been placed online since the introduction of Internet-based trading in 1998. By comparison, US investors are slow to adapt!

Who's trading online?

So who are the brave souls who are trading online? Five years ago, they were mostly the early adopters, who rush to try any new technology, and computer nerds (including your fearless author), but now the profile of the average online investor looks a lot like that of the average American. As the price of personal computers plummets, more households are able to get connected to the online world. The lure of controlling one's finances from the privacy of the home computer is a strong one. Investors continue to move their assets and make transactions online in a rush to avoid being left out of the bull market.

Watching their customers transfer assets to online brokers prompted two of the big names in full-service brokerage, Merrill Lynch and Morgan Stanley Dean Witter, to attempt to stay a step ahead of the money flow by offering Internet-based trading. Other large brokers, famed for their full-service reputations, are following in Merrill's and Morgan's footsteps. As of mid-2000, approximately $1 trillion in assets were held in online brokerage accounts, evidence that many online brokers are trying to diversify their revenue mix and move away from their heavy dependence on trading volumes.

■ **As more households** *connect to the Internet, today's online investor is typically an average member of the public.*

> ## Trivia...
> *Several large brokers, including Charles Schwab and Fidelity Investments, took the step of granting all their customers online access to their accounts. Quite a few people found out they were online investors when they opened a letter from their broker informing them of the web address for their portfolio and their account password!*

I interviewed an executive at a high-tech firm in the Silicon Valley for my *Barron's* column a couple of years ago who told me that his employer had cut off access to financial web sites from the office. Now there's a sign that online investing has grown: Managing one's portfolio has become a major cause of wasted time at the office. While employees used to use fake screens to hide the computer games from the boss, now they're hiding their stock trading habits.

A panoramic snapshot

JUST TO WHET YOUR APPETITE, here's a quick overview of the resources on the Internet that you can use to manage your financial future. I'll go into greater detail in the upcoming chapters.

Places to trade securities online

Online brokers can range from those that charge high commissions and provide you with a lot of research resources and hand holding on down to those with extremely low commissions and not much in the way of customer amenities. This book will help you decide what level of service you want, and give you an idea of how much you'll pay for it.

There are brokers that focus on a particular type of investment, such as options or bonds. You'll learn whether you're better off with several different accounts at "specialty" brokers, or one account at a "one-stop shopping" broker.

■ **The Internet** *offers a vast range of tools and services for investors – from online brokers to investment research sites to online banking – that can be used to help you plan your financial future.*

To get yourself an online brokerage account, you'll need to go through the fun-filled process of filling out piles of paperwork, then sending the broker some cash or other assets to get started with online trading. I'll show you, step-by-step, what you'll have to do.

Places to do your homework

Research sites are plentiful on the Internet, and the information you can uncover about a potential investment is vast. In spite of their ubiquity, investment research sites vary widely in utility. For instance, if you're primarily interested in buying mutual funds, you won't find a site that focuses on stock options terribly interesting. I'll take you on a tour of investment sites for every investing appetite.

Places to keep track of your portfolio

Keeping tabs on your portfolio value is easy if you have everything in one place. But most of us end up with a couple of different accounts, and with some assets held online while others are offline. How can you stay up to date on what you own, what it's worth, and how well it's performing?

If you use a personal finance program such as Intuit's Quicken or Microsoft Money, you can hit a button and check out your current net worth – assuming you've stayed on top of all the necessary data entry. Both of these programs have become more and more Web connected with every update, but the unfortunate truth is that they can't read your mind and automatically make the entries necessary to update your portfolios, especially if you're a frequent trader. But it's worth the effort for you to stay on top of the entries!

Every April, Uncle Sam wants to know how you've done. Most portfolio analysis programs and web sites help you figure out how much you'll owe in taxes based on your gains and their timing. Plan to set up a way to track your trading gains and losses from the outset.

Places to keep your cash

Online banking is a convenient way to move money from one account to another. But online banking goes well beyond merely keeping track of your checks and deposits. Now you can search to find the best credit card for your situation, the highest interest rate being paid for certificates of deposit (CDs), or the lowest interest rate asked for a home loan. I'll show you how to find a bank, open an account, and set it up to make transfers to your online investing account. We'll also take a look at banks that are offering online investing themselves.

Basic ways to find what you need

AT LAST COUNT, THERE WERE APPROXIMATELY eleventy-bazillion and eight sites on the Internet aimed at investors, give or take a couple hundred thousand. While you're reading this paragraph, another 435 or so will launch! OK, so those numbers aren't precisely accurate, but it can certainly seem that way to the newcomer to the online world. Let's take a look at a few ways to find financial sites using the popular search engines, online catalogs, and communities of investors.

Finding that site

Search engines. Portals. Directories. Argh! What are these creatures and how will they help you find your way around the online world?

Back in the early days of the World Wide Web, you had to know the exact combination of keys to type in to get to a particular online destination. Then a few enterprising entrepreneurs cooked up the idea of creating a directory of web pages much like a phone book, while a few others wrote up a search program so users could find web sites that contained specific words or phrases. These two ideas blossomed into Yahoo! and Alta Vista, respectively, both of which are still excellent places to go when you're trying to find a Web site. They have a lot of company now too. Though the word most often used in these search engines is sex, money-related searches are also popular.

Use quotation marks if you're looking for a particular phrase, otherwise you'll get a long list of sites that contain any one of the words you typed. When searching for "International Business Machines" I get over 60,000 possible pages to look at, as opposed to the 6 million I get if I don't use quotation marks.

Some sites – Alta Vista, Lycos, MSN, Snap, and Yahoo! – also qualify as portals. A portal crams a lot of tools on one page: A search engine, a link to an email account, and quite a few other items. I have a portal site as my home page when I first start up my browser. Portals also have links to current news, stock tickers, weather, and other interesting items, making them incredibly useful when you log on to the Web with that first cup of coffee in the morning. They also allow you to enter a list of stock ticker symbols so you can see what's going on with the companies you're tracking.

SEARCHING THE WORLD WIDE WEB

I use all of these top ten search engines when I'm on a research mission. Each organizes the search results in different ways, and you'll find your favorite after exploring for a while. You may, as you explore, settle on a search engine that's not on this list, but here are some great places to start:

Search engine	Web address	Key feature
Alta Vista	www.altavista.com	Results organized by type: Web page, video, audio, etc.
Ask Jeeves	www.askjeeves.com	Ask a question, get well-organized answers.
Dogpile	www.dogpile.com	Searches web sites and newsgroups, plus a joke of the day.
Google	www.google.com	Easy, fast, simple interface.
Lycos	www.lycos.com	Results are listed by popularity.
Metacrawler	www.metacrawler.com	Sends your search to 12 engines at once.
NBCi.com	www.nbci.com	Editors and users rate sites for usefulness.
Northern Light	www.northernlight.com	Organizes results into folders.
Search.com	www.search.com	Start your search in a particular category.
Yahoo!	www.yahoo.com	Locates web sites, news, and online events.

When you set up an email account, you may be approached by a password or credit card thief. The usual scheme is that you'll be told, "There's something wrong with your sign-up information," or "A virus hit our main computer, would you please give us all your information again?" You'll be asked for your user ID, password, credit card information, and possibly your social security number as well. Some of the scammers are incredibly sophisticated and have created web pages that almost look official. CompuServe and AOL members are especially vulnerable.

Never give your password to anyone online!

If you heed only one bit of advice from this entire book, make it this: DO NOT give out your personal information to anyone who approaches you via email. These thieves send out thousands of emails, hoping to snare a few trusting individuals. If you feel funny about being asked for your password or your credit card number, don't supply it. Save yourself a lot of trouble.

Directories of sites

Beyond search engines and portals, there are some great directories of investing and financial information on the Web. The directories provide listings, and sometimes reviews, of sites that are organized by topic. Besides those on the list opposite, the portals I mentioned above all have financial directories with web addresses that are too arcane to reproduce here. In any case, think of them as road maps for your online explorations.

Talk about it

Another resource available online are forums where other investors talk about their strategies. You can learn a lot on these forums, but be careful: Some of the bulletin boards and chat areas are magnets for people who plant rumors about a company, trying to manipulate the stock price.

There are two ways that investors interact online: One is by posting messages on bulletin boards, and the other is in live chat rooms. You can post and read messages at your leisure, whether or not your correspondents are online at the same time. Interacting in chat rooms, however, involves talking directly with others who are online simultaneously, and progresses only as quickly as the participants can type (and read).

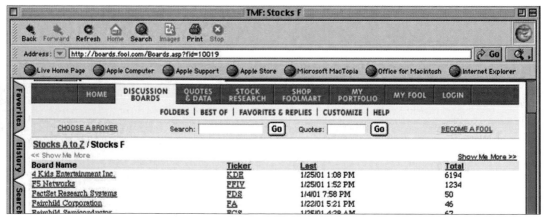

■ **Discussion boards** *are a means of communicating online by writing messages. They can be a useful source of information and provide an opportunity to learn about other investors' opinions.*

FINANCIAL FACT-FINDING

These top ten financial directories organize financial information by topic, acting like an online version of the Yellow Pages. You can peruse lists of brokers, banks, data suppliers, research sites, and so on. Many of these directories contain reviews and rankings as well.

Site name	Web address	Key feature
AOL Investing	search.aol.com/cat.adp?id=68	Has thousands of links, arranged by category.
CyberInvest	www.cyberinvest.com	Has a terrific collection of online investing guides.
Dow Jones Business Directory	businessdirectory.dowjones.com	Has reviews from the *Wall Street Journal* with links to money-related sites.
FinanCenter	www.financenter.com	Helps you create your own ranking of brokers and banks.
Gomez Advisors	www.gomez.com	Has scorecards ranking banks, brokers, insurance providers, etc.
Investor Guide	www.investorguide.com	Has articles, quotes, and news clips, as well as links.
Looksmart Money	www.money.looksmart.com	Click on Categories to get links to other sites.
MoneyClub	www.moneyclub.com	Has links organized by channel. Includes investment club directory.
MoneyWeb	www.moneyweb.com	Includes links to education resources as well as the usual financial suspects.
Yahoo! Finance	quote.yahoo.com	News, links galore, and real-time quotes.

TRADING VIEWS AND IDEAS

Do you like to engage in conversations with other investors, drink a cup of coffee (or something stronger!), and join in? Here are my favorite discussion boards on the Web, all of which include articles on investing, portfolio trackers, outspoken individuals, and their own particular points of view.

Site name	Web address
ClearStation	www.clearstation.com
Investors Forum	go.compuserve.com/investors
Motley Fool	www.fool.com
National Assn. of Investors Corp.	go.compuserve.com/naic
ProphetTalk	www.prophetfinance.com/prophettalk
Quicken.com Message Boards	www.quicken.com/boards
Quote.com Community	www.quote.com/quotecom/community
Raging Bull	www.ragingbull.com
Silicon Investor	www.siliconinvestor.com
Smart Money Forums	www.smartmoney.com/intro/forums/
Yahoo!	messages.yahoo.com

I'll admit to a personal preference for bulletin boards over chat, but your experiences may vary.

An annoyance prevalent on bulletin boards is the number of advertisements that are posted, which I simply skip – but they take up space. I'll admit that I browse the forums when I'm researching a company, but I take the advice with a grain of salt. The greatest values I've gotten out of the discussion areas are learning about online resources, such as a news or research site, and hearing about breaking news that I can verify with the company in question.

■ **Participating in online chats** *and discussions can be entertaining as well as illuminating – but be wary of unscrupulous users who may be out to misinform you.*

A simple summary

✓ Online trading has outgrown its original niche and has become mainstream.

✓ You can do more than just trade online. You can also turn your computer into your financial partner, using personal finance software, research, and portfolio analysis packages.

✓ Search engines can help you wade through the mass of information online and zero in on what you need.

✓ Financial directories provide lists of investing and news sites organized by topic. Try one of these if you're not exactly sure what you're looking for.

✓ Talk to other investors via message boards and live chat, but watch out for stock touts and spammers.

Chapter 2

Reasons to Invest Online

BASED SOLELY ON THE FACT that you're reading this book, I'm going to assume that you're interested in becoming an online investor or in becoming a more skillful online investor. There's more to investing online than simply finding a web-based broker and hitting the Trade button frequently. Read this chapter for a lot of reasons to invest online – and a few that might talk you out of it.

In this chapter...

✓ **Control for the educated investor**

✓ **Round-the-clock information**

✓ **Low fees (most of the time)**

✓ **Is online trading for you?**

INVESTORS ARE WISING UP TO THE CONVENIENCE, CONTROL, AND LOWER COST OF TRADING ONLINE

Control for the educated investor

THE INTERNET HAS REVOLUTIONIZED INVESTING by bringing tools to the rest of us that were formerly available only to professionals or to the very wealthy. And just when those of us who have been following the industry for most of the last decade think it can't get any better – it gets better. An information provider will start publishing another gem of a database, allowing the average investor immediate access to tools and data that used to take hours to use.

Trade what you want, when you want

You get home from work, pour yourself your favorite beverage, and go check on your investments. Back in the olden days, you'd have to make yourself a list of things to discuss with your full-service broker, assuming you remembered to make the phone call the next day.

Now you can just open your browser, read the news, do some research, see who's saying what about whom in the chat rooms, all from the privacy of your home. Then you can go to your online broker's site and set up the trades you'd like to make when the market opens.

What should you trade? That leads us to a logical starting point: The concept of asset allocation.

Asset allocation – does it hurt?

Asset allocation is probably a phrase you've heard before but may have tried to avoid. It can sound complicated, but really all it means is to have a strategy for spreading your investments around different sectors of the market and across different types of investments. There are plenty of worksheets that help you figure out what your asset allocation model should be, based on your goals, your expected rate of return, and your point in life.

Trivia...

Back in the dark ages of the 80s, I used to write a report for my boss analyzing our company's competition. This task involved days squinting over microfiche, scribbling numbers on various pieces of paper, assembling tables, and making calculations, then sending the whole lot over to my secretary to make it readable. Now I can perform the same analysis in about 15 minutes and produce a beautifully formatted table quickly as well. I try not to think about the wasted hours. It hurts just to think about the word microfiche.

If you expect a high rate of return from your investments, you'll have to be prepared to take a lot of risk. So you might lose a large chunk of your nest egg if you put too much of your portfolio in high-risk investments.

Let's say you're 35 years old, married, and have two lovely children, ages 5 and 2. You'd like to retire at age 65. You currently have $80,000 in your portfolio and another $15,000 in a money market fund. Drop it into the retirement planner on Quicken's web site and – snap – it suggests that you spread your investments as follows:

- Domestic bonds   18 percent
- Large cap stocks   41 percent
- Small cap stocks   16 percent
- International stocks   25 percent

This type of analysis once came only with a high price from a full-service broker. It wasn't so long ago that I paid $150 for an analysis of my investments that wasn't much more informative than the reports you can get now for free.

Knowing what you own and how it's classified is an important piece of information as you head online. I'll talk more about this in Chapter 4.

UNDERGOING ANALYSIS

There are a lot of places online, as well as in packaged software programs, that take you through the asset allocation process. Try a few of these to see what they recommend for you:

Web address	Key feature
www.quicken.com	Planner focused on investing for retirement.
www.AmericanCentury.com	Mainly aimed at the mutual fund investor.
www.fidelity.com	Different planners depending on your current savings strategy.
moneycentral.msn.com	Simple asset allocator based on expected returns.

Round-the-clock information

THE INTERNET NEVER SLEEPS. This is a double-edged sword, considering that we humans do need to rest from time to time. You can use your computer, however, to collect information, news, data, and gossip to assist your investment decisions whether you're awake or not. And with the current trends toward after-hours trading and globalization, giving investors the opportunity to trade outside the usual market hours, as well as in foreign markets, you could wire your eyeballs open and trade 24 hours a day. I wouldn't recommend that, but a triple-shot cappuccino does help on days when sleep is inconvenient.

Up-to-date portfolio balances

Not that long ago, around 1995, a huge innovation emerged when a couple of online financial sites allowed investors to set up their *portfolios* and track the total value on a day-by-day basis. If you logged on on Friday, for example, you'd see how much your portfolio was worth as of the end of the day on Thursday. Prior to this startling innovation, you

■ **Keeping track** *of your investments has never been easier, thanks to online broker services that update the value of your portfolio as soon as prices change.*

had to create a spreadsheet file or use a personal finance program that either downloaded stock prices or let you update them by hand to generate the value of your portfolio.

Today, most online brokers update the value of your portfolio with up-to-the-minute prices. If you're truly compulsive, you can set up a service that shows you the value of all your portfolios simultaneously, just by bringing up a web page. Keeping an eye on the value of your portfolio, and on the performance of each investment within it, is a habit you'll have to develop to take advantage of changes in the market as well as changes in your own investing goals. Chapter 8 is devoted to the variety of ways you can keep track of your holdings.

DEFINITION

Your portfolio is a list of the stocks, mutual funds, options, and other investments that you own at a particular point in time. You'll want to track the date you purchased the investment, the number of shares, how much you paid for it, and the commission you paid the broker.

■ **Dozens of online brokers** *enable you to keep up with events on the stock exchange as they happen. By accessing their web sites, you can chart changes to stock prices as if you were on the trading floor.*

Breaking news

The latest scoop isn't just for news anchors any more. Thanks to an incredible array of sites for financial news hounds, you can read a press release five minutes after it goes out over the wire – if you know where to look. The Web is dishing out news that used to be available only to professionals, who would then dole it out to select clients (along with a commission-generating trading pitch, of course). I'll talk a lot more about financial news in Chapter 7.

Real-time quotes

Not so long ago, investors had to pay for *quotes* that were 20 minutes old. Now there are dozens of places where you can watch the price of a stock change in real time, right when it happens.

Some brokers and web sites can show you price information for NASDAQ stocks in great detail, including the number of shares being offered or asked for at a specific price.

DEFINITION

Quotes *tell you the price someone in the market just paid for a particular stock. On some stock exchanges, for instance on the New York Stock Exchange (NYSE), you're given a single price that shows the amount paid per share during the most recent transaction. Other exchanges, such as the NASDAQ, display two prices for each quote: The bid, or the price a potential buyer is willing to pay, and the ask, which is the price a potential seller wants to receive.*

In the last couple of years, more and more web sites and online brokers have given their users access to Level II quotes (see below). These screens can take a while to learn to read, but for frequent traders, they're an important – actually an essential – tool. I'll talk more about them in Chapter 7.

QUOTES AND LEVELS

Quotes are supplied in a variety of flavors, from one-at-a-time to long lists of symbols. You can look at them in a table format or request that the prices roll across your screen as they're updated. There are three levels of quotes you can get on NASDAQ stocks.

Quote level	Used by	Features
Level I	Retail brokers Most web sites	Displays best (highest) bid and best (lowest) ask price – just two prices per stock.

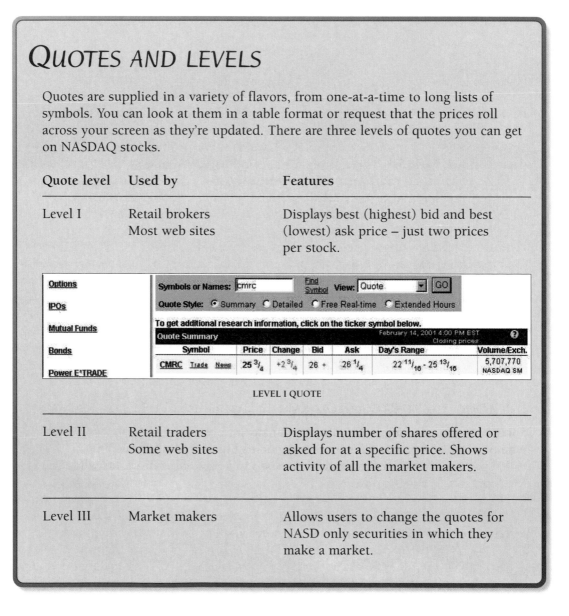

LEVEL I QUOTE

Quote level	Used by	Features
Level II	Retail traders Some web sites	Displays number of shares offered or asked for at a specific price. Shows activity of all the market makers.
Level III	Market makers	Allows users to change the quotes for NASD only securities in which they make a market.

Low fees (most of the time)

THE NUMBER ONE FACTOR DRIVING *the growth of online trading in the early years was, frankly, lower costs than those offered by full-service brokers. The group of hardy souls that first braved the murky waters of trading stocks online were computer savvy and willing to put up with ugly screens and arcane commands to save on commissions. Be honest with yourself now: Isn't it the thought of saving $100–$200 per transaction one of the main reasons you want to invest online?*

Online commissions versus live broker fees

Recently, I bought 300 shares of a stock through my full-service broker. A couple of days later, I decided to buy some more through one of my online accounts. The full-service commission was $180. The online commission was $20. Since this particular stock was trading at $14 when I bought it, the full-service commission cost me as much as 11 shares of the stock! I ended up transferring those shares out of the full-service brokerage account and into the online account, just so I could control them all in one place and save on commissions when I decide to sell at some point in the future.

Online commission charges per transaction vary from $0 to about $40 these days, with the industry average hovering at about $18. Some brokers are adjusting their fees in an attempt to find a happy medium between earning money on commissions and earning revenue from asset management.

There are other fees associated with trading, though, including charges for maintaining the account, issuing checks, transferring assets, and so on. I'll talk a lot more about what brokers charge, and the services they offer, in Chapter 9.

Low fees, high execution prices, and what it all means

Some brokers make money by passing your stock transaction on to a market maker, who pays the broker a small amount, say one-eighth of a point, for using it. This is called payment for order flow, and it can cost you a piece of your profits when it happens. Here's how it works.

Let's say you enter an order to buy 100 shares of XYZ Company at $20 per share. Your broker might send your order to a market maker, who happens to have a large pile of XYZ stock to sell at $19¾ per share. So they sell it to you at $20, and split the 25 cents per share (the spread) between the broker and the market maker. What does that do to you? It effectively raises the cost of your transaction by $25, or 100 shares times 25 cents.

Payment for order flow wasn't invented along with online brokerages, but it's been a major source of income for some brokers. When you see ads for a broker that proclaim, "We don't take payment for order flow!" they're telling you that they don't skim this fraction of a point off the top, and they're trying to get you the best possible price.

Payment for order flow is becoming less of an issue as the regulatory agencies jump into the act and try to minimize it, but the practice is still out there and it can affect your overall profitability. Effective July 2001, a new SEC regulation requires brokers to tell you whether they engage in the practice of payment for order flow.

Is online trading for you?

ONLINE TRADING SOUNDS GREAT, *doesn't it? But it could be a revolution you should avoid. If you don't have the time or discipline to put into managing your investments, perhaps you should stay away from investing online. There are some other traps online to watch out for, as well. Let's take a look.*

Can you do the homework?

As we've discussed above, the resources are many for online investors, but there's one resource only you can control: Your time. Do you have enough of it to devote to your portfolio? That's a question only you can answer. You have to be ready to react quickly to shifts in the market, changes in your goals, and the ups and downs of your own personal finances.

If you just can't spend a minimum of 30 minutes to an hour a week taking a look at your investments, you might be better off having a full-service broker who will stay on top of things for you.

Are you impulsive?

This is the flip side of not having enough time to stay on top of your portfolio: What if you overreact to every little piece of news? You might end up making unnecessary trades, turning the potential for long-term gains into short-term losses. Two professors at the University of California, Davis, Terrence Odean and Brad Barber, studied the behavior of a group of online investors from 1995 to 1997, and published their results in a study entitled, "Boys Will Be Boys: Gender, Overconfidence and Common Stock Investment." They concluded, "After going online, investors trade more actively, more speculatively, and less profitably than before. It is difficult to reconcile these results with rational behavior." They also noted, "Greater overconfidence leads to greater trading and to lower expected utility."

What does that mean in plain English? Investors who go online, change their investing style, and end up buying and selling frenetically, also end up with lower gains than if they'd stayed offline.

Beware of the tendency to get seduced into trading frequently just because you can, and just because it's so cheap.

A simple summary

✓ By investing online, you take control of your investments thanks to online tools that bring information to you that was formerly available only to professionals. Learn what they are and how to use them, and you're well on the way to being an educated investor.

✓ Go through the process of asset allocation before you embark on the online investing journey. You need to know where you are now before you start making significant changes.

✓ The Internet makes it possible for you to know what you're worth as of this very second, with real-time quotes and portfolio balance updates. You can also grab news relating to your investments as it breaks.

✓ The big lure of online investing is that it appears to be much cheaper than making trades through a full-service broker. You can save hundreds of dollars in commissions, but make sure you're not giving it up in payment for order flow.

✓ Online trading might not be for you if you don't have the time to devote to your portfolio, or if you're impulsive and prone to panic.

Chapter 3

Necessary Equipment

WHILE IT'S POSSIBLE TO BE A SUCCESSFUL online investor without owning your own computer equipment, you'd give up a lot of control, customization, and privacy. You might already own a computer you're happy with, be ready for an upgrade, or be in the market for your first home system. In this chapter, I'll talk about the hardware and software you'll need to get started, and I'll recommend other goodies that will help you stay on top of your investments.

In this chapter...

✓ Hardware: What you really need

✓ Software for online efficiency

✓ Other useful tools

THE RIGHT SOFTWARE WILL HELP YOU TO MANAGE YOUR PERSONAL FINANCES MORE EFFECTIVELY

Hardware: What you really need

THE FIRST TIME I EMBARKED *on a computer-buying mission was in 1982. I recall listening to a sales rep who earnestly described the capabilities of the $25,000 microcomputer on display. As she was talking, I was thinking, "I wonder when she's going to start speaking English again." Not only was she speaking in an unrecognizable dialect but none of the attributes of the computer made any sense to me.*

■ **Buying a computer** *is an investment in itself, so it's important to consider factors such as hard disk speed, memory, monitor size, and price before you make your purchase.*

Since then, I've managed to purchase dozens of computers, and I have mastered the arcane language of computer geek speak. I can throw around jargon with the best of them, but I'll spare you that kind of abuse here. Bill Machrone, former editor-in-chief of *PC Magazine*, used to say, back in the 1980s and on up until about 1995, "The system you want will cost $5,000." Costs have come way, way down – you can probably get what you want for under $2,000 now, including a monitor and printer!

Let's get down to the basics of what you'll need in a system for managing your finances and investments. It's simpler than you'd expect, although you can add on all kinds of equipment depending on the other uses you'll have for your computer.

Buy the fastest computer you can afford.

There are two types of speed you want to look at: One is the speed of the computer's "brain," or processor, and the other is the speed of the hard disk, where you'll be storing all your data. Resign yourself to the fact that whatever you buy will be obsolete within months, but that's just the way it goes when buying computers!

DESKTOP OR LAPTOP?

LAPTOP

A fundamental decision you'll have to make before you go shopping is whether you want a portable system or one that will stay at home. This is a question only you can answer, so consider it carefully. If you travel a lot and want to monitor your investments from the road, a laptop or notebook computer is probably right for you. Another advantage of a laptop is that you can bring it to work with you so you don't have to use your employer's computer to watch your finances. This protects your privacy considerably, though it might also annoy your employer.

A desktop system is much more flexible than a laptop computer, since you can switch the components around as you like. Want a great big monitor? Great, no problem, just unplug the small one and plug in a new one. If you don't like your notebook's monitor, you're pretty much stuck. Keyboards on notebook computers tend to be small. Definitely take the opportunity to try before you buy.

If you'll be running games or using your computer for graphic design, you'll probably be happier with a desktop system. If all you'll be doing is managing your finances, dealing with email, and doing a little word processing, you could get by with a laptop as your main machine.

Laptop computers are, in general, more expensive than a desktop with a similar configuration. The smaller the package, the pricier it is.

DESKTOP SYSTEM

The basics: Storage, memory, monitor, keyboard

Buying a computer has never been easier. When I think back to the intense anguish I experienced while purchasing my first computer, the venerable IBM PC with less memory than is currently left in my skull, I have to head for the medicine cabinet.

I hesitate to recommend an ideal configuration in a book, though. Things change so quickly that a system that is state-of-the-art as we go to print will, sadly, be obsolete by the time you read this. But here are some general guidelines.

If your main purpose for buying a computer is managing your investments, your needs are actually fairly simple. You'll need a hard disk, which is where your data and programs are stored. Try to find one with the smallest number in the access time statistics; that means you'll be able to load programs and save data faster than a computer with a larger access time figure. You'll see a two-digit number with the abbreviation "ms" (which stands for milliseconds) after it – that's the access time. Typical access times are 18ms, 25ms, and 29ms. Remember: For disk access times, the lower the number the better.

■ **Think about** *where you plan to put your computer system, as this may have a bearing on the size of monitor and the types of accessories you choose.*

Just to confuse you, another number you'll see listed is the speed of the computer's processor. This is the chip that does all the computations. In this case, you'll want to buy the computer with the fastest processor that you can afford, unless you are a very patient person. This number is typically expressed as a three-digit number with the abbreviation "Mhz" (which stands for megahertz) after it. Typical processor speeds are 600Mhz and higher. If you're buying a Macintosh, look for a G3 or G4 processor (though by the time you read this, it could be up to G7 or higher!). Remember: For processor speeds, the higher the number the better.

PC or Macintosh? Frankly, it doesn't matter much because most of the tools you'll use are accessible from your web browser. Your decision will be driven more by the other things you want to do with your computer. If you're interested in running high-end technical analysis software, though, you should get a PC rather than a Mac due to software availability.

Another important component is the monitor, or screen, that you'll use to watch your net worth grow. The ideal monitor depends on where you'll put the computer and how much you want to spend. The minimum monitor size you should consider is 15 inches, which is measured diagonally across the screen. The larger the monitor (up to a point), the more you can see at once. If you wear reading glasses (like Yours Truly), you'll appreciate the ability of your computer to increase the font size, so a larger monitor will help fit more on the screen at once. As you browse the Web, you'll find graphics and tables and other fascinating pages, and a larger monitor helps you see it all at once rather than having to scroll around to view the items off the edge of the screen.

The perfect voice-activated computer is still in the works, so for now you'll need a keyboard to type your commands to the computer. Try a few out before you buy. Do you prefer one that feels like a regular typewriter and makes a loud clacking noise as you press each key, or would you rather have a quiet keyboard that barely registers its existence as you flail away on it? If you suffer from carpal tunnel syndrome, or any kind of repetitive stress injury, check out the keyboards that are split in the middle and have a slight rise to them. They look funny, and take an hour or so to adapt to, but they go a long way toward relieving pain in your hands and arms.

INTERNET

www.cnet.com

www.zdnet.com

These are great sites for comparing computer systems and components. Both let you search through reviews and find the best prices online.

Media players, backup devices, and printers

It's hard to buy a new computer that doesn't have a CD drive any more, which is just fine with me. Most software you buy will be shipped on CD-ROMs, making installation incredibly easy. Some systems have a DVD drive as well as a CD drive – or a single drive that serves a dual purpose. CD drives are also given a speed rating, and this time you want a high number. Typically the speeds are expressed as a two-digit number followed by x, such as 24x or 48x.

You'll be saving a lot of data on your computer's hard disk, and the sad truth is that many hard disks, in time, fail. You can lose that hard-earned data if you haven't

■ **Most computers** *now have built-in CD drives, so installing CD-ROM software is easy. Check the speed rating of these drives before you buy.*

copied it, or backed it up, on another format. Backup devices include writable CD drives, tape drives, Jaz drives, and Zip drives. These items can add $100–$300 to the cost of your system, but they can save you a lot of time and heartache. You can always copy your important data files to a diskette, but that can be a time-consuming process. These backup devices are sold with programs that make it easy for you to create copies of your important files.

ZIP DISKS

Printers that generate full-color reports are plentiful these days, and can also be used to print photos. Beware of the really cheap printers (under $200) because many of them have ink cartridges that are expensive to replace.

While you're working on your computer, you can be entertained with your choice of music, either played in your CD drive or downloaded from the Internet. Unless you're a stereo aficionado, the mid-range speakers offered by most computer shops will do the job. The low-end speakers sound a little tinny.

You can go wild adding other goodies to your computer, but to keep your investments in line, these are the basics. Oh yes, to get you hooked up to the Internet, there's one more thing . . .

Modems and other black boxes

Most computers today are equipped with built-in modems. Of course, you want the fastest possible connection you can get. A modem uses your telephone line to dial into a computer network that links you to the Internet. A typical modem speed is 56K, which means that approximately 56,000 bytes of information (roughly equivalent to a character on your screen) can be transferred per second.

MODEM

There are faster ways to log on, of course. To take advantage of these methods, you'll need to have a network card installed in your computer, then make arrangements with either your cable TV company or your local phone company for a higher speed connection.

Your cable company can sell you a special modem that connects your network card to the cable system and then connects to the Internet. Telephone companies offer direct subscriber lines, or DSL, connections, which can use existing telephone wiring in your house to provide high-speed access. There are occasional problems with each of these methods, but the payoff is huge: Access speed of up to 50 times that of a 56K modem.

Both cable and DSL connections are more expensive than dial-up connections, but they're a lot faster. You can also stay connected 24 hours a day if you'd like – as mentioned before, the Internet never sleeps! If you want to take advantage of real-time portfolio updates, streaming quote services, and technical analysis and charting on the Web, you'll be much happier if your connection is fast.

It doesn't hurt to have more than one type of connection available, just in case one is unavailable when you need it most. I use DSL, with dial-up as a backup should my DSL service take an unexpected "vacation."

Firewalls and other security issues

No doubt you've read the horror stories about computer viruses wiping a computer clean, or hackers breaking into a computer and stealing a list of credit card numbers. How can you protect your computer from being the subject of a future horror story?

If the tests described in the box below tell you that you've got a security problem, you have two alternatives for eradicating it. Well, three actually, but the third one is to unplug yourself from the Internet and never go back, and that's not a productive resolution.

SAFEGUARDING YOUR COMPUTER

If you're connected to the Internet using cable or DSL, you should find out how your computer looks to the outside world. There are several web sites that purposely try to break into your computer just to show you whether it's secure from outside attacks. Check out these web sites to make sure your connection is secure:

Site name	Web address	Kay feature
Secure-me	www.secure-me.net	Intensely probes your computer to find any security holes.
Gibson Research	www.grc.com	"Shields Up" is a program that tells you if anyone on the Internet can crawl into your computer.

The first alternative is to install a software program that protects your computer. There are several commercial ones out there such as Norton Utilities Personal Firewall and ZoneAlarm. The former can be purchased from any computer store or downloaded at http://www.symantec.com. ZoneAlarm comes in two flavors: a free version, and a Pro version at a small fee. Both can be downloaded from http://www.zonelabs.com.

The second, more costly but more secure, alternative is to buy a firewall device that sits between your cable or DSL modem and your computer. Most hardware firewalls are simple-looking boxes, festooned with blinking lights, but what they do is block any attempt at getting past the box and into your computer. An added benefit to a hardware firewall is that many of them can be used to share a DSL or cable connection among up to four computers in the same location. Selecting and installing a hardware firewall is a topic that's a bit too complex for this book, though.

If security tests show that your computer is at risk, don't ignore the warning. Protect yourself before you do anything else. I mean it. Though the risk is small that an unscrupulous hacker will locate your individual system, it's not so small that you can just cross your fingers and hope you'll be OK.

Going wireless

One of the most intriguing recent trends in online investing is *wireless* connections to your portfolio. As we go to print, more and more online brokers and financial data providers are enabling access to their systems from Palm Pilots, BlackBerry wireless devices, cell phones, two-way pagers, and other "magic" boxes. (Well, they look like magic to me.)

Watch the financial pages for special promotions. Brokers are giving away web-enabled cell phones when a customer opens a new account, for example. Though wireless devices can't replace a desktop or laptop computer in terms of analysis

■ **With a wireless device,** *you have the advantage of being able to receive important information immediately — wherever you happen to be.*

> **DEFINITION**
>
> *A wireless device lets you access financial information, email, and some web sites without having a physical line connecting you to a phone or network. It uses two-way radio technology rather than telephone lines for hooking you up to your online resources.*

LOOKING INTO WIRELESS CONNECTION

Wireless access to online investing is rapidly evolving, and prices, both for the devices themselves and for online services, are coming down fast. Here are some of the companies to check out if you're considering a wireless device:

Company	Type of device	Web address	Phone
Casio	Cassiopeia handheld	www.casio.com	800-962-2746
Compaq	iPaq handheld	www.compaq.com	800-345-1518
Ericsson	Cell phone	www.ericsson.com	212-685-4030
Handspring	Visor handheld	www.handspring.com	650-230-5000
Hewlett-Packard	Jornada handheld	www.hp.com	800-752-0900
Motorola	Cell phone, two-way pager	www.motorola.com	800-331-6456
Nokia	Cell phone	www.nokia.com	888-665-4228
Palm	Palm handheld	www.palm.com	408-326-9000
RIM	BlackBerry handheld	www.rim.net	519-888-7465
Qualcomm	Cell phone	www.qualcomm.com	619-587-1121
Samsung	Cell phone	www.samsung.com	800-726-7864

and portfolio management, they can keep you connected to your trading system even when you're away from your home base. You can set up alerts so that when a stock hits a new high or low, reaches a particular price, or has news items that hit the wire, you'll be instantly notified.

If you're a frequent trader and need to stay constantly connected to your portfolio, wireless access is a must-have tool. For buy-and-hold investors, it's not as important, unless you just like having a pocket-sized device that beeps at you once in a while.

Software for online efficiency

OK, NOW THAT YOU'RE ALL SET UP with your computer and your connection to the Internet, what next? You'll need an Internet service provider (ISP) so you can log on and look around.

Signing up for an online service

If you have a 24-hour connection to the Web (as described above) such as cable or DSL, you already have an ISP built in. But if you're using a dial-up modem to connect to the online world, your new computer will probably have icons for several possible services to which you can subscribe.

Which one will work best for you? Find out who has a local number first, so you won't be racking up the phone charges while you're exploring online. Check to make sure that local number will allow you the fastest possible online access too. If you're in a rural area without a local number, or if you travel a lot within the United States, find out if you can dial in using a toll-free number. Most of the time you'll be charged an additional fee to use the toll-free number, but it could save you a lot in phone bills.

How much time do you think you'll spend online? You can sign up for an unlimited access plan with some ISPs that's a few dollars a month more than one that gives you just 15 or 40 hours a month of connect time. You might prefer a local company to one of the national ISPs (such as America Online or Netcom), so make a few phone calls and check out the current rates and specials before committing to a particular service.

I'm sure you've seen ads for "free" ISPs, and I think it's a good idea to have an account with one of these companies – but only as a backup to your regular connection.

The "free" ISPs make you look at ads in exchange for your connection, which can slow down your browsing, and take up real estate on your screen as well. Just in case your regular connection crashes, though, you'll want to have another way to get online.

Browsing around

Getting around on the Web requires a program called a browser, which displays web pages and helps you move from one to another. The two most popular browsers are Netscape Navigator and Microsoft Internet Explorer. A browser should be a quiet partner as you navigate the Internet rather than a factor that gets in your way.

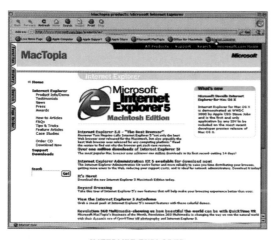

INTERNET EXPLORER

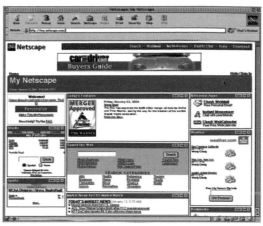

NETSCAPE

Whatever browser you use, be sure to check the publisher's web site frequently for updates. The technology of getting around the Web is constantly evolving, so it's best to have the latest version.

I use both browsers interchangeably. There are some things I prefer about Internet Explorer, for instance the ability to preview on screen how a page will look before I print it. Netscape Navigator includes a customizable sidebar that is displayed on the left side of the screen that is updated as the day goes on. The sidebar can show whatever you want active – stock quotes, portfolio updates, your buddy list, and many more items.

Some online brokers have programmed in specific bells and whistles that work better with one browser than the other. In general, I've found that many broker sites say that they've been optimized to run under Internet Explorer, which just means that some of the flashing graphics will load faster with that program.

No matter which browser you pick, make sure you've got the version that lists its cipher strength as 128-bit. This specification means that your browser has the top level of security built in. Since you'll be using your computer to help you with your finances, you'll want the most secure connection you can get!

Both Netscape Navigator and Internet Explorer are usually installed on new computers, so you won't have to go looking around for them online. Your ISP may have also given you a browser that has its brand name all over it (for example, America Online uses a customized version of Internet Explorer). Don't be afraid to experiment!

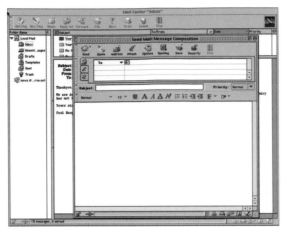

■ **Email software** *is often provided by your ISP, and is supplied by popular browsers. Alternatively, you can download programs from the Web for free.*

Email software

Electronic mail isn't just for chatting with the kids any more. You'll use email to stay in touch with your online broker and to receive alerts and account statements as well. Your ISP, whether America Online or any other service, usually has you choose your email address when you first sign on. You'll want to use that as your main address for communicating with your online broker.

Your ISP may have also provided you with software for reading and writing electronic mail. The main browsers have a program built in, or you can use a program like Microsoft Outlook Express (part of the Office suite), Eudora, or JustMail. Eudora and JustMail can be downloaded from www.downloader.com (type "email client" in the search box), and they're free.

Do yourself a favor and set up folders so you can sort your email. I have folders for each of the brokers I use, plus a few other folders for other business topics, online shopping, and personal mail.

Many of the web sites I'll be talking about later in the book require you to set up a user name and password. They'll ask you for your email address and will usually ask you if it's OK to send you promotional material from time to time. I always say no to this question, but that doesn't keep me from getting a mailbox full of junk.

To protect my main email address, I've set up a second account with a free email service called Hotmail. I use my Hotmail address when registering at financial web sites, and I've turned on the spam filter. Junk mail goes straight to the trash, and I don't even bother looking at it.

Other useful tools

YOU HAVE TO KNOW WHEN to hold 'em and know when to fold 'em. Keeping track of your net worth is an important component of being an effective and successful online investor. How can you track how your investments are performing if you've got a bank account, several stock portfolios with multiple brokers, a 401(k) through your employer, and that trust fund set up by Grandmother? Here's a look at four packaged software programs that help you manage your portfolios, among other things, and access up-to-date pricing data via the Internet.

Personal finance software

The two big names here are Intuit's Quicken and Microsoft Money. Every fall, these publishers roll out their latest versions. Quicken and Money have turned into extensions of the web browser, so if you have accounts that are accessible electronically, you can minimize your data entry chores by downloading the information directly from the broker or bank. Not every broker or bank is connected yet, but E*Trade and numerous others are wired into both programs. What that means is that you'll need to take some time to set each individual account up within the program. But once you do, you can bring in transactions (such as checks written, deposits made, stocks bought and sold) during the electronic update process rather than having to make all the entries manually.

Both programs do a good job of giving you a handle on your capital gains as the year goes on, which, of course, depends on how well you've kept up with entering transactions. Should you use one of these programs? I'd say yes, for about 90 percent of you reading this book. It comes down to a style preference and whether the brokers and banks with whom you do business link to a particular program. Demos are available online, so you can get a feel for how the programs work, at www.quicken.com and www.microsoft.com/money. Money and Quicken cost about $60, plus or minus $20, depending on which version you purchase and the vendor you choose.

The very wealthy, and those with extensive assets beyond stocks and bonds, would do well to take a look at Financial Navigator (www.finnav.com). It's a complex program, though, so it helps if you've got a staff to deal with the accounting details. The program can handle whatever you throw at it in terms of asset type. You can even keep track of your mineral collection and your antique cars (not to mention your homes scattered around the globe). Bringing online data into Financial Navigator involves the purchase

INTERNET

www.quicken.com

www.microsoft.com
/money

Online demos of Quicken and Money can give you a feel for how the programs work.

of one or two additional modules: The latest version of StockWeb, for current quotes and news, and the latest version of Access, for historical data. The great thing about Access, which none of the other programs can do, is that it will retrieve prices for your portfolio from any past date you specify. The personal edition of Financial Navigator will set you back $395, and the add-ons are $149–$249 per module.

NAIC's Portfolio Record Keeper (PRK), developed by Quant IX Software ($69–$79 for NAIC members, $99 for nonmembers), is a venerable piece of software – it was first released in 1985 – with several useful reports and the ability to track a wide variety of investment types. The Performance Report calculates an annual internal rate of return, and you can track each account individually or collectively. Other reports display diversification analysis, and the tax reports are also informative. It suffers from the usual problem: Getting data into the program. Unlike Money and Quicken, though, PRK requires that you do all the transaction data entry by hand, and importing current prices takes several steps. PRK offers a great deal in terms of tabular analysis, but it leaves a lot of the work up to you. It's much more complete than any web-based portfolio tracker I've seen, in spite of the data entry problems. If you don't care for the soup-to-nuts coverage of Quicken, Money, or Financial Navigator, you might be happy with PRK.

Tax preparation software

More and more Americans are using tax preparation software to file their returns. And the IRS likes the trend because it makes the agency's job easier to do. If the Feds prefer returns that are filed electronically or on the paper-saving 1040ES forms, doesn't it make sense to cooperate? Those of you with complex financial lives would, of course, do well to consult a tax professional. But for those with humbler finances (or those who simply prefer to do it themselves), it makes sense to use specialized software to assemble a return, rather than try to build one with a calculator, pencil, eraser, and a lot of colorful mutterings.

I've been reviewing tax software since 1991 and have used it for my personal and business tax returns since 1984. I've switched back and forth between the two top programs, TurboTax and TaxCut, several times in the last decade and a half. Intuit publishes TurboTax (www.turbotax.com), which ties neatly into Quicken and minimizes the data entry required to finish your return – assuming you've been keeping track of all your transactions as they occur. TaxCut (www.taxcut.com), published by Kiplinger, can read Money files directly. Both programs use an interview format to gather data and enter it into the appropriate form.

Self-employed individuals, including day traders, especially those taking the Business Use of Home deduction, should use the business version of each program (TurboTax for Home & Business or TaxCut for Your Business) to get additional forms and assistance.

If you are receiving distributions from a retirement account, both programs walk you through the appropriate 1099 form, though TurboTax goes a little deeper into the esoterica of the codes used and what they mean. When I attempted to make a deliberately erroneous entry on the SEP deposit line, both programs noticed and let me know, in no uncertain terms, that I was making a mistake.

There's a lot of help available in both programs; their CD-ROMs are packed with tax tidbits, deduction finders, and lists of IRS publications. There are links to the publishers' web sites, where you can get the latest version of the software or gain additional insight into your tax situation. If your return is relatively simple, you can even prepare it online.

A simple summary

✔ When buying a computer for managing your investments and trading online, try to get the fastest processor you can afford, as well as the most RAM.

✔ If you travel frequently, and need access to your finances while you're on the road, seriously consider using a laptop or notebook computer as your main machine.

✔ If it's available and you can justify the expense, invest in a high-speed connection to the Internet, such as DSL or cable. The bare minimum you should consider is a 56K dial-up modem.

✔ Choose an Internet service provider with a local number or toll-free access number to keep your phone bills down.

✔ Use personal finance software, such as Intuit's Quicken, Microsoft Money, or Financial Navigator to stay on top of your net worth. If you want a high-powered portfolio manager, try NAIC's Portfolio Record Keeper.

✔ Tax software, such as Intuit's TurboTax or Kiplinger's TaxCut, will help you figure out what you owe Uncle Sam. These programs interview you, enter the data, and make the calculations.

Chapter 4

Understanding Your Financial Self

To know where you're going, you need to know your starting point. You also need to have a handle on the resources available to get you from here to there. Take a good hard look at your finances and at your attitude toward money and wealth. Peter Lynch, longtime manager of the Fidelity Magellan fund, once said, "Everyone has the brainpower to follow the stock market. If you made it through fifth-grade math, you can do it." In this chapter, you'll be taking an objective view of your current financial position and working out your strategy for the future.

In this chapter...

✓ Your financial profile

✓ Understanding your financial parameters

✓ Create and set goals

THE BETTER YOU KNOW YOURSELF, THE WISER YOUR INVESTMENT DECISIONS ARE LIKELY TO BE

Your financial profile

DO YOU REMEMBER THE OLD FABLE *about the ant and the grasshopper? As summer progressed, the ant kept gathering food, storing it away for the coming winter, while the grasshopper partied and lazed around, certain there would always be plenty to eat. When the snow fell, the grasshopper had to beg for crumbs from the ant.*

This fable is, as you surely know, a thinly disguised morality story about saving up for retirement. It's more fun to party and hang out in the sun during the fat months of summer – winter seems so far away. Advertisements lure us to buy that big TV or spend our savings on an exotic vacation. Hey, there's always the lottery, right? An anonymous wag once said, "Bulls make money. Bears make money. Pigs get slaughtered."

Everyone's heard of nurturing your inner child. Now it's time to locate and nurture your inner accountant.

Your strengths and weaknesses

Your success as an investor, whether online or offline, depends on your attitude. Are you a can-do person, always looking for opportunity and ideas? Or do you assume you're going to make a mistake, so you completely avoid making a move? Don't pat yourself on the back if you're a can-do person – you might also tend to overdo. There's a happy medium that depends on your current stage in life and on a realistic assessment of your finances.

"Money ranks with love as man's greatest source of joy and with death as his greatest source of anxiety," said economist John Kenneth Galbraith. Many investors trip themselves up by acting emotionally – leaping into the market when the *bulls* are driving prices up, then jumping out when the *bears* prevail and prices fall. Count a cool head as one of your strengths if you can avoid panicking or overreacting to sudden moves in the market.

Take a look at your calendar now. Are you completely overbooked with business and social engagements? Do you have the time to devote to the homework you'll have to do to grow your portfolio? It takes more than a few clicks of the mouse to be a successful investor. Before you click that mouse, you must do the work of researching a stock, monitoring the news, knowing what will move the price of this stock, and having the big picture of your overall strategy in mind. If you don't have the time now, what can you carve out of your schedule in order to make the time?

KNOW YOURSELF

What kind of investor are you? In general, online investors fall into one of the following three categories:

1 **Conservative cyberinvestors:** The conservative online investor uses the Internet for its efficiency and access. Online accounts and investment news can be accessed quickly, 24/7. But this investor wants some personal attention and guidance along the way from a broker. Conservatives can be new to investing or experienced traditionalists. They trade less frequently than the other two types.

2 **Active onliners:** This group is comfortable with going it alone, being responsible for their own research and interactions in the cyber environment. These investors will trade on a consistent basis through holding some stocks for the longterm and some for the shortterm. Online most days of the week, active onliners do their research and monitor the market often.

3 **Electronic traders:** This group of active, aggressive speculators buys and sells most frequently to catch the upswings and downswings of the market, rather than hold positions and grow an investment. Day traders are the most active of this group. They make trades continuously throughout a day, potentially making large gains – and losses.

Tune in to your emotional maturity. You can play online all over the Internet, but don't play with your investments. Online investing can become a game – one you're likely to lose. There's a feeling of exhilaration when beating the market, but the thrill of victory can quickly turn into the agony of defeat if you treat investing as a sport.

Getting out of your own way

My friend Kim had one of the more interesting reactions to a financial windfall, in this case a surprise inheritance. "I don't deserve this," she said, "I should just give it all away." Fear is an effective inhibitor to financial success. A small dash of fear can inspire us to do a little more research or take a breath before leaping into a particular investment. But an overwhelming dose of it will prevent action. If you're crippled by fear of success or dealing with money, you should work your way out of this limiting mindset.

Many of us grew up with the message that there wasn't enough money, or that we had to scrimp and save and deny ourselves luxuries. We may believe that it's not OK to be wealthier than the generation before us, or that stepping up a financial notch would be an insult to our parents. You may have some internal messages about money that you don't acknowledge explicitly, yet they hold you back.

If you believe that "money is the root of all evil," how do you think you'll react to a surge in your personal wealth? Be aware of the ways you can sabotage your own success, and don't get in your own way!

Life stages and investment styles

The way you invest, and the items you choose for your portfolio, depend on your age and your attitude toward risk. If you're in your 20s, you can take a few more risks than you can if you're in your 60s since, presumably, you've got time to make up for any mistakes you might make. If you're close to retirement, you don't want to gamble the nest egg you've spent most of your life nurturing. At its simplest, asset allocation just means the percentage of your portfolio you put into the basic investment types, which are stocks, bonds, and cash. It gets more complex as you break the basic types down to more detailed components, such as the specific type of company for your stock investments – large, mid-sized, small, domestic, foreign – or the type of bond – tax-exempt government bonds, taxable corporate bonds. Even cash comes in different flavors!

Asset allocation protects you from having all of your investments in one particular piece of the market through a strategy that encourages diversification. Let's say you put all of your savings into small company stocks. If that one sector of the market crashes and burns, you're in big trouble. But if you put 20 percent of your savings into small company stocks and the other 80 percent spread over large company and mid-sized company stocks, the effect of a downturn in one sector wouldn't hurt you as much.

If you'll need your money within the next 5 years, you should consider low-risk investments such as bonds and money market funds. It's true, those investments don't produce high returns, but your money is protected and it's unlikely you'll lose it. In the short run, the stock market is considerably more volatile, so if your time frame is 10 years or more, you should have a larger percentage of your money in stocks. A short-term downturn won't mean that much in the long run. Check out the web sites below for their asset allocation worksheets. Each has its own particular philosophy and its own style of investments. By working through a couple of these, you'll get a general idea of where you should be right now:

- www.strong-funds.com/strong/Planner98/asset.htm
- www.fidelity.com (click on Planning and Retirement, then on General Planning)
- www.fs.ml.com (for Merrill Lynch customers only)
- www.armchairmillionaire.com (go through the Five Steps to Financial Freedom)
- www.investorama.com/calc/riskprofile.html

Understanding your financial parameters

LET'S SEE WHAT YOU HAVE available to invest now that you have a notion of how you want to invest. Your financial plan should include the following three categories of investing, so budget for the ones that fit you:

(*a*) Cash savings for immediate needs and emergencies. Start out with at least 3 months' expenses on hand, with a year's worth as your longer term goal. This is money that doesn't go into the stock market.

(*b*) Short-term investing for things such as a down payment on a house, a new car, a big vacation trip, or accumulating money to start your own business.

(*c*) Long-term investing for items such as retirement or your newborn baby's college expenses.

Your current income

This ought to be easy to measure – just look at your paycheck, right? Most employees have more going for them than just their salaries though. Make sure you know what your total compensation is, including profit sharing, company stock purchase plan, and incentive bonuses.

Does your employer offer a 401(k) plan? This lets you deduct some money from your paycheck before taxes are calculated, and put it to work in a selection of investments (usually mutual funds) that you can withdraw after you've retired. 401(k) plans are complicated enough that there are entire books devoted to their management, but if your employer offers one, go for it. Try to maximize the amount you can put into the plan because it all works for you

■ **By analyzing your current** *financial situation you will be able to budget realistically for investment and plan more effectively for the future.*

tax-free until you take the money out. In addition, almost all employers throw a little extra into the pot for you as an incentive to get you to save.

Other factors to consider are nonmonetary benefits such as medical insurance and life insurance. In most cases, you'll have money deducted from your paycheck to pay a share of the insurance premiums, but some (rare) employers foot the entire bill. These benefits are all part of your financial plan, so be aware of them and make sure your choices fit your current life situation. If you've recently changed marital status, for instance, review all your employee benefits as well as your tax deductions.

How deep are you in debt?

Your debts include the mortgage on your house, your car loan, and all those pesky credit card bills. The latter is about the most expensive money you can borrow, and you're paying for it out of after-tax income.

Pay off your credit cards first, and make a plan to keep your debts to a minimum in the future by developing a realistic budget – and sticking to it!

INTERNET

www.quicken.com/
shopping/debt

The Quicken.com Debt Reduction Planner will show you the best strategy for paying off your current debt and the amount of money that will be freed up when you reach your goal.

If you max out your credit cards and are paying just the minimum every month, do yourself a huge favor and stop it. Now might be a good time to take another look at your mortgage too. How does the rate you're paying compare to the current interest rate? You might be able to bring your payments down, which will leave more money available for your investments. Learn to live a less leveraged life and your monthly cash requirements will drop.

How much can you budget for investments?

Don't let your investment budget consist of the crumbs that are left over every month once you've paid all your bills and gone out to dinner every weekend. Pay yourself first. Try to set aside a fixed percentage of your monthly income for your investments.

If you're already contributing the maximum to your 401(k) and your company stock purchase plan, fantastic. Plan to contribute to an Individual Retirement Account as well; that money grows tax-free until you start to withdraw it (hopefully after you retire). Now set aside another chunk of change every month – 10 percent is a reasonable figure to strive for – and put it into an investment account before it winds up in your checkbook.

Not all of us are earning regular monthly salaries, as I'm well aware. I'm self-employed and my income can best be described as unstable from month to month. My plan, though, is that I have a certain set amount transferred from my business account to my investment account every month. After I balance my checkbook and plan for the following month's cash flow, I transfer 30 percent of what's left to my investment account. Part of this ends up paying my self-employment taxes every quarter, but I end up with a nice chunk of change to invest every month. Granted, I worked up to this 30 percent figure from the early days when I was lucky to save $100 per month.

The key to investing is to plan how much you'll put away rather than having it happen haphazardly.

How much risk can you handle?

Risk isn't necessarily synonymous with loss, nor does it guarantee a huge gain. Risk is, however, a part of any portfolio strategy because none of us is clairvoyant and able to see which of our investments will pay off and which will decline.

The younger you are, and the longer the time frame you're investing over, the more risk you can handle in your portfolio. As time goes on, and your goals draw near – retirement, college for the kids, that sort of thing – you'll start to move your riskier investments into ones that preserve your capital so you don't lose money. The less risk, though, the lower your return. An incredibly safe portfolio would consist of nothing but high-grade bonds. Your initial investment is safe, though inflation might eat away at your potential returns.

Asset allocation models, as mentioned on page 62, help you figure out what sorts of investments you should consider, given your time frame and your attitude toward risk. It's a trade-off between risk and potential return – and it's a choice only you can make.

Trivia...

Another aspect of asset allocation to consider is the time you've held a particular stock or fund. If you sell a stock within one year from the date you bought it, any gains you receive are taxed at your ordinary income rate. But if you hang onto the stock for more than one year, the most you'll pay in capital gains is 20 percent. Also consider the taxes you'll pay on dividends you receive, which are taxed at your ordinary income rate. For tax reasons, it might be better to pick a stock that you believe will grow 10 percent in value over the next year rather than one that doesn't grow, but pays 10 percent in dividends. If you're in a high tax bracket, 36 percent or more, you'll need to pay close attention to the tax consequences of your investments.

Create and set goals

WHY INVEST AT ALL? *Why not just do the grasshopper thing and fritter away every penny of your income? You already know the answer to this one, even though frittering sounds pretty good sometimes. Who wants to live from paycheck to paycheck? There will come a time when you don't want to work at all or when you'll want to drop a chunk of change that you can't generate out of current income.*

Think ahead and decide whether your goals are long term – 10 or more years out – or shorter term – 2 to 5 years in the future. Consider your plan and decide whether you're disciplined enough to follow through.

Making investment goals keeps you on track. This is especially important with online investing, which can become entertainment or an escapist adventure. A goal-oriented financial plan consists of:

- Setting a goal
- Developing a strategy for achieving that goal
- Taking logical steps toward the goal
- Honestly assessing your short-term results
- Following through with the plan

Here are a few goals to consider. Feel free to make up your own. Think, plan, do – and keep going!

Retiring in comfort

I don't know about you, but as I grow older, I appreciate the perks my increasing income allows me. I don't want to give those up when I decide to stop working. Actually, I'm sure I'll want even more. How much do you figure it'll cost to support you in the style to which you'd like to be accustomed? Be sure to factor in travel!

Your investing goals today should definitely include creating income after you stop working. Many of the sites mentioned above, including Quicken.com and ArmchairMillionaire.com, have terrific retirement planners that will give you some guidelines. Most online brokers have numerous financial calculators and retirement planners available to their clients. The one-stop shopping brokers will tie the calculators to your portfolio and recommend changes in your holdings to meet your goals.

■ **Enjoying retirement** *means being able to live comfortably once you stop work, to take vacations, pursue hobbies, and make the most of your free time – all of which requires sound financial planning.*

■ **The expense of educating your children** *can be easier to bear if you invest in a college savings plan, since you can make substantial tax savings if you are a high earner.*

Sending the kids to college

When setting up a college savings plan, check into a 529 Plan. Earnings in a 529 Plan account grow federal income tax deferred. When assets are withdrawn for qualified expenses such as tuition, room and board, books, and required supplies, federal income taxes are payable by the student, typically at a lower rate than higher earning parents would have to pay. Fidelity Investments (www.fidelity.com) and CollegeSavings.com (www.collegesavings.com) offer online management of 529 Plans.

Buying that airplane or great big diamond

J. Paul Getty once said, "If you can count your money, you don't have a billion dollars." Saving and investing is much more interesting when our goals are immediate and personal.

I had a goal a few years back: I wanted to get my pilot's license. I did some research into how much it would cost, then added 25 percent to the budget, and set about putting the money away. At the time, for me, a mutual fund made sense for this money, so I tucked the funds away every month until I reached my goal. Then I signed up with an instructor and learned to fly. I managed to pay for my lessons without dipping into my lesson fund, and left the money alone. Since I'd picked a winner of a fund, the money grew at a rate that surprised even optimistic me, and now I plan to use my lesson money (plus growth) as a down payment on an airplane.

The key to a shorter range goal, such as a big diamond, a small plane, or a long trip, is to have a realistic idea of how much it will cost, then decide on an investment strategy. You can be safe with fixed income investments such as short-term bonds or a CD, or you can hope for a higher return with a riskier outcome. The sooner you need the money, the less risk you can take.

Trivia...

Investing to send your kids to college takes on a different flavor from the goal of retiring. For those of us who had children prior to turning 45, our kids will attend college before we retire. Though I'm encouraging my kids to get top grades and simultaneously excel in sports, I can't count on a scholarship award. More's the pity; I'd much rather spend the money I've set aside for their bachelor's degrees on something frivolous for myself!

A simple summary

✔ Know thyself! What's your total income, how deeply are you in debt, and how much can you put away for your investment goals?

✔ Develop a winning attitude toward your investment strategy. Educate yourself to the point where you believe in what you're doing.

✔ If you are in debt, especially credit card debt, take immediate steps to pay it off and plan to keep future debts to a minimum by working out a realistic budget.

✔ Think hard about your current stage in life and what you want to do with the money you invest. As you set your goals, and the time frame for them to come to fruition, you can put together an asset allocation strategy that balances risk and return.

✔ Make sure that you pay yourself first every month.

PART TWO

LEARN HOW TO READ THE MARKETS EFFECTIVELY

SETTING UP SHOP

A S YOU SET OFF DOWN THE ROAD toward financial freedom, you'll need to sort through the zillions of *web sites* available to find the investments that will work best for you. The Securities and Exchange Commission is looking out for you by requiring that companies disclose pertinent financial details to potential investors.

The Internet is packed with information for investors. I'll show you what you can invest online, how you can *track the investments* you've got, how you can *follow the markets*, and *maximize your portfolio value*.

Chapter 5

Setting Up an Investment Account

THOUGH THE ADVERTISEMENTS blaring at you from your television set, radio, computer monitor, and newspaper may lead you to believe that you can open an account and trade stocks in 2 minutes, in truth it's not that easy. It's not the long laborious proposition it used to be either – you don't have to sit down with a total stranger and reveal your entire financial life. But you'll need to have some basic information on hand before you start to fill out the forms and an idea of what kind of investments you want.

In this chapter...

✓ **The basics**

✓ **Flesh-and-blood or electronic broker?**

✓ **How much financial savvy do you need?**

✓ **Types of investments**

IF YOU ARE TO REALIZE YOUR GOALS, IT PAYS TO DO SOME HOMEWORK BEFORE SETTING UP AN ACCOUNT

The basics

THESE NEXT FEW PARAGRAPHS *may seem so basic to you that you might wonder why I'm mentioning them. Over the course of the last decade, however, as I've taught classes on personal finance and online investing, I've met a surprising number of students who didn't know exactly what is necessary to open an account with a United States-based brokerage. So let's start, as the song from* The Sound of Music *says, at the very beginning.*

Your tax ID (Uncle Sam wants to know what you make)

If you're opening an account as an individual, you'll need your social security number. If you're opening a joint account, either with a spouse or domestic partner, you'll both need your social security numbers handy. Perhaps you're opening an account for your child or another minor – in that case, you'll need the minor's social security number.

If you didn't apply for your child's social security number at birth, you'll need to get an SS-5 form and either mail it or take it in. You can download the form from the Social Security Administration's web site, www.ssa.gov, or call 1-800-772-1213 for more information.

If you're setting up an account for a trust, you'll need to obtain a separate tax ID, since the trust exists as a different legal entity as far as the government is concerned. So what's the deal with the tax ID, anyway? Well, Uncle Sam wants to know about any gains you make from your investments. The brokerage has to report your transactions – and then so do you – on your tax return.

United States citizenship or proof of legal residence

During the application process, you'll be asked whether you're a United States citizen, or a legal resident. United States citizens who are not residents of the United States may not be able to open accounts with some online brokers. This will depend on the way their legal teams interpret United States' securities laws.

Non-United States citizens who do not reside in the United States may not be able to open dollar-based accounts with most United States-based online brokers, but this situation is changing rapidly. Many United States-based brokers have formed alliances with European, Asian, and South American brokerage firms, giving their clients international access to investing. Internationalization is an ongoing process that is improving access to investment vehicles as well as to brokerage accounts.

An address

Now, this item may sound basic, but brokerages don't like to use post office boxes as addresses. They don't mind mailing your statements and documents to a P.O. box, but you'll need a street address to sign up for an account initially. The street address requirement is also tied to taxation: The state you live in determines which state will be the recipient of income taxes on your investments. A P.O. box does not imply legal residence, so the broker will want a street address.

Having something to trade

Once you fill out all the forms, you'll need to fund the account. You can do this by sending in a check for at least the minimum required by the broker, which can range from $100 to $25,000, or by transferring stocks or mutual funds you hold elsewhere into the account. A growing trend for online brokers is an electronic link to your checking account. Once that's established, you can fill out a form online that moves money to your brokerage account. If you mail a check, allow at least 5, and up to 10, working days before you'll have access to your money.

Transferring stocks or other assets from an existing account into your new account is a little tricky. To accomplish this task, you'll have to print out some forms or request them from your new broker. Fill out these forms carefully; a wrong number will set your transfer request back considerably. The forms go from your new broker to your old broker, who then transfers the assets for you. The old broker will probably charge you for the service. It could take a month for the transfer to happen, so don't expect to be trading immediately.

Cash or margin account?

While filling out your new account forms, you'll be asked whether you want to open a margin account. Trading on margin means borrowing money from your broker to buy stocks. The rate of interest offered is usually lower than, say, a loan for a vacation home, but you'll still have the expense of interest payments that will offset your investment gains. What you want to do is make more money from the margin account than it costs you in interest payments. As you borrow more from your broker, typically the rate of interest will drop. With a margin account, you can also borrow against the value of the securities in your account, allowing you to own more assets than you can afford with your current cash balance. But when the market drops and the value of your stocks goes with it, your broker can ask you to pay back all your margin debt, which is known as a margin call. This may force you to sell stock – at a loss – to pay your broker back.

Should you decide to trade on margin, you have to pay attention to your loan balance and the possibility of a margin call. Don't ignore your portfolio, especially when the market is down.

Flesh-and-blood or electronic broker?

ONCE YOU'VE DECIDED to open an online account, you'll have a wide variety of brokers from which to choose. I'll go into detail on several dozen brokers in Chapters 10 and 11, but one consideration as you make your choice is the broker's physical presence. Here's what some of the buzzwords mean that you'll be hearing.

Bricks and mortar

A bricks-and-mortar broker is one with a lot of offices and real live account representatives who like to talk to you on the phone or see you in person. You make a phone call and tell the broker what you want to buy or sell, and the human on the other end of the line does what you ask – and probably tries to talk you into a few other investments as well! Bricks-and-mortar brokers are usually full-service, high-commission operations, though some discount brokerages also qualify in this category as well. Typically you do little or no business with a bricks-and-mortar broker from your own computer. This group is rapidly shrinking as even the full-service brokerages begin to offer online trading to their customers.

Clicks and mortar

This type of broker has both electronic operations and physical offices with brokers you can visit in person. As far as convenience goes, this is the type of broker I prefer. If I get a stock certificate for some reason, I can take it over in person and deposit it into my account rather than mailing – and risk losing – that valuable document. There might be a time when the broker's web site crashes and having a human available is a big help. Typical brokers in this category include Charles Schwab, Fidelity, and TD Waterhouse.

Clicks only

Online-only brokers, such as E*Trade and BUYandHOLD.com, don't have offices you can pop into, but they offer extensive online services as well as trading via Touch-Tone phone. You can set up online cash transfers into and out of your brokerage account, and you never have to talk to a human if you don't want to. An interesting trend lately is that some online-only brokers are trying to establish physical offices, thus moving into the clicks and mortar category from the electronic side.

■ **The type of broker** *you use depends on your preference. You may find it more convenient to choose a broker who can be contacted both electronically and in person.*

How much financial savvy do you need?

FRANKLY, YOU NEED TO BE COMFORTABLE *doing some arithmetic and understanding the calculations you make to be a successful investor. You'll also need to know the basics of how a business is run so you can figure out the components of a company's financial statements and how changes in the economy might affect an individual firm. Being able to read a graph that shows price changes over time or a pie chart illustrating percentages is a useful skill as well. Does this mean you have to have an MBA? Well, no – but it means you ought to acquire some knowledge about the financial world so you can be an effective investor.*

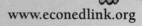

INTERNET

www.econedlink.org

www.federalreserve.gov

Check out the EconEdLink, a program offered by the National Council on Economic Education, for an online guide to economics. And keep an eye on the Federal Reserve by logging onto its web site.

Some basic financial concepts

When it comes to analyzing a company's stock price and its potential for growth, you'll need to understand at least the following terms that apply to individual companies:

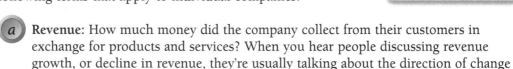

(a) **Revenue:** How much money did the company collect from their customers in exchange for products and services? When you hear people discussing revenue growth, or decline in revenue, they're usually talking about the direction of change in the firm's revenues over time.

(b) **Net Income:** How much does the company have left after it's paid all its expenses, including its tax bill? Often a company that's growing quickly will have higher revenue from one time period to the next, but its expenses might more than make up for it. Watch for companies that trumpet their revenue growth while trying to hide a drop in earnings.

(c) **Earnings Per Share (EPS):** How is the company's income allocated to its stock? EPS is the company's net income divided by the number of shares of stock outstanding. Stock analysts figure the price of a stock is the value investors place on the company's ability to earn a certain amount of money per share. You'll see major swings in the stock price if the EPS is higher – or lower – than expected.

IMPROVING YOUR KNOWLEDGE

If you'd like to learn more about the financial world – and who wouldn't? – there are some web sites where you can read about financial and investing concepts at your own pace.

Site name	Web address	Key feature
InvestSmart	library.thinkquest.org/ 10326/index.html	Describes itself as a site for high school students to learn about the stock market, but it's a good introduction to novice investors of any age. The market simulation is a great spot to test your knowledge.
National Discount Brokers University	www.ndb.com (click on the NDB University icon in the border)	Has 24 clearly written lessons about everything from budgeting to investing to estate planning.
Investopedia	www.investopedia.com	Has a financial dictionary, articles about investing, and financial topics that are updated several times a week, plus a series of lessons focused on investing.

d) **Price to Earnings Ratio (P/E):** How is the company's income compared to its stock price? This is one of the most often quoted figures you'll hear when a particular stock is discussed. To calculate the P/E Ratio, you divide the current stock price by the company's most recent annual earnings per share figure.

e) **Market Capitalization:** How much do investors say this company is worth? Multiply the number of shares of stock outstanding by the current price of the stock to arrive at this figure. For example, if a company has 1,000,000 shares of stock and the current price is $20, then that company has a market capitalization (usually called market cap) of $20,000,000. You'll hear companies categorized as large cap or small cap; which is a reference to the market capitalization.

Volatility: How much does this company's stock price fluctuate compared to the overall market? This figure is usually called a stock's beta, and the calculation itself is relatively complicated. A beta of 1 means the stock's price moves exactly with the overall market. A lower figure, say 0.8, means the stock is more stable, fluctuating 20 percent less than the market as a whole. You'll see a lower beta with certain industries such as utility companies. A higher beta, say 1.4, means the stock price fluctuates 40 percent more than the market, which happens with many technology stocks.

That wasn't so bad, was it? Now we'll move on to topics that describe the entire economy.

Who is Alan Greenspan and why should you care?

Factors outside of an individual company's ability to make money affect its stock price. One major influence on the stock market is the Federal Reserve Bank, which is the central bank, created in 1913, of the United States.

It's made up of 12 regional banks, and its seven-member Board of Directors, of which Alan Greenspan is currently the chair, sets interest rates and makes a variety of decisions that affect monetary policy. Every time the Federal Reserve Board, usually just called the Fed, meets, the stock market shudders a bit trying to anticipate whether interest rates will go up or down.

Types of investments

ONLINE BROKERS HAVE OPENED *the way to invest in many kinds of assets from the privacy of your personal computer. You'll find brokers who specialize in a particular type of asset, for instance bonds or futures, but most let you trade stocks and mutual funds.*

Stocks: Own a piece of a company

A share of stock is, in essence, a piece of a corporation. When a company incorporates, it's technically a separate legal entity. Part of the incorporation process is issuing stock. One person can hold all of the stock, or shares can be sold to many people. Let's say a new company issues 1,000 shares of stock, and two people each own 500 shares. That gives those two people a 50 percent interest in the company. When the company is profitable, the stockholders can receive dividends based on how much of the company they own.

■ **Stocks are among** *the various assets traded by brokers. There are two types of stock that you can buy, common and preferred, and each has different benefits for the investor.*

Larger companies can have billions of shares of stock outstanding. When they go public, or start trading their stock on one of the exchanges, anyone with the money can buy a piece of the company. When you buy stock in a company, you share in its profits and losses.

There are two types of stock a company can issue: Common stock and preferred stock. Common stock, which means you own a piece of the company "in common" with other shareholders, is the most prevalent type of stock. When a company makes money or outgrows its competition, common stockholders benefit as the stock price goes up (capital appreciation) and when the company issues dividends.

The second type of stock, preferred stock, usually pays higher dividends than common stock but doesn't give the stockholder ownership rights in the company. Generally, the price of preferred stock is more stable, and should the company go bankrupt or out of business, preferred stockholders will be paid back before common stockholders. Investors usually buy preferred stock because of the dividends. Some preferred stock can be converted to common stock, either at the stockholder's request or when directed by the corporation's board of directors.

Mutual funds: Own a fraction of a bunch of companies

Mutual funds pool money from a large number of investors, then professional managers put together a portfolio of assets with the intention of outperforming the market. One advantage of investing in mutual funds is that you are automatically diversified even if you don't have a huge amount of money. There are thousands of mutual funds to choose from, each with its own particular focus. For instance, you could invest in a fund that buys only stocks in European companies, or tax-free bonds, or high-tech startups. You can buy into a high-risk fund with potentially high returns, or a lower risk fund with lower returns. Some funds are designed to track a market index, such as the S&P 500 or the Dow Jones Industrial Average.

It's important to research mutual funds carefully, and to take a look at the fees and maintenance charges you'll pay. Those fees will chip away at your investment gains.

Options: Which way do you think the market will go?

When you buy an option, you're buying the right to buy or sell a specific number of shares of a stock at a specific price on a specific date. Sounds complicated, right? Well, frankly, it is. Options trading is not for the timid! Your potential gains are high, though, if you consistently pick winners. Here's a short primer on how it works.

INTERNET

moneycentral.msn.com/
investor/finder/
predefstocks.asp

moneycentral.msn.com/
investor/finder/
welcome.asp

Learn how to screen for stocks by first checking out pre-defined filters. And check out the stock-filtering program at MSN Money Central to find companies with particular characteristics, such as industry and market cap, to see the range of performance results. You can filter by price/earnings ratio or by earnings growth too.

INTERNET

screen.morningstar.com
/FundSelector.html

This site at Morningstar (www.morningstar.com) has a terrific mutual fund screening tool, which rates mutual funds by performance. By playing around with this tool, you'll learn all the ways a mutual fund can be evaluated, and maybe find a few that are worth your investment.

There are two basic options strategies: Calls and puts. When you buy a call, you have the right to purchase the stock you've chosen at a fixed price before the option period expires. For instance, let's say the stock of XYZ Company is currently trading at $50, and you think it will go up in the next few months. You might buy the right to purchase 100 shares of XYZ at $65 (strike price) in 90 days, and pay $5 per share for that option. You can trade the option itself up to the date it expires; the price of the option will fluctuate depending on the price of the underlying stock as well as the volatility of the movement of the stock price. The option price also depends on the time remaining before the option expires, the rate and timing of dividends paid by the company, and the strike price. What if the stock price doesn't go up? You lose what you paid for the call. If it does go up, let's say to $80 per share, you have the right to buy the stock for $65 and sell it at $80, so you immediately gain $15 per share.

> ## Trivia...
> Options trading began in 1973 when the Chicago Board of Options opened. That year, one million options contracts were traded. Nowadays over one million options contracts change hands daily.

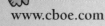

> ### INTERNET
> **www.cboe.com**
>
> Most options trading in the United States takes place on the Chicago Board Options Exchange, or CBOE. The CBOE's web site includes an education section that explains how options work as a part of an investment strategy.

Puts are the flip side of calls. When you buy a put, you're subscribing to the notion that the stock's price will fall between now and the time the option expires. If the stock price goes up rather than down, you lose what you paid for the option. But if the price per share drops below the strike price you've specified, you can trade the option itself for more than you paid for it. You can also sell the stock at your strike price and buy it back at the current price. For instance, if you buy a put option for XYZ at $60, and the stock price drops to $50 on the expiration date, you can exercise the contract and make $10 per share.

Investors use options to hedge their bets on stocks that they've purchased, which are called covered options, or on stocks that they don't currently own, which are called naked options.

Whew! I could fill a book just with options trading strategies, which can range from conservative to wildly speculative.

Bonds: You're the banker

When you buy a bond, you're loaning money to the seller in exchange for a fixed rate of interest over the life of the bond. At the end of the period, you get your initial investment (principal) back, plus you get interest payments every 6 months.

Corporations and government entities sell bonds. Bonds are safer investments than stocks, with fixed rates of return and payback of your principal, and they can also be traded before their due date. Most asset allocation models recommend a higher percentage of bonds in your portfolio as your retirement date approaches, mainly to preserve your capital while still getting some kind of return on your investment.

An investment strategy that provides regular income is a bond ladder. Let's say you have $1,000,000 to invest in bonds. When you build a ladder, you spread that money out over ten different bonds that expire 6 months to a year apart.

If you build the ladder carefully, you can time the interest payments so that you receive income every month. As the bonds expire, you get your principal back, and then buy another bond with an expiration date beyond the last one in your portfolio. Some brokers, such as E*Trade and Schwab, have ladder building programs that help you select from available bonds at the time you're in the market.

INTERNET

www.bondagent.com

BondAgent is offering Bond University (click on Learning Center on the home page). The Bond Terminology Glossary is an A to Z list of words you'll hear bandied about as you explore investing in bonds further.

Annuities: Invest now, collect later

Annuities, traditionally sold by life insurance companies but now extending to some online brokerages as well, let you put aside money and hang onto the earnings, tax-deferred, until you start making withdrawals on or after age $59\frac{1}{2}$. You can also roll over a lump sum payment from your retirement plan into an annuity if you leave your employer. There are a variety of options both for funding and for receiving income from annuities. You can make one single lump sum deposit, or make regular deposits over time.

INTERNET

www.annuity.com

Check out a range of annuities and annuity calculators at this site, which brings together quotes and information about annuities offered by several dozen insurance companies.

Rates of return on annuities are somewhere in the range of high-investment quality bonds (which have lower interest rates than riskier bonds), so they're not high-flying investments, but they can grow tax-free.

Futures and commodities

Futures markets are essentially ongoing auctions of products that are called commodities. A commodity is typically an agricultural product, such as wheat, in which one lot pretty much looks like another and is difficult to differentiate. The futures markets were created to level out the usual boom and glut cycle inherent in agricultural products, and now include trading of metals, petroleum, foreign currencies, and stock indexes as well.

There are two types of futures contracts, one in which the item being traded will be physically delivered at a future date; and one in which a cash payment is made without delivery. Someone who expects the price of a commodity to increase would buy futures contracts, hoping to be able to sell them later at a profit. This is called going long. A trader who expects prices to decline would go short, or sell contracts, hoping to buy them back at a lower price. The month in which delivery or settlement is expected is specified in the contract.

INTERNET

www.orionfutures.com/
fut101.htm

Futures broker Orion Futures Group offers Futures 101, an online course in understanding futures and commodity trading.

A growing number of online brokers are offering futures trading, but most of the online activity in this area is happening with specialized brokers.

A simple summary

✔ To open an investment account, you'll need to furnish your tax ID and your physical address. Proof of citizenship or legal residence may also be required.

✔ Effective investing requires a basic knowledge of financial concepts, such as revenue, price to earnings ratio, and market capitalization, and a willingness to keep learning as your skills improve.

✔ Online brokers give you access to stocks, mutual funds, options, bonds, annuities and futures, though most brokers specialize in just a few of these different types of investments.

Chapter 6

Setting Up Your Analytical Tools

B Y NOW, YOU'VE FIGURED OUT your budget and how much you'll be able to set aside every month for your investments. It's time to get comfortable with the stock markets and with reading about financial trends. We'll start with watching the economy as a whole and drill down to analyzing individual firms.

In this chapter...

✓ Watching the market

✓ Why the past matters

✓ Researching a company's financial health

✓ Following the professionals

TIME SPENT ANALYZING MARKETS, TRENDS, AND COMPANIES IS AN INVESTMENT IN ITSELF

Watching the market

YOU HEAR IT EVERY DAY ON THE NEWS, "The Dow was up today," or "The NASDAQ continues to fluctuate." And when you buy or sell a stock, typically the trade takes place in one of the stock exchanges that acts as a clearing house, gathering buyers and sellers in one place. What are these averages and exchanges and what do they mean to you and your portfolio?

The New York Stock Exchange (NYSE)

The New York Stock Exchange was founded in 1792 as the New York Stock and Exchange Board, 25 years after the signing of the Buttonwood Agreement, which is considered the basis for the stock market. The Buttonwood Agreement was the basis for paying a broker a commission for enabling the trading of securities. The Bank of New York was the first company to have its stock listed, or made available to exchange, on the NYSE. For a company to be listed on the NYSE, it has to meet a series of requirements, such as number of stockholders (at least 2,000), market value of the company ($100 million in most cases), and pre-tax earnings of at least $2,500,000. The company has to be capable of turning a profit before it can be listed on the NYSE, which is why you see so many brand-new companies, which are still running at a loss, getting listed on other exchanges.

Listed companies can trade stocks, bonds, and warrants on the NYSE. Different stocks are traded in different areas of the exchange, and though much of it is automated so that a computer is matching up the bids from buyers to the offers from sellers, there are still people who go to the floor and shout out their orders.

The American Stock Exchange (Amex)

The Amex was officially formed in 1921, just in time to participate in the great upswing of the market in the 1920s – and in the crash of 1929. The Amex existed in a less formal format prior to 1921 but counts its birthday from the time it moved indoors, so traders no longer conducted their business under the trees.

Smaller companies than those listed on the NYSE can get their stock listed on the Amex, and even companies that haven't yet posted earnings can join Amex. The initial stock price has to be at least $3 a share. Trading takes place through specialists, who are in charge of dealing with exchanges of a particular company's stock.

Amex members have a wide variety of tradable equities available. They can trade equity options as well as stocks, bonds, and warrants, and they can trade other securities such as holding company depository receipts (HOLDRS) and equity hybrid securities. The Amex also lets investors trade in index shares such as the NASDAQ 100 Index Tracking Stock. Also located in New York City, the Amex is a short walk from the NYSE.

HOLDRS represent ownership in the common stock of a group of specified companies that are in a particular industry. Equity hybrid securities are a cross between a stock and a bond and have characteristics of both. Each hybrid is a partially paid-in capital, similar to a stock, and a loan to the company, similar to a bond. There are HOLDRS available in 14 industries, from biotech to wireless, that are traded on the Amex.

A HOLDR is not quite the same as a mutual fund because the list of stocks and ratio of shares in the HOLDR owned remain the same. The price fluctuates as the price of the stocks in the HOLDR change.

The NASD Automated Quotation (NASDAQ)

The National Association of Securities Dealers (NASD) opened the NASDAQ in 1971, and though it's the youngest of the major stock exchanges, its volume is greater than the NYSE and the Amex. The NASDAQ and Amex merged in 1998, but they still maintain separate operations. Unlike the NYSE and the Amex, trading on NASDAQ is almost completely automated, so there aren't any specialists yelling and screaming on the market floor. Only equity shares are traded on the NASDAQ

Very small companies and start-ups can be listed on the NASDAQ, which is why so many Internet "dotcom" stocks are traded there. When a company makes its initial public offering on the NASDAQ, the price of each share must be at least $1, and it's not required to have turned a profit yet. There are a number of large companies that qualify for the other exchanges but stay on the NASDAQ because of the way trades are automated.

INTERNET

www.amex.com

www.nasdaq.com

www.nyse.com

Learn more about these exchanges and their histories at their informative web sites. These sites also include valuable investor information, such as the risks of trading in fast-moving markets.

Other exchanges

As mentioned in Chapter 5, most options are traded on the Chicago Board Options Exchange (CBOE). Its web site, at www.cboe.com, explains how investors can use options as insurance against major swings in a stock's price. The CBOE was formed in 1973 to reduce the chaos that previously characterized the options trading market. It started small, with options on just 16 companies available, but it now has not only corporate options but also interest rate options and index options.

■ **Check out** *the International Federation of Stock Exchanges web site. It's an ideal place to learn about international exchanges and how they compare to our (relatively) familiar US markets.*

For investors who want to trade in stocks in very small companies, or stocks that are priced at under $1 a share, the Over the Counter Bulletin Board (OTCBB) is the place to go. The OTCBB opened on a pilot basis in 1990, was formalized in 1997, and doesn't have listing standards for companies traded. It cooperates with the NASDAQ to provide quotes and to execute trades but operates separately. Check it out at www.otcbb.com.

The International Federation of Stock Exchanges (FIBV) maintains a web site (www.fibv.com) with information about its member exchanges. A summary of each exchange's requirements, in Excel spreadsheet format, can be viewed at www.fibv.com/stats/infobour.xls.

Why the past matters

MOST PEOPLE FIND GRAPHS AND CHARTS easier to interpret than a block of numbers. A favorite tool for investors and other crystal ball gazers is historical price charts. These charts can be arranged to show closing prices of the stocks you're studying by day, week, or month. You can also take a look at how the price of a stock changes throughout the trading day.

Historical price charts are presented in many formats. You enter the equity's ticker symbol, then customize the chart to display the period you want to study. Most charting sites also let you compare an equity's performance to an index, industry average, or another individual equity.

Long-range charts (monthly, yearly)

If you're considering an investment over the long term, you'd be wise to see how it performed over at least a 5-year period. A stock you're thinking of holding for 2 or 3 years is worth studying for a similar historical period, mainly to see if you can find seasonal variations in the price so you can time your purchase.

For instance, many retail companies have an upswing in sales in December, due to holiday gift buying, then a drop in January and February. The market reacts to the relative strength of the company's sales compared to past years. If a retailer has a particularly good December, its stock price will

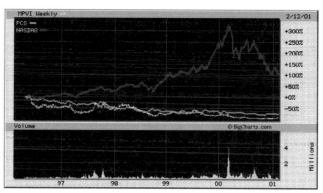

■ **Long-range charts** *enable you to check out how a stock has fared over the past 5 years. You can also compare the stock with various markets, such as the NASDAQ, shown here.*

go up. Then when the post-holiday slump hits, the stock price might drop off a bit. It might be a few months before the stock price of the company comes back to its December levels. You'll see seasonal swings in many stock prices if you take a look at the price performance on a monthly basis over a 3- to 10-year period.

Avoid buying a stock during its seasonal peak but pick up a few shares when it tends to be low.

Short range (weekly, daily)

Weekly and daily price charts give you a clear picture of how volatile a stock price can be. You can get a clear picture of seasonal changes in a stock price, or how investors have reacted to news about a company's earnings, dividend announcements, etc. You can't fit as long a time period on a short-range chart though, so typically you'll see, at most, 2 years' data on a weekly or daily chart. If you try to jam much more on, it will look pretty squished and be difficult to read.

Intra-day charts, tick-by-tick

To stay on top of the minute-by-minute changes in a stock price, you can view charts that show how the price changes from one trade to the next. These are called intra-day charts, and they'll show what's going on with a stock that you're getting ready to buy or sell. Several sites now offer real-time intra-day charts, so you can see what's happening as it happens, though the sites that display constantly updating, or streaming, charts usually charge a monthly subscription fee. At the free sites, you'll have to click on your browser's Refresh button to get the latest prices, which is slightly inconvenient – but cheap!

WEB SITES THAT OFFER CHARTS

Web address	Key feature
www.bigcharts.com	Offers price history of up to 30 years on many stocks.
finance.yahoo.com	Yahoo! Finance offers real-time tick-by-tick charts free of charge.
moneycentral.msn.com/investor/charts/charting.asp	Microsoft's Money Central Investor provides daily and weekly charts that include symbols that clue you in to when a company has posted a dividend or earnings announcement.
www.prophetfinance.com	Offers price history of up to 30 years on many stocks.
www.windowonwallstreet.com	Window on Wall Street (WoW) is a subscription service that brings together a huge historical data set plus technical analysis and interactive charting, along with streaming quotes and portfolio analysis.

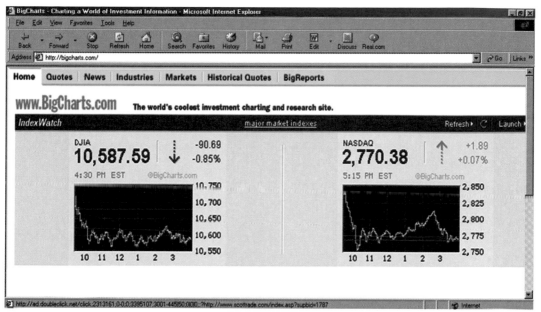

■ **Real-time intra-day charts** *enable you to chart the ups and downs of stock prices as they change between trades, so that you know exactly what's happening as you prepare to buy or sell.*

One service offered by many online brokers is a streaming real-time ticker that you can customize to display the latest prices of a group of stocks you want to watch. If you keep your online broker's site up in one window on your computer all day, the streaming ticker is a great tool to use.

Trends and forecasts

The main reason we study the past is to get a clue about the future. Armed with knowledge of how the price of an equity has behaved in the past, we'll want to make an educated forecast of what will happen to it as the march of time progresses. Forecasting is a combination of science and art, and even the best crystal ball gazers are happy to have half of their prognostications hit the mark.

Most charting sites, including BigCharts (www.bigcharts.com) and ClearStation (www.clearstation.com), give you the option of generating *moving averages*.

Moving averages are a good introduction to trend analysis, though they're just one tool in a very rich set. I'll go into more detail about technical analysis techniques and forecasting in Chapter 16.

DEFINITION

A moving average is a useful tool for showing general price trends over a period of time, smoothing out the highs and lows. You can calculate a moving average for a particular period of time, say 15 days, by adding up closing prices for the previous 15 days and then dividing by 15.

If you do that for a long series, say a couple of years' worth of data, you can get a picture of price trends. An exponential moving average gives additional weight to the more recent data. Many web sites let you choose the number of days to include in a moving average calculation.

Researching a company's financial health

COMPANIES THAT OFFER THEIR STOCKS *to the public are required to provide an enormous amount of financial information, which is a mixed blessing. You'll have a lot of reading to do if you decide to pore over the company's annual report.*

Annual reports are required by law, and include financial statements and an auditor's report, along with a detailed description of the company's operations and comments on what they plan to do in the upcoming year. The Securities and Exchange Commission (SEC) requires companies to file a variety of additional reports throughout the year, such as the 10-K, which contain even more detailed financial information than many annual reports. The financial web sites we use for analyzing corporations take the data from annual reports and 10-Ks and enter them in a database, allowing investors to compare companies and analyze their performances relative to the industry as a whole.

So what's in an annual report? Companies are required to publish, in this order:

1. A summary of the previous year's highs and lows (with an emphasis on the former).

2. Information about the company in general, including its history, products, and line of business.

3. A letter to shareholders from the President or CEO.

4. An in-depth discussion about the financial results and other factors within the business.

5. The complete set of financial statements (balance sheet, income statement, statement of retained earnings, and cash flow statement), including explanatory notes, which are often more revealing than the statements themselves.

6. Auditor's report assuring the accuracy of the results.

7. Other information on the company's management, officers, offices, new locations, and anything else the company decides to share with its stockholders.

So what do all these financial statements mean? And how are they dissected to provide worthwhile information for investors?

Financial statement primer

The profit and loss statement (P&L), also known as the income statement, is the report most investors focus on. Publicly traded companies have to publish a P&L every quarter and at the end of every fiscal year. There are three sections to a P&L:

(1) Revenues, which state where the company made its money.

(2) Expenses, which describe how much the company spent to support its money-making activities.

(3) Earnings, before and after taxes.

This last section, earnings, is often called the bottom line, and many investors focus their attention on that figure and how it's changed since the previous statement.

PROFIT AND LOSS ACCOUNT

	CURRENT PERIOD	PREVIOUS PERIOD
Sales	2,200	2,050
Cost of sales	1,700	1,600
GROSS PROFIT	500	450
OPERATING EXPENSES		
Office supplies	46	42
Bad debt charges	24	20
Rent	15	14
Salaries and wages	245	194
Sales and marketing	30	22
Delivery	20	18
Heat, light and power	12	11
Depreciation	45	35
TOTAL OPERATING EXPENSES	437	356
OPERATING PROFIT	63	94
Interest payable	20	15
Exceptional costs	10	0
PROFIT BEFORE TAX	33	79
Taxation	7	16
PROFIT AFTER TAX	26	63
Dividends	12	10
RETAINED PROFIT	14	53

■ **The profit and loss statement** *records the difference between revenue and expenses for the period it covers, revealing how well a company has performed.*

Examining the components of revenue and breakdown of expenses is a good exercise, and can explain a lot about shifts in a corporation's strategic direction.

An often overlooked financial statement is the balance sheet, which is a snapshot of what a company owns and owes at a particular point in time. There are also three sections to this report:

1. Assets, which include cash, money owed to the company by its customers (accounts receivable), investments, buildings, and equipment, along with prepaid expenses.

2. Liabilities, such as loans and bills that have not yet been paid (accounts payable).

3. Shareholder's funds, which includes the book value of the company's stock, plus any earnings the company has reinvested in staying in business.

The reason this statement is called a balance sheet is that assets are equal to the sum of liabilities and shareholders' funds. It's possible for equity to be a negative number if a company's liabilities are larger than its assets. That can happen when a company is starting up, changing direction, or simply having a lot of trouble staying afloat.

A careful reading of the balance sheet will show the potential investor whether this company has enough cash to stay in business. It might have a fantastic looking P&L due to increasing sales but be so far in debt that it might not be in business much longer.

The statement of cash flow is another requirement. Though the numbers on the cash flow statement usually appear on the P&L and balance sheet, they're arranged to show you just how much cash the company has generated for a specific period of time, usually a quarter or a year. An influx of cash is displayed as a positive number, while an outflow is a negative number. As with the other two required statements, there are three sections:

1. Cash flows from operating activities or the day-to-day business of a company. Many of the figures in this portion of the cash flow statement can be traced to the P&L.

2. Cash flows from investment activities such as interest on savings accounts or purchases of stock in other companies.

3. Cash flows from financing activities such as a stock offering.

■ **The balance sheet** *shows everything that a business owns (its assets) and all that it owes (its liabilities), providing a picture of a company's performance at the precise moment it is drawn up.*

BALANCE SHEET

	CURRENT PERIOD	PREVIOUS PERIOD
FIXED ASSETS		
Tangible	170	150
Intangible	10	10
Investments	5	5
TOTAL FIXED ASSETS	185	165
CURRENT ASSETS		
Inventory	208	185
Debtors	337	254
Other	18	16
Cash	2	10
TOTAL CURRENT ASSETS	565	465
CURRENT LIABILITIES		
Creditors	80	109
Accrued expenses	20	18
Dividends payable	12	10
Taxation	7	16
Overdraft	60	0
TOTAL CURRENT LIABILITIES	179	153
LONG-TERM LIABILITIES		
Bank loan	15	30
Mortgage	25	30
	40	60
TOTAL ASSETS LESS LIABILITIES	531	417
Shareholders' funds		
Share capital	220	120
Retained profit	301	287
Other reserves	10	10
TOTAL SHAREHOLDERS' FUNDS	531	417

CASH FLOW STATEMENT

Operating profit
Depreciation
Increase in inventory
Increase in debtors
Increase in creditors
OPERATING CASH FLOW

Interest paid

Dividends paid

Exceptional costs

Taxation

Capital expenditure

CASH FLOW BEFORE FINANCING

FINANCING
Increase in overdraft   – 15
Decrease in bank loan   – 5
Decrease in mortgage   100
Issue of share capital   140

                                       ‾‾‾‾ – 8 ‾‾‾‾

MOVEMENT IN CASH

■ **The cash flow statement** *provides a good indication of how well cash, the lifeblood of any company, is being managed.*

Insider trading

Companies are required to report quite a bit of their internal workings, such as who owns large blocks of stock, to the SEC. Anyone classified as an insider, such as a member of the board of directors or a top-level officer, must tell the SEC how much stock he or she owns and must disclose any purchases or sales of stock. By reading up on the way insiders feel about their own company, you can often gauge whether the stock is a good idea for you as an investment.

Let's say you're analyzing a company that looks pretty good on the P&L, but it has some huge debts on its balance sheet. Then when you take a look at insider behavior, and see that half of the board of directors has sold large chunks of stock in the last few months, you might realize that this company is headed for a fall.

Insiders have to file a form with the SEC whenever they buy or sell stock in their own companies. There used to be a fairly large time lag between the time a stock transaction took place and when it was disclosed, but that's shrunk to a matter of days now. Web sites that allow investors to look at insider transactions bring this information to the public rapidly and in easy-to-read formats. It wasn't so long ago that I used to have to extract months-old data from microfiche (remember microfiche, anyone?), so the easy availability of insider trading statements both thrills and depresses me. The SEC's electronic data gathering, analysis, and retrieval system (EDGAR) automates the collection, validation, indexing, acceptance, and forwarding of submissions by companies and others who are required by law to file forms, and this data is available online shortly after it's filed. There are hundreds of these forms filed daily, so having a few web sites handy that help you search and sort the data is a must in any investor's toolkit.

Who else has invested?

The odds that you'll be one of the bigger shareholders in a particular company are rather small. But you can find a list of the major owners of a stock. Find out who else is in the pool before you jump in, and stay informed while you hold the stock, too. If big shareholders are continuing to buy, then the odds are good that they expect the stock price to continue to go up. If you see them bailing out, it might be a good idea to pass on your investment for a while.

Mutual fund managers don't buy small stakes in the companies they've chosen. They tend to swallow up huge chunks of stock so they can be involved more intimately than those of us who buy stock in smaller increments.

If you invest in mutual funds, it's worthwhile knowing whether one of the funds that you hold also has a stake in an individual stock you're considering. For example, let's say you own $50,000 worth of a particular fund and you find that

INTERNET

www.lionshares.com

How can you find out who else owns a chunk of the company? Head on over to LionShares and check out its Institutional Ownership Reports. You can see the top stockholders in a company and find out how much of the company they own. The tables also show how much of the institution's portfolio is tied up in this particular stock, and whether it has bought or sold recently.

WEB SITES THAT OFFER INSIDER DATA

Site name	Web address	Key feature
SEC	www.sec.gov/edgarhp.htm	Posts the forms it receives from insiders quickly, but the format leaves much to be desired.
EDGAR	www.edgar-online.com	Offers nicely formatted reports and online alerts, but some require a fee. Has easy-to-search free access to annual and quarterly reports.
FreeEDGAR	www.freeedgar.com	Type in a stock ticker symbol, then select from the list of reports, including interesting information like salaries for top officers.
InsiderScores	www.insiderscores.com	Ranks the behavior of insiders to let you know which ones are worth following. For companies with over $50 million in market capitalization, the site evaluates how effective a particular insider is with regard to the timing of his or her trades. Using the scores calculated by insiderscores.com, you can decide which insiders are worth following.

5 percent of the value of its holdings are in XYZ Company. If you're considering buying shares in XYZ, you should know that you already indirectly own $2,500 worth.

Investor sentiment

In theory, a stock's price at any given point in time is a reflection of how investors feel about the company. If a company is producing solid returns, investors are usually buying shares, and the stock price goes up. Conversely, if they perceive weakness, their sentiment drops, and they may sell their shares off, causing the stock price to decline. Any out-of-the-ordinary occurrence, such as a management buy-out, death of a key board member, or a change in corporate structure, can alter investor sentiment, causing the stock price to leap or drop in response.

Are you interested in investor sentiment for the market as a whole? Check out LowRisk's (www.lowrisk.com/sentiment.htm) investor sentiment table, which shows, week by week, what visitors to the site think of the current market. You can be part of the calculation by playing their Guess the Dow contest every week.

One way to measure investor sentiment is to calculate whether more money is going into buying a particular stock, or if the money is flowing away from that company. One interesting technical analysis indicator is the Chaikin money flow oscillator. The underlying calculation is based on the closing price of a stock relative to the prior day's close, and the number of shares traded that day (by volume).

If the number calculated is positive, that's a signal that investors are paying higher prices for the stock over the previous period, which is a sign that the price is expected to continue to rise. If it's negative, then the opposite is true and it's a sign that the price is expected to decline.

See how it works at StockCharts (www.stockcharts.com) by adding a Chaikin money flow indicator to a graph. You'll find it in the drop-down box in the Indicator Windows section, below the displayed graph.

Following the professionals

THERE ARE THOUSANDS OF PEOPLE *who actually get paid to study certain sectors of the market, and pass on their wisdom to the collected masses (that's us). These professionals often work for investment banks or financial publications, and many investment web sites summarize their recommendations, which are usually reported on a five-point scale: Strong buy (one point), buy, hold, sell, or strong sell (five points). Standard and Poor's, a well-respected group of financial analysts, uses a five-star system: buy (five stars), accumulate, hold, avoid, and sell (one star). When you see tables comparing stock recommendations, don't let the difference in the scales confuse you!*

Who are the analysts and why do they matter?

Since analysts are usually much closer to the company than you are, they're probably privy to some internal gossip that you'll never hear. Dozens of companies send me detailed press releases about their operations, mergers, and new products in the

■ **Video conference calls** *between analysts and company executives provide a good opportunity to eavesdrop – some web sites allow you to dial in and join the call, or simply listen in to pick up tips.*

mistaken belief that I write articles analyzing individual businesses for *Barron's*, so I often see the sort of information they disclose to analysts. There's a lot they say that doesn't make it out to the rest of the world!

You can access much of the information sent to analysts on the Web. For press releases, either keep an eye on each individual company's web site, or search through Business Wire (www.bizwire.com) for up-to-the-minute postings.

Analysts are often invited to join conference calls with company executives, and recently several Web sites have allowed individual investors to be part of the fun. Bestcalls (www.bestcalls.com) lets you set up a list of stocks, then notifies you of upcoming conference calls. You can dial in to join the call using the information provided on the site, or just hook up your speakers and listen in over the Web. You can even search through the archives for recordings of past calls.

INTERNET

www.briefing.com

www.multex.multex investor.com/

Briefing.com brings together analyst ratings from a huge list of sources so you can see the consensus view of a particular company. It updates its list three times a day. The Multex Investor provides "The Analyst Corner" in which analysts discuss their most recent ratings and give individual investors a chance to ask questions. Find out why they praise or trash a particular stock.

Upgrades and downgrades

Every day, analysts revise their opinions of companies they're tracking. These opinion shifts can provide you with important information about a company's direction. For instance, if Standard and Poor's drops a company's rating from Buy to Hold, you'll want to find out why and take a look at that stock's position in your portfolio.

Calibrating and ranking analysts

With the thousands of analysts out there, who should you believe? Which publications, authors, analysts, and columnists do the best job of recommending stocks that increase in value? Keep in mind that sometimes a recommendation from a top analyst can be a self-fulfilling prophecy, but not all analysts attract such a powerful following. You also want to avoid pump-and-dump schemes in which a purported analyst writes a strong recommendation for a stock, hoping it'll make a short-term jump in value so he or she can cash out quickly. Check up on the analysts at Validea (www.validea.com), which ranks them from top (five light bulbs) to bottom (one light bulb). You can look at the top journalists, magazines, online sites, and television commentators, or search through the company list to find the most talked-about stocks. Before you follow an analyst, check out how often that analyst's predictions come true.

A simple summary

✓ Most stock transactions take place on one of the stock exchanges, which exist to provide an efficient way for buyers and sellers to get together.

✓ Different exchanges have varying requirements for companies that want to be listed, and they process the transactions in different ways.

✓ Stock price charts give you a visual summary of how a particular equity has performed.

✓ On the Web, you can define an amazing number of parameters for your charts, pinpointing just the type of analysis you want.

✓ Publicly traded companies are required to divulge quite a bit of information. The forms they use, designed by government committees, are difficult to read and interpret, but there are numerous web sites that will come to your rescue. You can read the raw reports or subscribe to a web site that lets you search a database and find out just what you want.

✓ Find out who else is interested in the company by checking out insider trading, institutional holdings, and investor sentiment.

✓ Stock analysts and pundits can give you additional insight into a company's prospects and its suitability for your portfolio. Be sure to check up on whether the analyst's record is any good.

Chapter 7

Setting Up Your Own News Agency

EVEN AS RECENTLY AS THE EARLY 1990S, investors had limited ways of getting news about the equities they were holding, let alone the equities they were considering. Thanks to the Internet, investors can log on and develop their own virtual newsrooms, staying on top of current pricing and breaking stories. As I type this, there's a stock ticker streaming across my screen, giving me current prices for my watch list. Going in-depth for current news or placing a trade is just a click away. Here's how you can track what's happening right now with your portfolio and watch list.

In this chapter...

✓ Current prices: The stock ticker

✓ Company news

✓ Ongoing research

THE GOOD NEWS IS THAT YOU CAN KEEP ABREAST OF FINANCIAL GOINGS-ON AS THEY HAPPEN

Current prices: The ticker

WE TALKED A LITTLE BIT about current stock prices and real-time quotes in Chapter 6, but now I'll go into the subject more deeply.

Finding a ticker symbol

In the olden days (the 1980s), when you perused the newspaper in search of the previous day's price information, you saw the company names in impossibly tiny print, abbreviated, and missing many of their vowels. Online, you're prompted for a ticker symbol, which consists of one to five letters that sometimes appear to bear no relation whatsoever to the company's name.

Occasionally ticker symbols are used as a marketing device – for instance, YUM is the symbol for Tricon Global Restaurants, a spin-off of PepsiCo, which owns Taco Bell, Pizza Hut, and Kentucky Fried Chicken. It's considered remarkably cool to have a one-letter ticker symbol. AT&T is simply T, Agilent Technologies snagged the letter A when it spun off from Hewlett-Packard in 1998, and Venator, formerly Woolworth, is known as Z.

Locating a ticker symbol used to involve having a stock market guidebook in your possession, which was usually out of date by the time you received it thanks to new stock issues, consolidations, and other market moves. Now you can look up a symbol online from databases that are kept up to date. The quote services we'll talk about below have ways of searching for ticker symbols by company name. If you're looking for a mutual fund ticker symbol, type in the name of the company that manages the fund (such as Fidelity or Vanguard), then scroll through the list until you locate the fund in which you're interested.

In general, stocks that trade on the NYSE have one- to three-letter symbols, while Amex stocks have two- to three-letter symbols. NASDAQ stocks have four- to five-letter symbols, and OTCBB stocks have five-letter symbols. If you're looking outside the United States, foreign exchanges carry a prefix or suffix, depending on the exchange. For instance, the company with ticker symbol A in Canada would have the symbol C:A.

You'll find that your favorite ticker symbols will stick in your memory, so you won't have to look them up all the time. Or you can add the symbols to a quote list, as I'll discuss below, giving you quick access to a collection of symbols.

Trivia...

Symbols were first created in 1844 by telegraph operators trying to transmit prices rapidly, but now you see them scrolling across your television screen or a monitor at the airport. They're called ticker symbols because for many years prices were reported on a ticker tape – a long, thin piece of paper that scrolled out of a clacking machine in a stockbroker's office.

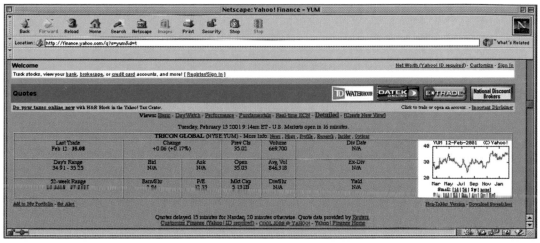

■ **Ticker symbols** *can be located using online databases that are regularly updated. Generally, you type in the company name, and the database will search out the corresponding symbol.*

The ticker tape indicates the number of shares traded at a particular price. For example, XYZ 500 54-½ would be translated as 500 shares of XYZ traded at 54, down ½ a point from the previous trade. If the report was XYZ 1K 54 ¼-¼ then the trade was 1,000 shares at 54-¼, down ¼ point. K is the usual suffix for thousands of shares.

Stocks that trade on the NASDAQ and OTCBB have two prices that are displayed in a quote: Bid and ask. The bid price, which is lower, is the price a trader is currently willing to pay for the stock. The ask price is the price a trader wants to sell the stock at. The difference between the bid and the ask is called the spread.

Delayed quotes: They're everywhere, they're free!

Sometime around 1997, online data providers realized that the Internet-using public loved picking up stock quotes, so they started handing out free stock quotes like candy. Believe it or not, prior to 1997, investors had to pay $5–$20 per month just for intra-day quotes. Now they're a commodity.

Quotes come in three flavors:

1. Historical

2. Delayed 15 to 20 minutes

3. Real-time

I discussed historical quotes in Chapter 6. The other two categories of quotes are updated constantly throughout the trading day. You can get free delayed quotes just about everywhere now – scrolling across your AOL Instant Messenger buddy list, for example. The lag time between when the trade executes and the price is updated on your screen varies from 15 to 20 minutes. This lag time isn't a major factor for long-term investors or for those who aren't in the market on a particular day or for people watching slow-moving stocks. Delayed quotes are pretty passé though, and most quote providers are offering free real-time quotes these days.

Real-time quotes

Real-time quotes come in two flavors: Snapshot and streaming. With snapshot quotes, you define a list of equities you want to track, which are then displayed in a table format. You hit the Refresh or Update button whenever you want the latest prices.

Streaming quotes are updated constantly, either at an interval that you set (for example, every 2 minutes) or whenever a trade takes place and changes the price. As with snapshot quotes, you define the equities you want included in your electronic ticker tape, and how often you want the prices updated.

If you're a frequent trader and have to have the latest price information, you will need to have streaming real-time quotes as one of your investing tools.

Data providers are offering snapshot quotes as a freebie now, replacing delayed quotes as a giveaway. You usually have to pay for streaming quotes, though, either by having an account open with an online broker who offers them as a perk or via a monthly fee to a data provider. Most of us can make do with snapshot real-time quotes, though. CNN and CNBC viewers are treated to streaming real-time quotes across the bottom of the screen during the trading day, but the stocks they display may not be in your portfolio.

Constant display all day long

If you have a fast computer and a high-speed connection to the Internet or directly to your broker, you may be interested in quotes that go one step beyond streaming. Trades on the NASDAQ and OTCBB are sent through market makers, each of whom maintain an order book.

Real-time quotes on the NASDAQ and OTCBB are available on three different levels:

1. Level I: Real-time bid and ask prices.

2. Level II: Real-time quotations by a market maker. Each market maker may be handling multiple orders on a stock at any given moment. When you look at

ACCESSING QUOTES

You can pick up delayed quotes online just about anywhere. Most brokers offer free snapshot real-time quotes. Here are some places to get quotes without having a brokerage account:

Quote provider	Web address	Delayed	Real-time	Streaming
BigCharts	www.bigcharts.com	Free	N/A	N/A
Esignal.com	www.esignal.com	Free	Fee	Fee
FreeRealTime	www.freerealtime.com	Free	Free	N/A
MoneyCentral	moneycentral.msn.com	Free	Free	N/A
PCQuote.com	www.pcquote.com	Free	Fee	N/A
Quicken.com	www.quicken.com	Free	Fee	Fee
Quote.com	www.quote.com	Free	Free (limited)	Fee
StockSqueeze	www.stocksqueeze.com	N/A	Fee	Fee
Thomson Investor	rtq.Thomson.com	Free	Free	N/A
Yahoo! finance	finance.yahoo.com	Free	Free	N/A

Level II quotes, you can see how many orders are outstanding at a particular price.

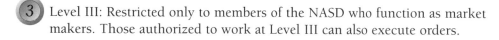

3 Level III: Restricted only to members of the NASD who function as market makers. Those authorized to work at Level III can also execute orders.

One trend that developed during the year 2000 was increasing access to Level II quotes. These displays look like the control center for a space shuttle, but once you learn to read them, they're fascinating.

Company news

GETTING THE LATEST DIRT ON A PUBLIC COMPANY *is easier than ever. All of the quote services mentioned above allow you to search by ticker symbol, locating recent news releases, earnings reports, management changes, and product announcements. Most online brokers also connect to financial news feeds, so you can find out what's going on just as fast as your out-of-work full-service broker. Here's what you can expect to find online.*

General information

Once an equity is part of your portfolio, getting the news is relatively easy. Your online broker or portfolio management program (which I'll discuss in Chapter 8) will have easy links to the latest news. But if you're just checking a company out, trying to decide whether it's worth your hard-earned money, you'll need to have a news service handy that you can search to find out what's happening. Use one of the portals that I mention in Chapter 1 as your market overview.

So what's online when it comes to financial news? As it turns out, just about everything. Here are some typical headlines from Reuter's Financial News (www.reuters.com), which supplies news to numerous other sites:

- *a* Allegheny Ludlum Announces Price Increases.

- *b* Human Genome Sciences Board of Directors Approves Two-For-One Stock Split.

- *c* ESI Announces Fiscal 2001 First Quarter Sales and Earnings.

- *d* Riverstone Networks Files Registration Statement for IPO.

- *e* Millennium Chemicals Terminates Equistar Sale Effort.

- *f* Allied Holdings, Inc. Third Quarter Results Impacted By Firestone Recall.

- *g* L&H Announces Management Change.

As you can see, companies are fond of announcing everything and anything. If you've signed up for conference calls (mentioned in Chapter 6), you can even tune in remotely to announcements companies make and virtually sit alongside the journalists who write many of these articles.

Make a habit of scanning the news for the competitors of the equities in your portfolio.

Yahoo! Finance (finance.yahoo.com) lets you set up watch lists so you can track quotes and news about publicly traded companies. It pulls news in from several dozen sources, so it's a great spot for one-stop (free) shopping.

News flashes

When news breaks about a stock in your portfolio or about a company you're watching, you might be the type of investor who wants to know immediately. In that case, set up a

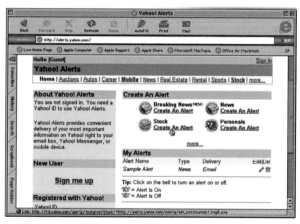

YAHOO! ALERTS

News Alert. If your online broker doesn't provide it, Yahoo! comes to the rescue again. Head over to http://alerts.yahoo.com/ and create a Yahoo! account, if you don't already have one. Then click on News and Create an Alert. Type the ticker symbols you're following into the box, then tell Yahoo! how to notify you of news. You can download and install Yahoo! Messenger, which will then pop up and beep at you when you receive a news alert, or you can just have the news item sent to your electronic mailbox.

Yahoo! also lets you set stock price alerts so you can be notified when a stock trades above or below a price you've entered. From the main Alerts page, hit Stocks and enter the pertinent ticker symbols and prices. This is an easy to use, free service.

Getting in on day one: Initial public offerings

How can you keep tabs on companies that aren't yet public but are about to start selling stock? Some online brokers supply initial public offerings (IPOs) to their clients, but getting the scoop on companies that aren't yet public can be difficult if you don't know where to go.

Alert-IPO (www.alert-ipo.com) lets you search through a database of upcoming IPOs and set up a list of up to 20 issues that you can easily track. The sort of information you can get before a company goes public includes its newly established ticker symbol, the report the company had to file with the SEC about its current financial state and management team, the proposed price per share, and the name of the underwriters. Underwriters are investment banks and brokerages that help a company go public by offering the stock to the public, usually earning a hefty fee along the way.

To get in on IPOs yourself, you need to know when they'll go to market. Companies often announce offering dates, then back off and change the date if the market is acting up (or, more likely, down!). It helps a great deal to have a large account with your broker so that you're closer to the front of the line when a new stock offering is made.

Research IPOs carefully, and be wary if a broker seems to have a lot of shares of a new company to hand out. That could be a sign of a low-quality offering.

You might consider waiting until the lockup period, or the time between the initial offering and when company insiders are allowed to trade (usually between 3 and 24 months, with 6 months being the most prevalent), before you leap in. When a lockup expires, the insiders (who often hold large blocks of stock) can start to sell their shares. You usually see a drop in stock price on the lockup expiration date, so you can pick up a bargain then. Alert-IPO has a list of lockup expiration dates that you can search.

Why did the stock price do that?

Here's an unfortunately all too common experience of mine: I get up in the morning and pull up my portfolio. By the time I get to my computer, the United States exchanges have been in business for an hour or two. I look at one of my stocks and see that it's either dropped 10 percent or the price is suddenly soaring out of site. That's when I ask myself, "What the heck is going on here?" and run off to the news reports.

A news story, seemingly unrelated to the stock market, can have a major effect on investor sentiment.

Often the big change has nothing to do with the company in question but with one of its competitors. For instance, last fall, when one of the major PC makers announced a drop in earnings, stock prices for all of the other PC makers fell as if in sympathy. Investors feared that one company's performance was a prediction for the rest of the sector.

Roundups of the day in the markets are great educational tools for learning what moves a stock's price. Check out c|net's daily news report (www.cnet.com), which can be sent to you via email if you'd like. Briefing.com (www.briefing.com) offers a variety of reports from which you can select that will keep you up to date, sometimes on an hourly basis, on market movers and shakers.

Ongoing research

AS YOU GET MORE COMFORTABLE *digging around online for financial information, you'll put together your list of most-often-visited sites and services. You'll probably also find yourself most interested in a few sectors of the market and want to study those more in-depth.*

Creating a financial home page

A technology that has blossomed recently is account consolidation combined with quotes, news, and research. For those of us with multiple online accounts, such as online banking and online trading, a financial home page that features an account consolidator is a wonderful boon.

Once you tell the account consolidator where to find all your online data, by supplying it with your sign-on IDs and passwords, it brings your account positions, recent credit card charges, and banking transactions onto one screen. I won't pretend that this initial setup phase isn't tedious, but you have to do it only when you first sign up, and then when you add a new online account. What do you get? You get to collect all your portfolios in one place, and you get flagged when there's news on your holdings. You can see your checking account balance and the sum you owe on your credit card. When these consolidators were first introduced, they didn't cover many of the financial transaction web sites, but they're getting better all the time (see the table on p. 114).

> ### Trivia...
> *I've got my computer set up so that the home page on my browser shows me the current value of my various online accounts. Being inherently lazy, I like this a lot: It saves me the trouble of visiting multiple web sites to get an overview of how my holdings are performing.*

Which piece of the pie is the hottest?

> **DEFINITION**
>
> *Sector analysis is a way of analyzing companies by industry group. For instance, all the automobile manufacturers are grouped together, and their statistics are reviewed as a whole. You study the characteristics of a group of companies, then decide whether you'll invest in one of the members of that group.*

As you get more familiar with the stock market, you'll start to see that companies in certain industries are usually on the top of the Most Active lists, or the New Highs list for the day. One way to uncover other companies in which to invest is to check out the competition within an industry. This is called *sector analysis* and is a powerful tool for anyone in the market.

It's a good idea to take a look at your portfolio and make sure you're not concentrating on just one or two sectors, so that you spread out your risk. (Check out the portfolio analysis discussion in Chapter 8.) You also want to review which sectors are performing best to make sure you haven't missed any investing opportunities.

CHOOSING A CONSOLIDATOR

The following chart shows some of the better account consolidation web sites. You'll see that there are three main suppliers of consolidation services, each serving slightly different markets. It's worth your time to make sure your major online accounts are covered by the consolidator you choose. Also, be sure to check out the original consolidator sites (eBalance, Yodlee, VerticalOne) and run through their demos and lists of financial partners, just to see if you like their styles.

Site name	Web address	Details
BankRate	www.bankrate.com	Powered by eBalance.
eBalance	www.ebalance.com	Supplies many web sites; check their site for the full list.
MoneyCentral	moneycentral.msn.com	Powered by Yodlee.
Motley Fool	www.fool.com	Powered by eBalance.
OnMoney	www.onmoney.com	Powered by VerticalOne.
Quicken.com	www.quicken.com	Powered by Yodlee.
USA Today	www.usatoday.com	Powered by eBalance.
VerticalOne	www.verticalone.com	Supplies many web sites, check their site for the full list.
Yodlee.com	www.yodlee.com	Supplies many other web sites but you can also do your account consolidation here.

Market Guide (www.marketguide.com) provides a list of the top performing sectors for the previous day and week. Click on the What's Hot folder tab, then on the Sector link in the left-hand column for the most recent list. It breaks the market down into 12 different sectors, and then takes it to a finer level in their industry lists.

Yahoo! Finance presents research by sector at http://biz.yahoo.com/ research/indgrp/. Click on an industry and you'll get a table of the companies in that industry group in order of performance. You can check out individual companies by clicking on a ticker symbol. Yahoo! gives you another way to get to this table as well: If you're looking at a company's research page, which you get to by entering a ticker symbol in the main Yahoo Finance page (http://finance.yahoo.com), you'll see a box entitled Earnings Estimates and Recommendations. In the bottom right-hand section of that box, there's a line that says Industry, followed by the company's rank. Click on the industry name, and you'll see information on competing companies.

Hoover's, a longtime investment research firm, offers industry research and commentary on their site (www.hoovers.com). Click on the Companies and Industries folder tab on their main page to read their most recent analysis.

Check out the best industries in terms of recent performance in graphical format at BigCharts (www.bigcharts.com). Click on the Industries tab then select the time frame for your ranking – from 1 week to 5 years. You'll get the top ten industries for the time period you've selected, then when you click on an industry name, you get the top ten stocks in that industry. This is one of my favorite places to do sector research.

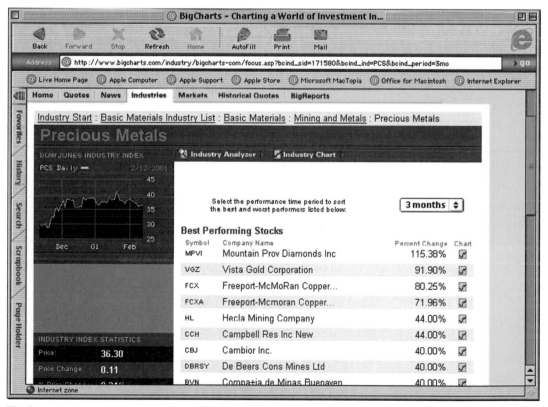

■ **There are numerous** *sites that will help you analyze industry groups, rather than individual companies. By spreading your investments over several sectors, you spread your risk accordingly.*

International markets

The Internet has not only turned individual investors into stockbrokers, it's also made the world a lot smaller. You can use your web browser to give you a front-row seat in the international investing arena as well as the domestic. Not so long ago, you'd find 2- to 3-day old data in your newspaper regarding international stock performance, but now you can get the latest news as it breaks.

The *Financial Times* (www.ft.com), the peach-colored paper that covers international finance, has an online version that's a must-visit for the international investor. With sections devoted to the United Kingdom, Europe, and Asia, the site brings you breaking news as well as quotes and analysis. It also compares international markets, so you can see how one exchange is performing compared to another.

Bloomberg (www.bloomberg.com) and CNNfn (www.cnnfn.com) are also full of international information. Bloomberg provides world market updates, equity indexes, and currency rates. Choose the country in which you're interested from the drop-down list on the home page. CNNfn offers up timely, original news stories on Asian and European markets. Click on World Markets in the left-hand column to go to its international page, or just go straight to http://cnnfn.cnn.com/news/worldbiz/.

INTERNET

www.validea.com

Who's doing the best job analyzing a particular sector? Validea ranks the analysts according to how well their recommendations have performed over the last three months. Click on Sources then choose a sector from the drop-down box and find out who's giving the best advice.

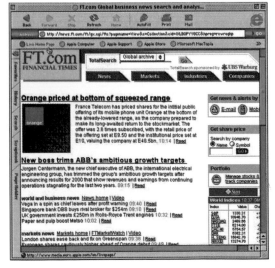

FINANCIAL TIMES

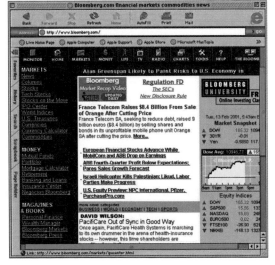

BLOOMBERG

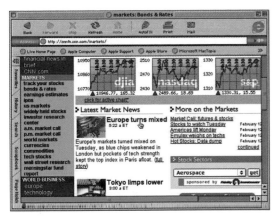

CNN

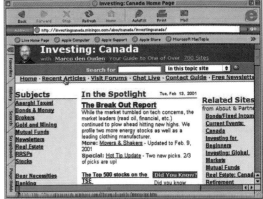

THE MINING COMPANY

How's it going in Canada, eh? Canada Stockwatch (www.canada-stockwatch.com) has been tracking information about Canadian companies since 1984, and it has moved its publications from paper to pixel. The information it presents is gleaned from news releases and other documents released by the companies themselves, which is reformatted for presentation on the Web. You can also take a look at quotes from Canadian exchanges while you're there, along with price/volume charts and insider trading data for every public Canadian company. Analysis of Canadian companies is provided by The Mining Company (investingcanada.miningco.com).

A simple summary

✓ Use your computer to bring you breaking news and stock quotes.

✓ Delayed quotes are ubiquitous and free, and real-time quotes are becoming more accessible (and cheaper too!).

✓ Set up alerts for the stocks you hold or are watching closely so that you're informed of breaking news immediately.

✓ By signing up with an account consolidator, you can create a financial home page that shows you your current portfolio value as well as news alerts and up-to-the-minute quotes.

✓ Take time to study industry sectors and international markets to make sure you're adequately diversified.

Chapter 8

Setting Up Portfolio Monitoring Tools

Most online brokers will show you your current positions, and a few will give you some analytical tools so you can track your progress. And the portfolio trackers built into most online brokerage sites are fairly rudimentary, plus they don't solve the problem of managing multiple accounts for you. So let's take a look around at online methods of watching your portfolio.

In this chapter...

✓ Track what you have: Portfolio analysis

✓ Test portfolios

✓ Online statements

NO MORE LABORIOUS CALCULATIONS – A FEW CLICKS ARE ALL IT TAKES TO TRACK YOUR PORTFOLIO

Track what you have: Portfolio analysis

AT ITS MOST BASIC LEVEL, portfolio analysis is simply listing everything you have and comparing the price today to the price you paid for it. Add it all up and you'll see whether your overall portfolio strategy is a winner – or a loser.

Naturally, you can make analyzing your portfolio a complicated proposition as well. Most investment professionals would recommend a mix of equities in your portfolio, depending on your current financial status and your attitude toward risk.

The real goal of effective portfolio management is maximizing your gains from your investments. To do that, you have to make sure your portfolio is in tune both with your eventual goal and with the current state of the market.

Even the most basic online brokerage accounts give you a portfolio-tracking screen. This screen allows you to view a full list of your account holdings along with information about each item, such as its current price, its total value, and what profit or loss you're showing since the time you bought it.

Key features to look for when you're deciding which portfolio analysis site or program to use include:

1. Tracking the original cost of the investment against its current value.

2. Creating subtotals by market segment (for example, company size) and industry (for example, automobiles or technology).

3. Linking to research, news, and price charts for each publicly traded company in your portfolio.

4. Tracking all of your investments – not just stocks and mutual funds, but bonds and options as well, if you hold those.

Web sites with great portfolio analysis capabilities

If your broker offers only a basic portfolio tracking service, you can still have the benefits of sophisticated tracking for free. Tracking services are offered at many financial web sites through Internet service providers and search engines. The financial directories listed in Chapter 1 give you a good list of up-to-date portfolio management web sites, and the News and Account Consolidation sites mentioned in Chapter 7 all include portfolio trackers that range from simple to complex.

Some free portfolio trackers on the Web come with advanced features that allow you to view and rank your stock holdings in various ways. For example, you can view your overall gains and losses from the time you opened the account, the day's gains or losses and price movements, and fundamental data about the items in your portfolio such as the present price/earnings ratio (P/E).

Customization is a key benefit to these portfolio-tracking web sites. You can decide which of your holdings to track and choose from among a variety of reports.

Many of the portfolio-tracking sites have been mentioned elsewhere in this book, but here's a rundown on some of the better portfolio analysis and management pages.

Quicken.com

At www.quicken.com, there are two portfolio reporting screens: Basic and Advanced. Both give you access to current news, quotes, and charts for each of your holdings, and as mentioned in Chapter 7, you can use the account consolidation feature to import your

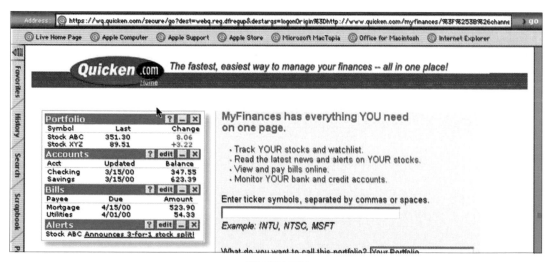

QUICKEN.COM

data quickly. (The import feature does not bring in the original price you paid for each investment, however, so you'll have to do some data entry. More on entering data in a few pages.) You can set up a lot of different portfolios here, and get a running total of your holdings at the bottom of the screen. The basic portfolio screens show you your gains and losses for the day and since your initial purchase, and a total for the day. The Enhanced portfolio compares each individual stock with its industry and displays rates of return for 1, 3, and 5 years. You can sort the list in different ways by clicking on a column, which will let you get subtotals by industry, for example.

MSN Money Central

At moneycentral.msn.com there's another terrific portfolio manager, which lets you look at your returns in a graphic format as well as in tables. The Portfolio Review is a powerful tool that provides a one-page summary of your portfolio's performance, asset allocation, transaction history, and best and worst performing stocks.

Moving data around from table to table is easy: You simply drag and drop it. You can decide which columns to include in the tables, too. When entering purchases and sales, Money Central will help you by supplying end-of-day prices as long as you know the date of the transaction.

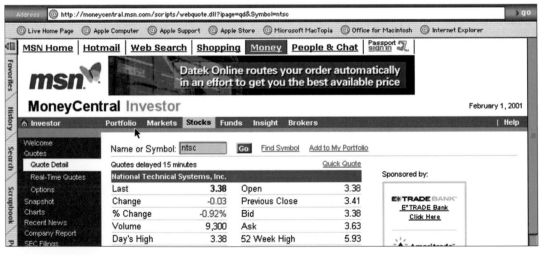

MSN MONEY CENTRAL

Wall Street City

Easy access to fundamental and technical data has been added to the portfolio analysis page at www.wallstreetcity.com. It also has a price projection page, showing you expected prices for the near term and intermediate term (1 week to 4 months in the future) for each of your holdings.

WALL STREET CITY

The rankings page shows how your portfolio as a whole ranks according to 11 different characteristics, and the DCipher My Portfolio button on that table creates an essay that describes your performance.

The ranking and DCipher combination can be either a wonderful or a humbling experience! In any event, you'll learn a lot about how the pros would evaluate your stock picks. This site also has a terrific stock screener.

Programs you can download

The web sites I've mentioned do a great job of giving you an overview of your stock and mutual fund portfolios, and they provide interesting reports that go into varying levels of depth. If you want additional number-crunching capabilities, download one of the following programs or get a couple and test them out. They all grab up-to-date prices through your Internet connection, and slice and dice your holdings along different criteria than the web site-based portfolio packages.

You can use many downloadable programs for a few weeks to a month before paying, so you'll get to see whether the style of the program works for you.

INTERNET

www.wsj.com

If you have a lot of international stocks, the portfolio manager at Wall Street Journal *Interactive, a subscription-based service that gives you the text of the* Journal *as well as* Barron's *and other Dow Jones publications, can handle it for you. You can add a link to the* Journal's *powerful Briefing Book feature to your portfolio; customizing the columns shown on the report is easy to do.*

Reeally!

Published by ManticSoft (www.manticsoft.com), Reeally! is a tool that helps investors improve the overall performance of their portfolios in a unique way. One problem faced by many investors (notably the Beardstown Ladies) is figuring out portfolio performance when additional investments are made over time, such as monthly deposits to a 401(k) program or dollar-cost-averaging strategies in mutual fund investments. Reeally! is designed to track, measure, and compare investments, translating performance of diverse holdings into a true rate of return. The program lets you analyze your investments in a wide variety of ways. As long as you keep up with the data entry side, Reeally! can guide you through different takes on calculating how your investments are doing.

■ **Downloadable programs** *equip you with a wide range of analytical tools. Try before you buy to find the program that best suits your style of investing.*

Reeally!'s performance calculations are based on what the developer calls a true rate of return. This figure takes into account irregular flows of cash into and out of a particular asset, and is expressed as an annualized rate, which simplifies comparisons. Graphs and calculations are based on asset-price files; the more often those files are updated, the more meaningful the graphs. Reeally! can track short positions, margin reserves, option trades, futures contracts, bonds (in the Professional version), and fixed assets. Updating price files can be done manually or by using Mantic's free add-on, DataFeed, available from the web site. For complex portfolio tracking, Reeally! is definitely worth downloading and checking out. The full version costs $150 ($525 for the Professional version), and the publishers are open to customer requests for additional features.

Captool Individual Investor

This program for Windows is flexible in terms of the types of investments it can handle: Stocks, bonds, mutual funds, certificates of deposit, options, commodities, GNMAs, annuities, real estate, zero-coupon bonds, partnerships, and others. It calculates a return on investment based on internal rate of return and lets you compare your investment performance against various market indexes. The screens look like spreadsheets, and Captool lets you compare portfolio performance to the overall market and also keeps track of estimated taxes based on tax-rate tables that can be customized for each portfolio. Captool's analysis features include more standard financial measures: Relative strength and financial ratios for stocks, yield to maturity and duration for bonds. At $249, Captool Individual Investor is a flexible way to examine your portfolio using standard methods of analysis.

There's a collection of free portfolio analysis packages out there as well; as a user, you just have to put up with a few banner ads in exchange.

StockVue

A free portfolio analysis package by NQL, Inc. (www.nqli.com), StockVue lets you set up portfolios of unlimited size, with subcategories set according to your specifications. You can have a portfolio with mutual funds, US and Canadian stocks from all available exchanges, as well as fixed-income securities. (Categories help you determine subtotals for the portfolio valuation report.) You can set up a scrolling ticker window that displays the most recent stock prices, even if you don't have StockVue open. StockVue also connects directly to Microsoft Office, so you can create and print additional reports using Excel or Word if you'd like. The program collects price information and charts from several financial web sites, and also puts together fundamental data and analyst recommendations (if available) for each security. You can also pick up EDGAR reports and other SEC filings. As you enter security symbols into the portfolio for tracking, StockVue sets up a ticker at the top of the screen that updates continuously. You can even configure StockVue to work with your Palm Pilot, and link directly to several online brokers.

StockTick

Available for download from www.naconsulting.com, StockTick by NAC Consulting allows full use of the program free of charge, though registered users (who are asked to pony up $24.95) get access to printing and data export features. It will also email you a portfolio report if you so choose, and it has a great set of portfolio analysis features. As with StockVue, if you're on the Web browsing in another window, you can keep the ticker open all the time to keep an eye on your investments.

Portfolios and their contents are displayed in an Internet Explorer-like list on the left-hand side of the screen, and the details are shown in a spreadsheet-like display in the larger window on the right. Clicking on a column header quickly sorts the table, and you can develop an investment history as you use the program, comparing portfolio values from one period to another.

Personal finance packages

There are two programs that dominate the personal finance market: Intuit's Quicken (www.intuit.com) and Microsoft Money (www.microsoft.com/money). Quicken and Money have turned into extensions of the web browser, so you can minimize your data entry chores by downloading the information directly from your broker or bank.

Quicken has added reports that help you figure out your portfolio performance over longer periods of time – up to 5 years. You can group your investments into categories that can be tracked separately, or you can roll everything together for a "big picture" analysis. Quicken's Investment Alerts feature, which you can customize for each item in your portfolio if you'd like, links to the Quicken.com web site for up-to-date data. The 401(k) Advisor gives you recommendations of mutual funds to consider, taking into account your financial situation and the funds provided by your employer.

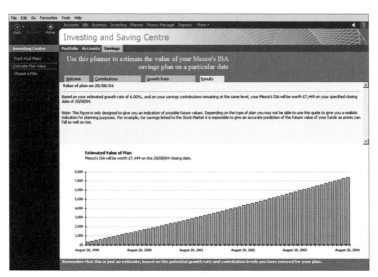

MICROSOFT MONEY

Microsoft Money's portfolio analysis features are linked to its asset allocation wizard, showing you how your investments are classified. The goal is to keep your portfolio properly balanced over time, and Money makes specific recommendations regarding what you need to load up on or dispose of in order to maintain that balance. The Lifetime Planner forecasts your current holdings and plans for further saving, so you can see whether you'll meet your long-range goals.

Both Quicken and Money can handle options, though you have to treat them like a regular stock when you make the initial entry. These programs include much more than just portfolio analysis, and they can help you put your financial life in order.

The ugly side of portfolio analysis: Data entry

I remain convinced that personal finance packages and portfolio analysis programs will gain full acceptance when the initial setup process and the ongoing data entry tasks are, if not eliminated, then at least considerably streamlined. There's an amazing duplication of effort in maintaining records. Can't all our computers just get along?

The number one problem with using one of these helpful programs is that someone (that would be you) has to enter every transaction into the database so that the reports make sense. If you just take a guess at the price you paid for those 100 shares of XYZ Company back in 1991, and you're wrong, all the calculations based on that figure will also be wrong. This goes back to record keeping: If some of your portfolio holdings exist only on paper, you'll have to refer to that paper when you're entering the data.

The old saying garbage in, garbage out is certainly applicable for portfolio analysis. Getting started is the hardest part of using one of these programs, and you'll just have to budget yourself the time to get it all done. The reward for your diligence? An accurate picture of your investments, leading you to smarter choices and higher returns. See? Not so bad after all.

■ **With portfolio analysis** *you'll need to gather together all your paper records of transactions so that you can enter the data correctly. This is a laborious process, but one that will ultimately benefit you.*

Test portfolios

YOU CAN TEACH YOURSELF *a lot about investing by setting up and following a test account. Some say that the best way to learn about investing is to throw your money into the market, make a few mistakes, figure out what went wrong, and avoid those errors in the future. I think that lesson is too expensive. A pretend portfolio lets you learn the same lessons without spending your own money. You can collect information about stocks you're considering, and figure out whether you can handle the ups and downs of the market. Another useful lesson is to watch a stock throughout a fiscal quarter, just to see how the market reacts to its performance expectations and earnings announcements.*

Do not just jump into the market, hope for the best, and learn from your mistakes. Instead, set up a test portfolio.

You can use one of the portfolio managers I discussed earlier in this chapter and just enter pretend trades when setting it up. This will give you some practice using a portfolio tracker, and with a little free experience you can decide which one works best for your style.

Testing the water (test portfolio setup)

Use your test portfolio to watch a variety of stocks. For instance, use one of the stock screening programs to locate a group of value stocks – those that have low price/earnings ratios compared to others in their industry. Follow the news on the stocks and see how they react to changing market conditions. You can also keep tabs on the stocks that wind up on the most active list all the time.

Set up a mock portfolio of technical stocks or watch a particular sector, such as automobiles. The possibilities are varied, and since it's not real money, you can track some stocks that you might consider too risky for your particular situation.

Use a test portfolio to track your employer's publicly traded competition. Set up a test portfolio and "buy" 500 shares of your stock as well as the stock of each of your competitors. You'll have a quick way to check up on the news, market capitalization, and financial performance data for your industry.

Playing with a trading strategy

Stock-picking games are fun ways to figure out how your strategy works compared to others. Here are some web sites that give you virtual cash to invest over a short period (usually a month) and offer interesting tools to work with while you play.

MarketPlayer

At www.marketplayer.com, each player is set up with a $1,000,000 pile of virtual cash, and the US resident with the highest percentage return (including dividends) after 4 weeks wins a real cash prize.

Click on Competitions then Competition Lineup to see which games are in progress and which ones you can join. One of the great features of this game is that it uses real trading data to set the prices for each transaction – some use end-of-day data only. In addition, you can sell short and trade on margin, testing somewhat riskier strategies than you might be willing to execute in real life.

E*Trade

This online broker (www.etrade.com) offers the E*Trade game in which participants start with $100,000 and try to end the period with the highest account balance. They've enhanced the game to allow short selling and options trading, and have also added quite a few extra reports that give you a good idea of where you stand overall. You can see what other players are doing by clicking on their names in the scoreboard. They offer a variety of prizes for the top 32 players.

Virtual Stock Exchange

At www.virtualstockexchange.com, there are dozens of games running at any particular point in time. You can join a public competition or set up your own private game and invite your friends and family to play along. This site includes message boards, so you can discuss your gaming (and real-life) strategies with others.

What if I'd bought Cisco at the IPO?

Though it's sometimes a depressing exercise, checking on what would have happened if you'd invested in a particular company at some point in the past can illustrate the value of getting into the market, and sticking around.

Trivia...

For a walk down memory lane, check out A Wall Street Century (www.awallstreetcentury .com). Sponsored by online broker BUYandHOLD.com, which is aimed at the long-term investor, A Wall Street Century lets you go back in time and invest your virtual money in companies that were listed on the stock exchanges between 1900 and 2000. One day of real time is a year in virtual time, so each segment of the game moves along pretty quickly. You're given a budget and a few hints about each company's performance from year to year. Prizes are awarded to the winners of each "era," which is roughly 20 years of elapsed time.

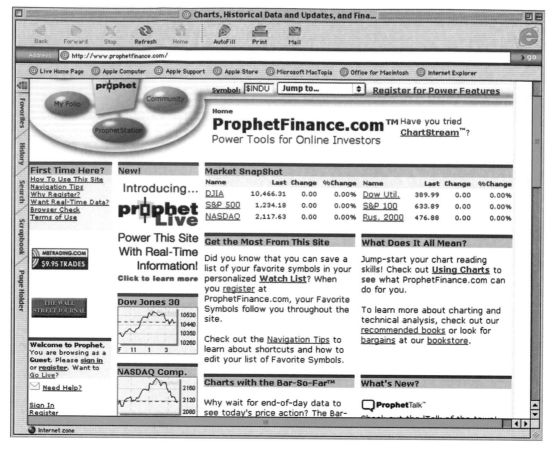

PROPHETFINANCE

ProphetFinance

At www.prophetfinance.com, there's a What If table under the My Folio button. You can fill in either dollars invested or shares bought for a particular stock, then enter the date of your hypothetical investment.

Depending on the stock you choose, be sure you have a box of facial tissues handy. If you enter a date when the stock market wasn't open, Prophet will find the nearest trading date and use the end-of-day data from that point. Prophet also includes an excellent portfolio analysis program, as well as charts, quotes, and research links.

Investorama

What if your parents had bought $100 worth of stock the year you were born? Investorama has a calculator at www.investorama.com/calc/birthday.html that shows that I'd have over $21,000 today if Mom and Dad had plunked $100 in a stock that returned the market average from the time I was born. Where's that box of tissues?

Online statements

ONCE YOU'VE OPENED A BROKERAGE ACCOUNT, you'll probably be swamped with paperwork. First there are the account agreements, then forms for making deposits, then confirmations of trades followed by monthly statements.

You can save a few trees, along with wear and tear on your file cabinet, by signing up for online notification of trades and statements.

Even if you choose online confirmations and statements, don't forget hard copy record keeping. Protect yourself by printing out the relevant items, especially trade confirmations and deposit receipts, and filing these records in a safe place.

Broker confirmations of each transaction, records of the cash you've moved into and out of accounts, dividend records, and regular account statements will come to you courtesy of your local postal service or through your computer if you opt for online reports. These are helpful in any dispute with the broker or the IRS.

Reading the reports: What does all this mean?

The quality of statements brokers supply varies from low – a minimum of information is transmitted, sometimes just current account balances – to high, in which your costs and gains are displayed as well as comparisons to major indexes.

The statements aren't all that useful except as a record of your portfolio history. You can get more recent updates online, after all.

When you're comparing online brokers, ask for a sample of their monthly statements. You will find some more informative and easier to read than others. If you're opening multiple accounts with a single broker, for instance an IRA as well as a taxable account, see how they consolidate the reports and if the results make sense to you.

Most monthly statements show the portfolio value at the beginning of the month, any cash transfers into or out of your account, and any equity transactions you've made.

Trade confirmations: How much did I pay for that?

In the last couple of years, brokers have greatly improved the timeliness and the readability of trade confirmations. If you were to place a trade with a full-service broker,

■ **Compare monthly statements** *issued by brokers with your trade confirmations. It's always better to find mistakes early and get them corrected quickly.*

you'd probably hear about the trade while you're still on the phone, then get a paper confirmation within a day or two.

You can get a trade confirmation with an online broker in a number of ways: Some will open an alert window on your computer, telling you that a trade has gone through, or send you an email with the quick details. Unless you instruct the broker otherwise, you'll get a paper copy of the confirmation mailed to you.

Don't throw out the trade confirmations of your purchases. You'll need to match them up with sales when you dispose of the stock. This will help you a great deal when you prepare your tax return after the sale, and also when you're keeping track of your realized gains, or how much money you've made from your investments.

Proxies online

When you own a stock, you're notified of the company's annual meeting and usually sent a list of issues to be discussed by the board of directors. Many of these issues have to be approved by a majority of the shareholders. If you can't attend the annual meeting in person, you can place your vote via a *proxy*.

DEFINITION

All voting by proxy means is that you indicate your vote on a paper ballot and mail the ballot in or dial the toll-free number to place your vote.

More and more companies are opting for online proxies, many of which are supplied through a company named ProxyVote (www.proxyvote.com). If the paper proxy says, "You can vote this proxy online," then fire up the browser and check it out.

You'll be asked for the control number from your paper proxy, and once you've entered it you'll be presented with a screen that mirrors the ballot. This is the easiest way to vote your proxies. You may be asked whether you want to receive your proxy electronically in the future as well.

A simple summary

✓ Track your portfolio's performance using a financial web site, your broker's home page, or personal finance software. Pick what works best for you, and use it religiously.

✓ Practice your investing strategies by setting up a test portfolio, or joining an online stock-picking game.

✓ You can opt for online statements and trade confirmations, but be sure to print out the important items and hang onto the hard copy to help you prepare your tax return.

✓ If you can't attend a company's annual meeting in person, you can opt to vote online by proxy.

PART THREE

DO YOUR RESEARCH TO FIND THE BEST PARTNER FOR YOU

YOUR ONLINE TRADING PARTNER

DON'T BELIEVE THE ONLINE BROKERAGE advertisements. Your success as an investor depends mostly on your *understanding* of the markets, not which button you push. Still, the brokerage you choose as your trading partner is an important decision. Before you fill out the forms and sign on, read this  section to understand the *types of brokers* out there, and the features you need to consider. The right brokerage for your neighbor might be all wrong for you.

There are brokers who strive to offer "one-stop shopping," and there are brokers who focus on a particular type of investment. *Which broker is right for you?* I'll walk with you as you step through the process of choosing the brokerage that best fits you and your investing style.

Chapter 9

Finding the Right Brokerage Firm

THE INITIAL PUSH INTO ONLINE TRADING was led by discount brokers, mainly Charles Schwab and Fidelity, who simply gave existing clients electronic access to their funds. Then along came upstarts like E*Trade and Lombard (now Morgan Stanley Dean Witter Online), and they stole customers from the traditional discount brokerages. Now there are well over 100 brokers vying for your online account. Which one is right for you? I'll describe in this chapter the steps you should take to analyze the universe of brokers, and give you a brief profile of dozens of online brokers in Chapters 10 and 11.

In this chapter...

✓ Types of brokers

✓ Key features to consider

✓ Online brokers rated

CHOOSE A BROKER TO SUIT YOUR OWN PERSONAL INVESTING STYLE

Types of brokers

JUST AS THERE ARE DIFFERENT STYLES of investors, there are different types of online brokers. Some firms target the active traders, who tend to look for rock-bottom commissions. Others go after investors who want data, reports, ratings, and a lot of help – and are willing to pay higher commissions to get all that. As the industry matures, it is likely that an increasing effort will be made by various brokers to target different segments of the online trading market.

There's no doubt that the online trading market will continue to grow as the Internet becomes an integral part of modern life – much as the telephone services did a century ago. While I expect to see continued improvement in features, notably order-entry screens with real-time portfolio updates, I'm also anticipating a decline in the numbers of Internet brokers out there. Consolidations and shakeouts seem all but certain in this crowded marketplace.

In the intense battle for customers, online brokers will continue to provide more features and services without charging more and, if it's possible, maybe charging even less. And the only sure winner in this will be the object of all this competition – you, the online investor.

In this chapter, I look at five basic categories of online brokerages: full service, one-stop shopping, cheap but clean, specialized services, and frequent traders. Read on to decide which style is right for you.

Full service with lots of personal help

Brokerages in this category are usually the online version of a full-service offline broker, created to staunch the flow of assets to the discount brokers. Offline, these brokers charge rather high commissions, usually a percentage of the value of the trade, but online their rates are in the range of $29–$40 per transaction. Several brokers in this group charge an annual fee based on the total assets in the account, which gives customers a certain number of free trades per year before an additional commission kicks in.

You get a lot of proprietary research from these folks, though, along with stock recommendations, tools for analyzing your portfolio, and calculators to keep your assets properly allocated. You can also talk to flesh-and-blood brokers whenever you want, and if your account value is high enough ($100,000–$1,000,000, depending on the broker) you qualify for additional perks such as initial public offerings (IPOs) and premium research.

■ **Online brokers** *cater for just about every style of investor. The more proprietary information and personal help you need, the higher the commission you are likely to pay.*

One-stop online brokerages

You can trade stocks, bonds, mutual funds, and options with this group of brokers, and you'll get access to charting, portfolio analysis, news, and research as well. Most of them include a good stock screener and mutual fund picker, and their commissions are reasonable (around $20 per transaction). Other features include bill payment, checking accounts, and credit cards. You can even shop for insurance or negotiate a mortgage at many one-stop brokers. These sites want to become your financial home base. Most of the brokers in this category also offer perks to high account balance holders as well.

You can talk to a human when you want to at most of these brokers. Financial planning tools such as how to save for retirement and the kids' college funds are available here too.

Cheap but clean, like Motel 6

The fees are lower for the brokers in this group, but you don't get as many goodies either. Most of the brokers in this category don't have their own research offerings, but they have links to other research providers around the Internet. Quotes and charts abound, but you'll have to deal with online help rather than human, and you won't get much in the way of advice. Commissions are low, around $12 per transaction.

These sites work for the self-directed investor who doesn't depend on a broker for research or portfolio analysis. You'll find some surprises at many of these sites, such as discussion boards and the occasional stock screener, but for the most part you're on your own when it comes to research. These brokers usually don't let you buy bonds, and the list of mutual funds available is limited in comparison to the first two groups.

Options and bonds

The original set of online brokers focused on stock and mutual fund trading, but those who include options, bonds, and futures in their portfolios might have had to look elsewhere. Most brokers who allow option trading have the simpler strategies – plain old puts and calls – automated, but if you're into the more complex strategies, such as spreads, straddles, and strangles, you'll have to find a specialized options broker.

The commission schedules for options trading are remarkably difficult to figure out in many cases, so make a few calculations before you jump in.

Some of the brokers in the three categories above make bond trading available electronically, but most of them make you go through a live broker to get into the fixed income market. The online bond market is a little trickier than the equity market. You can always jump onto just about any broker's web site and place a trade for AOL, for example, but you can't buy a bond unless there's a market for it with your particular online broker. And the list of available bonds changes from day to day. Brokers keep some of these bonds in their inventory, and sell from their stock on hand to their clients, or they allow their customers with large portfolios to place bonds on their market. If you're used to the instant executions you've experienced with stock transactions, you'll have to slow the pace for bond orders; though some markets move quickly, it could be the next day before you find out whether your order was executed.

Trading 20 times a day?

If you're a frequent trader, every fraction of a point will matter to you. You'll need to use a broker who lets you access up-to-the-second quotes, and one who lets you trade directly on an electronic communication network (ECN). The ECNs directly match buyers and sellers, and cut out the market makers who typically shave a little bit off and put it in their own pockets.

FINDING THE RIGHT BROKER

Type of brokerage	Name of company	Web address
Full-service brokers	Merrill Lynch Online JP Morgan Online Morgan Stanley Dean Witter Online	www.mlol.com www.jpmorgan.com www.msdw.com
One-stop online brokers	National Discount Brokers Charles Schwab DLJ Direct E*Trade	www.ndb.com www.schwab.com www.dljdirect.com www.etrade.com
Cheap but clean brokers	Datek Suretrade JB Oxford Financial Café	www.datek.com www.suretrade.com www.jboxford.com www.financialcafe.com
Options brokers	Wall Street Electronica Wall Street Access Mr. Stock	www.wallstreete.com www.wallstreetaccess.com www.mrstock.com
Brokers for frequent traders	CyBerCorp TradeCast myTrack	www.cybercorp.com www.tradecast.com www.mytrack.com
Bond brokers	Muni Direct BT Alex Brown's BondAgent TradeBonds	www.munidirect.com www.bondagent.com www.tradebonds.com

* Charles Schwab (www.schwab.com) and E*Trade (www.etrade.com) have bond trading capabilities, including calculators that help you build ladders.

Brokers who focus on peripatetic traders typically offer Level II quote screens and instantly updated positions screens and buying power calculations. You can chart price history to your heart's content, but these brokers are usually a little light on research offerings, assuming the customer will find fundamental data elsewhere.

Key features to consider

WHAT DREW THE ONLINE PIONEERS *into the digital world was the lower cost of trading, but the pricing structure has flattened out to the point that the brokers have to compete on services as well. Now, experienced online investors say that a broker's reliability and personal service are more important than the cost of a trade.*

When you're evaluating online brokers, go beyond the advertisements before you open an account. Do a little soul-searching and honest self-evaluation, and think about what else is important to you besides placing trades.

How often do you want to talk to a human?

Do you like a lot of personal service? If so, you should consider signing on with a broker who has a full-service component, or make sure the assets you'll use to open your new account are high enough to merit you special attention. Check out whether the online brokerage lets you talk to a human to place trades when there's a technical problem.

■ **If personal support** *is important to you, check out whether a prospective broker will be able to provide the level of attention you are looking for.*

When I'm reviewing brokers, I usually concoct a couple of questions and call around to see who responds best. I'll time how long I have to wait on hold, listening to a recording telling me how important they consider my call. Hey, if I'm so important, why doesn't a human pick up the phone?

Give this a try yourself – do you get stuck in voice mail hell when you dial the broker's support line, or do you get a courteous reply that actually answers your question? Check over the fee schedule to make sure there isn't a huge penalty for placing the occasional trade with a flesh-and-blood broker. And if you really like the human touch, consider opening an account with a brokerage that has a bricks-and-mortar office nearby.

SITES THAT SPECIALIZE IN RATING ONLINE BROKERS

Site name	Web address	How they rank
Barron's Online	www.barrons.com	Trade execution, ease of use, reliability and range of services, amenities, commissions.
Discount Brokers Rated	www.sonic.net/ donaldj/brokers.html	From least expensive to most expensive. Stockbrokers collect comments from web site visitors. Ranked html.
Gomez.com	www.gomez.com	Ease of use, customer confidence, on-site resources, relationship services, overall cost.
Keynote Index	www.keynote.com	Weekly list of response times and order execution speed.
Kiplinger's	www.kiplinger.com/ tools/brokerrank.html	Overall quality, fees, and services. Re-sort the list yourself based on your own criteria.
Money Magazine	www.money. com/brokers	Ease of use, customer service, system brokers response, products and tools, cost. Reweight for your own personalized ranking.
Smart Money	www.smartmoney. com./brokers/	Profiled three investor styles (do-it-yourselfer, navigator, delegator).

If you're fine with the idea of flying solo, scouring online help, or using email to get the answers to your questions, the universe of brokers you'll be happy using is much larger.

■ **If you're a confident emailer and online chatter,** *you may prefer to deal with all your account online, particularly if your broker is offering live chat with a customer service representative.*

Your comfort level

Are you an email junkie? Do you prefer picking your way through online guides when you have a question to picking up the phone? If so, you'll probably be fine dealing with the occasional query about your account online. Many brokers are now rolling out live chat applications on their web sites so you can type back and forth with a customer service representative. If you've managed to hold your own in a chat room, you'll handle receiving online customer service well.

Online investing is more appealing to the self-directed trader. If you don't trade very often, you'll probably rely more on investment advice than those who trade frequently. In that case, do some research and track your picks for a while before you leap in and put your money on the line. If you're a whiz at setting up a portfolio online and have no trouble searching through the news wires for hot items on your stocks, then you'll be fine investing online.

Trading on margin

I briefly discussed opening a margin account in Chapter 5, and if it's something you've decided to do, you'll need to check out the broker's margin rates carefully. It can be a challenge to compare the margin rates charged by different brokers because the rate depends on how big a loan you'll be carrying as well as the underlying *broker call rate*.

As you borrow more from your broker, typically the rate of interest will drop. With a margin account, you usually borrow against a portion of the value of the securities in your account (typically 50 percent), allowing you to own more assets than you can afford with your current cash balance. Some securities, especially recent IPOs in the high-tech sector, are so volatile that brokers will restrict the value of what you can borrow. As JB Oxford's web site says, "Any stock may be subject to more stringent margin requirements in light of such stock's volatility, sector volatility, market conditions, and/or other factors."

Should the market drop, and with it the value of your stocks, your broker can ask you to pay back some or all of your margin debt, which is known as a margin call. This may force you to sell stock – at a loss – to pay your broker back, unless you can inject some cash into your portfolio on short notice.

If you decide to be a margin investor, devote some energy to avoiding the panic of a margin call so you won't have to sell stock at a loss.

INTERNET

www.nasdr.com

www.sec.gov/consumer/ jneton.htm

For additional information on margin in the context of online trading, there's the NASD Notice to Members 99-11 (February 1999), available on the NASD Regulation web site, and the Securities and Exchange Commission's Tips for Online Investing, available on the SEC web site. The NASD Regulation site contains quite a bit of information on the topic of margin trading, though most of it is presented in bureaucratese rather than English.

Online brokers rated

AS THE ONLINE BROKERAGE MARKET *has grown, so has confusion over which broker is best for a particular consumer. Different evaluators use different scenarios and assumptions when ranking brokers, so it's no wonder that we all come up with such different answers. For instance, when I'm putting together my review for* Barron's, *I'm looking at the brokers through the eyes of a high-income, high-net worth individual who places, on average, six to eight trades per month and wants everything in one place. Other reviewers select criteria that generate a different number one.*

So don't just look at the list from top to bottom when you're checking out how a particular publication or web site ranked the brokers. Read the methodology carefully and see if the criteria used for that particular ranking fit your individual situation.

Places to talk about experiences with brokers

Another step to take before you sign up with a broker is to check out financial discussion boards and read up on other people's experiences with the different brokers. Keep in mind when you're browsing through messages that someone who has had a bad experience is much more likely to scream and yell about it than someone who is a perfectly happy customer, so you tend to see complaints rather than kudos on these boards. Still, forewarned is forearmed.

DISCUSSION SITES

Site name	Web address
Raging Bull	www.ragingbull.com
Silicon Investor	www.siliconinvestor.com
Motley Fool	www.fool.com
Yahoo!	messages.yahoo.com

■ **You can gain valuable insight into brokers** *by visiting financial discussion board sites and checking out what people have written about their personal experiences with brokerage firms.*

Check the dates on the complaint messages. If they're more than 6 months old, the odds are high that the broker has put some policies in place to minimize future negative comments of the same type. It's worth asking the broker a few questions if you see the same problem show up repeatedly on the boards.

Getting the dirt on a broker from Uncle Sam and the regulators

"Uncle Sam and the Regulators" sounds like the name of a country and western group, doesn't it? If complaints are on file about a particular broker, though, the tune they sing isn't so sweet.

The Securities and Exchange Commission (SEC) is the government agency charged with overseeing the stock markets and the brokerage industry. Set up in 1934, in the wake of the 1929 stock market crash, the Securities and Exchange Commission was empowered with enforcing the then-new securities laws, promoting stability in the markets and protecting investors. As they say on their fact-filled web site, "The SEC is concerned primarily with promoting disclosure of important information, enforcing the securities laws, and protecting investors who interact with these various organizations and individuals."

The SEC requires that publicly traded companies disclose a great deal of financial information, and it also makes sure that brokers are registered and follow certain rules. When you first sign up for an account with a broker, whether offline or online, you're presented with several pages of legalese that the SEC insists upon. It wants to make sure the broker isn't pulling you into investments that aren't suitable for your financial situation.

One reason the SEC is taking such a hard look at online brokers is this suitability question: When all your trades had to go through a live broker, there was someone at the firm to hold responsible if you were steered in an improper direction. Now it's all up to the individual investor to determine his or her own personal suitability for particular investments. The SEC publishes a wealth of useful information for investors at www.sec.gov. Be sure to check out their online trading pages.

The National Association of Securities Dealers is a United States-based securities industry self-regulatory organization, and its regulatory web site at www.nasdr.com is the place to go to find out if there are any actions being taken against a particular broker. You can't get the information instantly, though; you have to

INTERNET

www.nasdr.com

You can file a complaint online at the web site of the National Association of Securities Dealers if your broker did something you think is illegal.

fill out a form and ask for the report to be emailed or surface mailed to you. (If the report is larger than 1.5MB, the NASD won't deliver via email – it'll print the whole thing out and send it to your postal mail address.)

The SEC and the NASD web sites have improved greatly in the recent past, and though they're still filled with bureaucratese, some effort has been made to publish clear explanations of the regulatory process and your rights as an investor.

Both the SEC and the NASD sites are worth the time you'll spend reading over the information provided. Bookmark them and visit every month or so to see what's new.

A simple summary

✔ Different types of brokers serve the varying needs of investors. As the industry is maturing, the market is becoming more segmented.

✔ Once you know the type of broker you want – full service, one-stop shopping, cheap but clean, or specialist – you can focus on the brokers that serve that particular category.

✔ Be sure to check out customer service before you open an account. Make a couple of phone calls and ask a simple question.

✔ If you want to trade on margin, carefully evaluate the widely varying interest rates charged on the money loaned by your broker.

✔ The SEC and the NASD act as the regulatory overseers for brokerages. Check their files to see whether your broker is in trouble with Uncle Sam.

Chapter 10

The Best Brokers for Regular Investors

THERE ARE OVER 100 ONLINE BROKERS right now, and the constant barrage of ads often serve to confuse rather than help while you're deciding where to put your money. The previous chapters helped you understand your investing style and the type of broker you want to use. Now you'll read profiles of online brokers that do the job for stock and mutual fund investors. This chapter should help you narrow down the list to a few online brokers to check out in detail. Within each category, the brokers are arranged in alphabetical order. Each brokerage has its own online personality, not to mention services offered and commissions charged.

In this chapter...

✓ Full service with a lot of personal help

✓ One-stop shopping

✓ Low-cost brokers

DECIDE HOW MUCH HELP YOU NEED, AND FIND A BROKER THAT WILL MEET THOSE REQUIREMENTS

Full service with a lot of personal help

FULL-SERVICE BROKERS *are the online version of traditional full-service firms that charge fairly high commissions. You can set up a hybrid account to take advantage of the advice and financial planning offered by the full-service version and use the online brokerage to place your trades at relatively low fees.*

JP Morgan Online

This Internet-based trading and advice service (www.jpmorgan. com) is aimed at high net worth investors who want a combination of hand-holding and free rein when it comes to investment management.

To open a Morgan Online account, you have to deposit a minimum of $10,000 in an account, and pay a $2,500 annual fee. Clearly that fee makes no sense with a

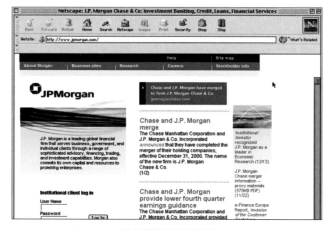

JP MORGAN ONLINE

balance of only $10,000, but for an account with over $500,000 or so, it's not such a big chunk of change. The $2,500 gives you access to Morgan Online's wealth management tools, which include asset allocation models for multiple strategies. You can make 24 free trades per year, but after that each transaction costs $30 (more if you have a block larger than 1,000 shares).

You can use Morgan Online's excellent portfolio evaluator and tracking program to keep tabs on all your investments, no matter where they're held. You can even import your portfolio holdings into a calendar, which will display the dates of earnings announcements, stock splits, and other items of interest.

The site includes a good employee stock option tracker that keeps tabs on the value of the options and lets you set trading alerts as well. The mutual fund screener is also excellent.

If any of your holdings, whether Morgan-based or elsewhere, are the subject of JP Morgan's proprietary research, you'll be alerted to the existence of a report when you look at the portfolio screen.

Merrill Lynch Online

Clients of Merrill Lynch Direct, at www.mlol.com, are given free access to numerous high-quality research reports. These include its weekly Focus 1 stock recommendations and in-depth analysis of various industries and corporations as well as unlimited free real-time quotes. ML Direct's portfolio reports are chock full of helpful information, including intra-day balances, so you can see where you stand immediately after placing a trade.

MERRILL LYNCH ONLINE

Other reports include portfolio performance, asset allocation, and unrealized gains and losses. The stock and mutual fund selection algorithms, though somewhat limited in scope, are flexible and give some intriguing results. You can personalize the site slightly by selecting items to display on the opening screen – for instance, news and account balances. The minimum to open a Merrill Lynch Direct account is $20,000, significantly higher than what most other online brokers require.

Morgan Stanley Dean Witter Online

This site, at www.msdw.com, is easy to navigate through, having a two-layer menu that allows you to get to just about any other spot on the site with a maximum of two clicks of the mouse. Account holders who have over $100,000 in assets can access Morgan Stanley research for free; others have to buy the reports individually. The portfolio and account balance screens are updated in real time, as soon as a trade executes, which is another plus. The site has great research, and a long list of equities that are tradable online. The Blue

MORGAN STANLEY DEAN WITTER ONLINE

Chip Market Basket, with which you can purchase $5,000 or more of a "basket" of ten stocks from the Dow 30 for a commission of $39.95, is an interesting way to invest a fixed dollar amount in a variety of stocks.

One-stop shopping

WHEN DISCOUNT BROKERS BURST *onto the scene in the early 1980s, they gave investors a lower cost alternative to the traditional full-service brokers. Now the discount brokerage sector has divided itself into a few more layers. This group, which covers most of the bases for the typical investor, wants to satisfy all of your financial needs, from online banking and bill paying to online trading and beyond.*

Discount options

Discount brokers offer a wide range of services. Here are some of the main contenders.

American Express

At www.americanexpress.com/trade, AmEx offers American Express Financial Advisors, whose mutual fund research is free to account holders, as are financial planning applications and an equity evaluator. Signing up for an account with AmEx (not to be confused with Amex, the American Stock Exchange) is a piece of cake – you can do it online, and once you're finished, you can make stock trades of up to $15,000 as long as you fund your account within 3 days. More online brokers should emulate the

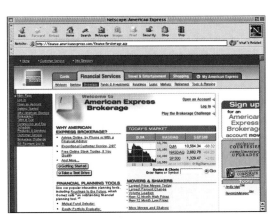

AMERICAN EXPRESS

portfolio analysis reports here, and the easy-to-read account balance screen. AmEx account holders with over $25,000 can make up to three free market buys per month, while those with over $100,000 can make up to ten free market buys or sells per month.

One feature I appreciate about the AmEx site's design is that the information displayed is set up to fit your screen. If you reduce the size of your screen, you still won't have to scroll left and right to see all the data as you would on many other web sites.

AmEx features a fine portfolio analysis report and easy-to-read account balances. The research available includes the usual suspects, but also gives you access to American Express's internal research, which is well written and worth a look.

CSFB Direct

Customers of CSFB Direct (www.csfbdirect.com) with over $100,000 in their accounts get free access to institutional research. There's a large range of assets that can be traded online. CSFB Direct give customers a wide variety of non-transaction services such as credit cards, cash management accounts, and online bill payment. This brokerage's services are aimed at customers who like the feel and range of services of a full-service broker, but would rather pay lower commissions ($20 per transaction). Formerly DLJ

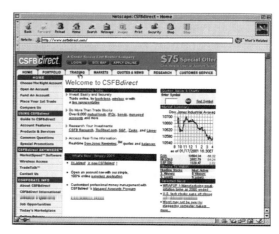

CSFB DIRECT

Direct, this brokerage is now owned by Credit Suisse First Boston.

E*Trade

The original hands-off all-electronic online broker, E*Trade (www.etrade.com) keeps adding reports and third-party research, and it has a terrific bond purchase area.

E*Trade is going after all of your financial business, with mortgages and insurance offerings as well as stocks, mutual funds, bonds, and options. Commissions drop as you trade more often.

Power E*Trade, offered to frequent traders, brings you real-time quotes and account balances as well as even lower commissions.

E*TRADE

Fidelity Investments

There are some terrific research tools featured by Fidelity Investments (www.fidelity.com), including one of the better mutual fund screening programs around. Its customizable interface, Powerstreet, is essentially a Lycos-powered home page with news and other features.

INTERNET

www.sia.com

The Securities Industry Association (SIA) is a trade group that the majority of online brokers have joined. You can see what issues they're working on and read up on proposed laws that affect your investments at their informative web site.

Powerstreet Pro is useful in giving investors an overview of the performance of securities on their watch list, including real-time quotes. A high-end service of Powerstreet, it is available only to people who make at least 36 stock, bond, or options trades in a calendar year. (Mutual fund transactions, however, do not count toward the total.)

Fidelity's retirement investing section helps you plan for the happy day when you quit working, and stays with you after retirement to keep tabs on your nest egg. It offers a lot of research, along with online bill payment and wireless trading. You can also step into a Fidelity office if you want to talk with one of the financial planners.

FIDELITY INVESTMENTS

National Discount Brokers

Trading screens supplied by National Discount Brokers (www.ndb.com) are packed with information for investors. You can opt to have your execution reports pop up through your browser. NDB features real-time portfolio updates and portfolio analysis reports that can keep you up to date on changes in asset values. NDB's Tax Center features "Schedule D-efense," which allows a customer to download account history

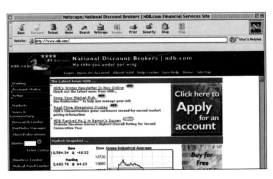

NATIONAL DISCOUNT BROKERS

into an Excel spreadsheet that performs Schedule D calculations. There's no proprietary research available from NDB, but the third-party collection it has put together is well organized and includes a Java-based charting application that features 11 technical indicators. NDB customers can place trades via Touch-Tone phone or live broker as well as on the Web.

High net worth customers — those who hold over $1,000,000 in assets at NDB — are designated concierge customers and are offered a wide range of additional benefits, including a dedicated help desk, access to IPOs, streaming Level II quotes, and reduced margin rates.

NDB has perks for frequent traders, including the Active Traders' Advantage with which you can make multiple trades in the same stock on the same side (all buys or all sells) for a single commission.

Quick & Reilly

With stock, mutual fund, option, and bond trading online, Quick & Reilly (www.quickandreilly.com) also includes online bill paying. It's owned by FleetBoston bank, and it keeps adding banking services to its offerings. You get access to IPOs, and its email customer service is usually prompt. It has over 100 investor centers scattered around the United States, so if you need to talk to a human, you can select a financial advisor and still make trades at the online discount rate. Customers also can sign up for free Internet access through service provider 1stUp.com.

QUICK & REILLY

Charles Schwab

Thanks to the way it gave all of its customers online access in the mid-1990s, Charles Schwab (www.schwab.com) has the largest market share in the business. This brokerage handles about 25 percent of all online trades. In the last couple of years, Schwab's enormous information technology department rolled up its sleeves, and the site has been considerably enhanced and streamlined.

CHARLES SCHWAB

Though Schwab's fees are still among the highest in the industry, it has one of the most complete packages of services available. You can trade just about anything you want here — stocks, mutual funds, options, corporate bonds, and treasuries, plus you have the ability to place several trades simultaneously.

Schwab offers quite a few research reports from the likes of Chase H&Q and Credit Suisse First Boston. The Research area offers Big Charts price/volume graphs displayed by industry, allowing you to compare 12 or more stocks at once. Velocity, Schwab's non-browser real-time trading program, is available to high balance account holders and frequent traders.

Muriel Siebert

A combination of online and offline tools and services is offered by Muriel Siebert (www.msiebert.com). There are stock and mutual fund screeners, unlimited real-time quotes, and after-hours trading.

MURIEL SIEBERT

You can customize your own trading portal with the mysiebertnet feature. Check out the morning call notes from Lehman Brothers. For a large block trade, Siebert will assign a broker to shop it for you and get you the best price. *Price improvement* strategies, which work to get you either a lower price for the buy side or a higher price for the sell side, are practiced at Siebert, though they can slow down the execution of market orders since they are passed by a live broker.

> **DEFINITION**
>
> *When brokers say they'll give you **price improvement**, they mean they'll work to get you either a lower price for the buy side or a higher price for the sell side when you place an order with them.*

Wall Street Access

Aiming itself at high-asset account holders, Wall Street Access (www.wallstreetaccess.com) says that its main benefit to investors is that it shops each trade to get the best possible price. Wall Street Access's average assets per account are among the highest in the industry, so it obviously appeals to investors who want a personal touch when placing trades. It is also favored by options investors (see the Options section in Chapter 11 for more information).

WALL STREET ACCESS

Through its partnership with Omega Research, publishers of ProSuite, TradeStation, OptionStation, and RadarScreen, you can place a trade immediately with Wall Street Access from your analysis program, getting you to the market immediately when you spot an opportunity.

Wall Street Electronica

This broker (www.wallstreete.com) prides itself on offering round-the-clock customer service. Indeed, every time I've called its customer service department during my online broker reviews over the last 6 years, a human has answered the phone promptly. The portfolio analysis program, especially the profit and loss table, is terrific. If you generate more than $1,000 in commissions, Wall Street Electronica will give you rebates. Spanish- and Portuguese-speaking customers can access the site in their native languages. Read more about Wall Street Electronica in Chapter 11, which discusses options trading, one of Wall Street Electronica's strongest points.

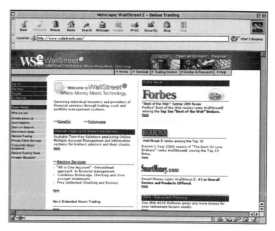

WALL STREET ELECTRONICA

TD Waterhouse

At www.tdwaterhouse.com there's a network of live brokers, giving you a flesh-and-blood alternative to web trading if you'd like. It offers a wide range of assets to trade as well as online banking services. A site upgrade that took place during the latter part of 2000 improved Waterhouse's ease of use considerably. The research amenities integrate quotes, news, charts, and reports for the ticker symbol you're examining, and it remembers the most recent ten stocks you've checked out so you easily can find the information again.

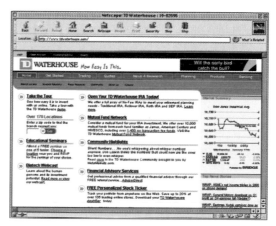

TD WATERHOUSE

Web Street Securities

This is the broker for you if you like to look at a lot of data. Web Street (www.Webstreetsecurities.com) gives you a live streaming ticker displaying the issues held in your portfolio. Account holders with more than $250,000 who

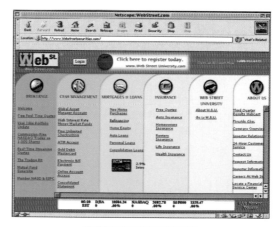

WEB STREET SECURITIES

DIVIDEND REINVESTMENT PROGRAMS

The cheapest way to buy stock is by purchasing it directly from the issuing corporation, bypassing brokers entirely. Then you sign up to have your dividends reinvested in additional shares of stock. This is called a dividend reinvestment program (DRIP), and it's offered by about 1,000 companies.

There are about 100 companies that let you buy stock at a slight discount (3 to 5 percent) from the prevailing market price as well. The downside? There are several. First, you have to own a minimum number of shares of stock already, between one and 50 depending on the individual company, before you can enroll in a DRIP. You can't control the timing of your stock purchases either; the company buys the stock for you on a set schedule, usually once or twice a month. You can buy only one stock at a time from each issuing corporation, so you'll have to open quite a few accounts to put together a balanced portfolio. Check out the details at www.dripinvestor.com, which includes a list of companies currently offering DRIPs.

make more than 25 trades per month qualify for Elite status and perks such as real-time streaming quotes (usually $29.95 per month), access to IPOs, and upgraded customer service. Live brokers are available 24 hours a day for Web Street customers, another perk.

Wingspan Investment Services

This service (www.wingspan.com) is offered by Wingspan Bank and supplies great portfolio performance reports and tax accounting tools. It lets you choose from three different levels of service, gold, premier, and ultimate, depending on your assets ($10,000 for gold on up to $100,000 for ultimate), which can net you reduced commission rates and additional services as you go up the ladder. You can chat with a customer service representative live, online during the week, and you can trade via Touch-Tone phone or a live broker. It's remarkably easy to move funds from a Wingspan bank account into the brokerage account (and vice versa) when necessary. You can also apply for a loan, stick some money into CDs, or get a credit card.

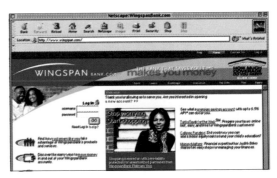

WINGSPAN INVESTMENT SERVICES

Low-cost brokers

IF YOU'RE ALREADY COMFORTABLE online and are just looking for a way to pay lower fees, a broker in this group can save you a lot of money. Don't look for a wide range of creature comforts, but if you're a frequent trader, you can save a lot of money in commissions.

AB Watley Web Trader

This low-cost broker (www.abwatley.com) charges just $9.95 per transaction, for which you get access to a well-designed trading screen. Watley provides a limit order pricing service, published by TradeWorx, that gives you an idea of whether a particular order will be filled at your specified price. You can set up an unlimited number of test portfolios at AB Watley and try out some trades before committing to them with real money. Though it doesn't offer proprietary research, there's access to the usual suspects (Zacks, Briefing.com, Market Guide, etc.) for free. You have to sign a margin agreement when you open an account here.

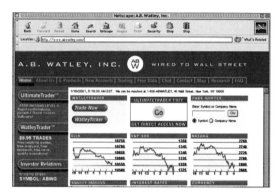

AB WATLEY WEB TRADER

Ameritrade

One of the largest online brokers and one of the heaviest spenders on advertising, Ameritrade (www.ameritrade.com) has a serviceable site that gets the job done at a reasonable price, charging an $8 commission on market orders. NetScreen, a stock screening tool, helps investors pick stocks based on fundamental criteria, and the site also includes a mutual fund screener. You can apply online and check the status of your application, and in most cases you can place trades the next day. Plan to do your financial planning and portfolio analysis offsite, though. Ameritrade invites certain high account balance holders to enjoy Premier status, entitling them to a dedicated broker team that can be contacted via a toll-free number.

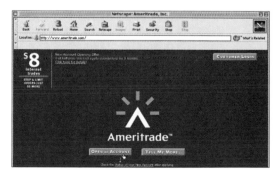

AMERITRADE

Brown and Company

With its $5 commission for market order ($10 limit), Brown and Company (www.brownco.com) is one of the cheapest brokers online. It focuses on high net

BROWN AND COMPANY

worth accounts – it's a minimum of $15,000 to open an account – and it wants prospective customers to declare that they're experienced traders. It provides links to third party research tools, but no proprietary information. Your list of holdings is updated in real time. You might get a rebate on commissions if you rack up more than $350 per month in fees. This site may be for you if you're not put off by the lack of amenities and portfolio analysis reports.

Datek

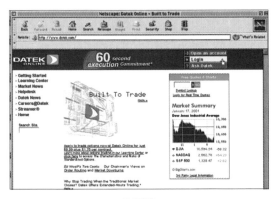

DATEK

A broker that appeals to frequent traders due to its low commissions and streaming quote ticker, Datek (www.datek.com) has information-packed trading screens. The stock screener lets you check out intra-day price movements, which appeals to hyperactive traders. Once you're comfortable trading here, you can opt to bypass Datek's confirmation screen, which sends your order to the markets a few seconds quicker. You can access transaction reports going back three years on Datek's site. You can't trade options here, and you'll have to do your tax accounting offsite as well.

Datek's order entry process is one of the best, with real-time quotes available and execution reports that are quick and informative.

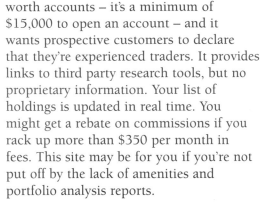

Financial Café

This broker (www.financialcafe.com) opened its virtual doors recently with an offer that's tough to refuse: unlimited free market-order stock commissions and fixed-rate options commissions (up to ten contracts) for only $14.75. The site is cleanly laid out, with easy navigation by clicking on file folder tabs.

Opening and funding an account is simple – you can transfer money into your account directly from your checking account, through the Web. The Trading Pad is the place for entering and monitoring trades.

It opens a separate small window on your monitor that can be run independently. Active customers can elect to bypass the review screen and go straight to the market.

You can qualify for the premium service by having $100,000 in your account and making over 24 trades per month. That also gets you free access to Stox.com's real-time streaming quotes, which usually cost $39.99 a month.

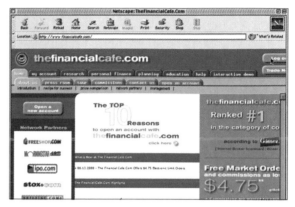

FINANCIAL CAFÉ

Third parties, such as Stox.com, Briefing.com, and Morningstar, supply most of the research offerings for Financial Café. But since your portfolio is not linked to these research items, you'll have to do a lot of extra typing to use these services (and also remember you'll need additional user IDs and passwords).

FirsTrade

Commissions at FirsTrade (www.firstrade.com) are posted at a low $6.95 per market order ($9.95 for limit orders). The site is basic and thus easy to navigate, but most services are aimed at experienced traders with access to outside research. Research functions are available from a drop-down list at the top of the screen and include links to outside services for most of the offerings.

Reuters Moneynet supplies the portfolio manager and charting. It has recently added stock and mutual fund screening tools and goal-planning tools as well as insurance and mortgages.

FIRSTRADE

JB Oxford

One of the first brokers to move into the online world, JB Oxford (www.jboxford.com) has stock and mutual fund screening tools as well as an IRA center, where you can learn about retirement planning and figure out what you'll need to sock away. When you first log on to a JB Oxford account, your current holdings with up-to-date quotes are displayed, and you can go directly to the trading screens from there.

JB OXFORD

Scottrade

Providing just the basics for the equity and options trader, Scottrade's (www.scottrade. com) menu is a list of items (such as trading and research) arrayed down the left side of the screen, offering quick access to what's available. Clients are assigned a personal broker, so they don't have to wait in a long phone queue when they have questions or concerns. With offices located all around the United States, Scottrade also offers access to live brokers. Commissions on trades placed through a live broker are $17 per trade, which is still quite a bargain. Margin traders also appreciate Scottrade's relatively low interest rates on margin debt.

SCOTTRADE

Don't sign up with an online broker until you've taken a look at the web site! Evaluate the broker's demo with your needs in mind.

Wang Investments

This is a workable site (www.wangvest.com) for investors who like low commissions, don't need much hand-holding, and are tracking the performance of

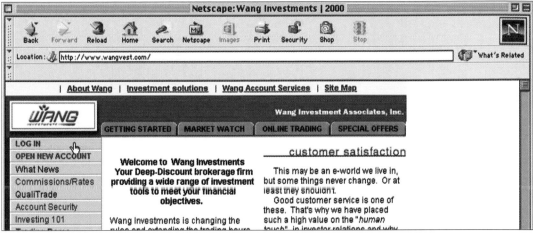

WANG INVESTMENTS

their portfolios elsewhere. Lehman Brothers and Standard & Poor's provide research reports. You can get real-time streaming quotes here, along with after-hours trading. Check out the stock and mutual fund screening tools. It's especially appealing for Chinese speakers who are active investors, because the entire site can be translated with the click of a mouse.

A simple summary

✔ Full-service online brokers serve up large helpings of proprietary research and stock recommendations at a price. They're looking for investors with large accounts.

✔ Brokers offering one-stop shopping entice you not only to trade stocks and mutual funds but also to apply for mortgages and auto loans.

✔ At the lower end of the commission spectrum are brokers who offer sites that are simple with fewer research resources available.

✔ Choosing a low-cost, "no-frills" broker may be your best option if are a confident investor and you trade frequently – you could save a lot of money in commissions.

Chapter 11

Brokers Serving Specialized Traders

BEYOND THE BASICS OF TRADING STOCKS and mutual funds, investors have additional options when considering brokers to serve their specialized needs. Though most of the brokers in Chapter 10's One-stop shopping section allow you to trade options and bonds as well as stocks and mutual funds, this chapter lists brokers who are particularly suited to specialized trading needs.

In this chapter...

✓ *Invest by dollar, not by share*

✓ *Options traders*

✓ *Bond investors*

✓ *Frequent traders and data junkies*

167

Invest by dollar, not by share

RECENTLY, THERE'S BEEN A NEW EQUITY investment model that hit the scene: Brokers that allow investors to "roll their own" mutual funds. One thing all these brokers have in common is a restricted universe of potential investments. Brokers such as BUYandHOLD, ShareBuilder, Foliofn, and UNX.com, utilize an equity investment model that allows investors to create their own mutual funds. You purchase a particular dollar amount, rather than a certain number of shares, of a chosen stock.

For instance, you'd buy $1,000 worth of XYZ Company rather than 100 shares of stock, and you can hold fractional shares. Let's say XYZ is trading at $17 when you enter your order for $1,000 worth – you'd get 58.824 shares. You can put a set dollar amount of stocks into what is called a basket at these sites. For example, assume you have $2,000 to invest. You could choose five high-tech companies, or blue chip companies, and spread your $2,000 evenly among them.

But there are restrictions. For instance, Foliofn has 2,500 stocks available at its regular fees; you have to pay a higher commission to trade in companies that aren't on the list. You're also restricted to certain trading time windows and have to accept the market price at the time of the trade. The idea is that if you're in it for the long run, a fraction of a point here and there won't make or break you.

shareBUILDER™

New! No Fee IRAs more info
Start a monthly retirement plan today

Set Up ShareBuilder Plan - Entry   Account: 1000-0000020071-01 Individual

ShareBuilder Plan Setup
A ShareBuilder Plan allows you to make automatic dollar-based investments in over 4,000 stocks and index products. Setting up a plan is VERY EASY and you can cancel or suspend it at any time.

What stocks do you want to invest in?
Enter a stock ticker and investment amount.

Enter Symbol	Amount to Invest	Reinvest Dividends
QQQ	$ 200 .00	☐
MAC	$ 200 .00	☑

Find ShareBuilder Stocks:
INDEX SHARES ▼ View
BASIC INDUSTRIES INDEX SPDR - XLB
CONSUMER SERVICES INDEX SPDR - XLV

NETSTOCK SHAREBUILDER

BUYandHold and NetStock Sharebuilder

These brokers introduced their easy-to-use web sites (www.buyandhold.com and www.sharebuilder.com) in late 1999. They let you build a basket of stocks one by one. The fees you pay are charged per stock and vary depending on whether you're making a one-time purchase or an automatic investment. Both sites allow investors to specify a particular dollar amount in a stock and then set up dividend reinvestment programs.

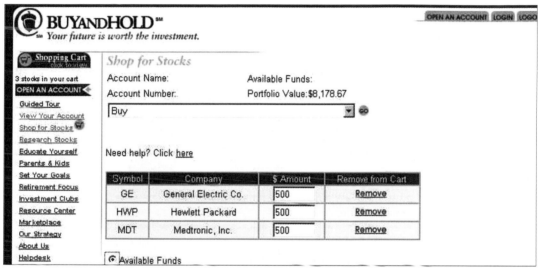

BUY AND HOLD

BUYandHOLD's position report shows your unrealized gains and losses and allows you to invest more in a particular security with one click of the mouse. For $2.99 per transaction (buy or sell), or $9.99 per month for an unlimited number of transactions, you can invest from $20 up in any of the stocks in their listing. NetStock charges a variety of fees, from $1 to $5 per transaction to purchase, but $19.95 to sell. Both brokers offer ways of setting up regular investments, and they make it relatively easy to sock away your money and to make regular monthly contributions to your IRA. They're also both setting up partnerships with banks and other online investing sites like mad. Check with your bank or credit union – you may already have access to one of these brokers.

Foliofn

Launched in spring 2000, Foliofn (www.foliofn.com) has taken the basket idea several steps beyond any other site. Rather than pay an individual commission, customers pay $29.95 per month or $295 per year to maintain an account. Each account holder can have up to three "folios" of stocks (additional folios may be established for $9.95 per month or $95 per year), each of which can contain up to 50 stocks. You can set up a list of, say, ten of your favorite telecom stocks and tell Foliofn to distribute $1,000 across them. One of the most intriguing features of Foliofn is its ability to rebalance your

Here are the stocks in the Dogs of the Dow FOLIO. You can change or add new stocks to this FOLIO when you buy it, customizing the FOLIO to fit your needs. You must decide if a FOLIO is right for you. We can't recommend any FOLIO to you because we don't know your financial needs or goals.

Dogs of the Dow

#	Symbol	Company	Proportion
1	CAT	CATERPILLAR INC DEL	10.00%
2	DD	DU PONT E I DE NEMOURS & CO	10.00%
3	EK	EASTMAN KODAK CO	10.00%
4	GM	GENERAL MTRS CORP	10.00%
5	IP	INTL PAPER CO	10.00%
6	JPM	J P MORGAN CHASE & CO	10.00%
7	MMM	MINNESOTA MNG & MFG CO	10.00%
8	MO	PHILIP MORRIS COS INC	10.00%
9	SBC	SBC COMMUNICATIONS INC	10.00%
10	XOM	EXXON MOBIL CORP	10.00%

FOLIOFN

portfolio should market moves throw it out of whack. You can also trade in stocks that aren't among the 2,500 or so on Folio*fn*'s approved list, but that will set you back $14.95 per trade, and you can't place limit orders. An idea that Folio*fn* has implemented that I'd like to see catch on is the ability to pay commissions by credit card, rather than having the fees deducted from your investment account. This is especially beneficial in IRAs or other tax-deferred accounts.

Universal Network Exchange

Universal Network Exchange (UNX), at www.unx.com, is open only to those investors the company determines are qualified to use its services. These investors usually are brought in by their financial advisers. If you're working with an adviser, check to see if you qualify for an account. Once you get past the gatekeeper, the trading system is designed to let you put together a fund weighted either in equal dollar amounts, by market capitalization of the companies you've chosen, or by some other user-selected criteria. You can trade any security on a United States-based exchange, and you're not restricted to trading "windows" either – the Universal Network Exchange scans ECNs to find the best execution price. You can even short-sell a basket. The net asset value of your portfolio is updated in real-time. The commissions are 2.5 cents per share for domicile accounts and 3.5 cents per share for delivery-versus-payment accounts, with a $10 minimum. There are no maintenance fees. At the moment, UNX.com isn't chasing the retail customer but is providing the engine for institutional investors and registered investment advisers.

Be sure you understand the basics of trading stocks before jumping in with your hard-earned savings!

The mainstream online brokers are, for the most part, prepared to help you learn how to trade stocks, and they offer you plenty of resources for finding out more. The rest of this chapter is devoted to more complex sorts of investments: Options, bonds, and direct access stock trading.

Options traders

MANY OF THE ONLINE BROKERS mentioned in Chapter 10 allow you to trade options, but not online. You have to call a human at many brokerages to place options trades. Several big name brokers don't allow you to trade options at all.

The trading experience on most of the online option trading sites is pretty basic. You enter the symbol for the underlying stock, and then choose a month and a strike price from a list. The symbol that defines the stock, month, and strike price combination is called the option chain. Most stocks have at least 24 chains, or series, to choose from, and some heavily traded stocks have hundreds. Plain old puts and calls or *simple option strategies* are available online at these brokers, and some also automate *complex option strategies*, such as spreads and straddles, as well.

You can place complex strategies even if they're not automated, but you'll need to know how to implement them and be able to make the appropriate entries yourself. Note that complex strategies involve at least two simultaneous transactions, which also subjects you to two simultaneous commission charges.

In general, to exercise or assign an option contract, you'll need to talk to a live broker.

Mainstream brokers

Many mainstream brokers, which cater to the stock and mutual fund investor, also offer options trading. Ameritrade and Accutrade, which use identical trading software, both coach you through the process of entering complex options trades if you select the Options Trading area then click on the Complex folder tab.

National Discount Brokers' (www.ndb.com) options trading area lets you look up the chain using a split screen; you type in the ticker symbol and hit the Ticker link and all available calls and puts are displayed in the bottom two-thirds of the screen. Check the box next to the symbol and you can get quotes on the chains in which you're interested. Find the one you want, and enter its symbol in the appropriate box on the trading screen.

DEFINITION

Simple option strategies *are puts and calls. When you buy a put, you're saying you believe the stock price will drop by a certain date (the expiration date). When you buy a call, you're saying you believe the stock price will rise by a certain date. If you don't have a long or short position in the stock itself, then you're trading in naked puts and calls.* Complex option strategies *include spreads, which are the purchase of a call or put and the sale of another of the same type on the same instrument; straddles, which involve the simultaneous purchase or sale of a put and a call at the same strike price; and strangles, in which the investor makes a simultaneous purchase or sale of a put and call, but with different strike prices.*

Charles Schwab

While Schwab (www.schwab.com) allows complex options strategies to be put in place online, you must first prove yourself worthy and obtain prior authorization, which has up to four levels, to be able to do it yourself. Otherwise, it pushes you to talk to a broker offline to place complex trades. Schwab's online option trading commissions are 20 percent less than those for broker-assisted trades. Some other brokers, such as Quick & Reilly (www.quickandreilly.com), also require investors to have prior authorization to place complex orders.

Wall Street Access and Wall Street Electronica

A feature that sets Wall Street Access (www.wallstreetaccess.com) apart from other online brokers is that it automates buy-write orders so you can make an equity and option transaction simultaneously. Frequent traders with Wall Street Access can earn discounts on data and analysis fees from Omega Research and DBC, who provide in-depth analysis software and historical data. Wall Street Electronica's site (www.wallstreete. com) has quite a few tools for options investors, including a profit and loss statement for options in your portfolio. Both Wall Street Access and Wall Street Electronica clients can place naked puts and calls as well as complex orders.

WALL STREET ACCESS

INTERNET

www.fiafii.org/tutorial/
index.html

www.investopedia.com/
university/options

The Futures Industry Institute and Investopedia offer online tutorials that will teach you about the complexities of trading options. Investopedia's tutorial is short and to the point, and it should take less than half an hour to read. You can move on to the Futures Industry's more extensive tutorial once you've digested Investopedia's information. Trading in options requires more extensive knowledge of the markets and the specific companies you're trading than does trading in stocks.

MAINTAINING AN INVENTORY

Maintaining an inventory of bonds is trickier than it might look to the casual observer. If you want to buy or sell a stock, you're trading an item that is essentially the same whether it was issued at the company's IPO or during a subsequent offering. Bonds, however, have specific characteristics that make each issuance unique, including the date the bond matures and the interest rate that will be paid to the holder over time.

Some investors purchase bonds when the company issues them and hang onto those bonds until they mature. Others trade bonds on the secondary market. Brokerages handle their inventory of bonds in different ways, so if you're looking for a particular company, interest rate, and maturity date, you might have to ask several different brokers if they have it in stock.

As the online marketplace for bonds develops and matures, including the creation of bond clearing houses that is currently underway, it will become easier for participating brokers to offer you the exact bond you want.

Bond investors

THE TURMOIL IN TECHNOLOGY *stocks no doubt has made some online traders appreciate Will Rogers' dictum that the return on capital counts less than the return of capital. Which, of course, leads you to bonds.*

Bond trading online isn't as ubiquitous as online trading of stocks and mutual funds – yet. Online brokers are still working out the kinks in maintaining an inventory of tradable bonds, so expect this area to develop in the next few years.

Bond Express

At www.bondexpress.com is the engine behind DLJ Direct's Fixed Income Center, E*Trade's Bond Center, Charles Schwab's BondSource, TradeBonds, MuniDirect, and BondAgent. You can search for current offerings by type of bond (treasury, muni, corporate, agency) and then build a ladder manually from the resulting choices. The advanced search engine lets you specify the industry when checking out corporate bonds, and it lets you exclude bonds by characteristic, such as whether or not they're callable. You can also buy T-bills and T-bonds at auction. The prices for the bonds vary slightly from site to site, depending on the dealer's markup policy.

The fees at E*Trade's bond site are quite a bit lower than DLJ Direct's, especially for larger orders. But compare several corporate bonds between the sites, and you'll find the prices to be the same. If you buy more than 20 treasuries or ten corporate or muni bonds in a single transaction from E*Trade, there's no fee; otherwise it's $20 for the former and $10 for the latter.

DLJ charges a minimum of $45. E*Trade acts as a principal, which means they own the bonds they're selling to you, so a markup is built into its price. DLJ Direct acts as an agent, selling bonds on behalf of the owner, and charges a commission on the transaction. After E*Trade's markup is added, its net cost might not always be lower.

Charles Schwab

The municipal bond portion is not included online by Schwab (www.schwab.com), though corporate bonds and treasuries are available. Charles Schwab is linking up with ValuBond, which provides a neutral platform that takes electronic feeds from multiple bond markets and puts them in a format for the retail investor. Investors search available inventory based on their personal criteria, then receive a listing of all the bonds that are being offered by many different firms, anonymously and listed by price. This lets users see what's out there and allows the offering institution to compete on the basis of price.

TradeBonds

This site, at www.tradebonds.com, though it contains the same basic information as other bond trading sites, is laid out in a way that's easy to navigate and includes research aimed at the fixed income investor. It doesn't charge a fee for trading anything but treasuries. MuniDirect asks you a series of questions, which you answer by clicking on radio buttons, before launching the search engine. It claims a cost advantage over other sites, but I wasn't able to compare similar issues to verify or deny that.

BondAgent

A subsidiary of BT Alex Brown, BondAgent (www.bondagent.com) offers a search engine that has several more frills than the others. You can specify the months that you want a coupon paid or restrict the search to new offers, for instance. You can also design a search and save it, making it easy to look for the same type of bonds on a future visit to the site.

The trading methodology doesn't exactly qualify as online trading in a strict sense, though; to place a trade, you have to send a secure email to BondAgent's trading desk with the specifics of your transaction, such as the bond CUSIP ID.

Morgan Stanley Dean Witter

Developed internally, Morgan Stanley Dean Witter's bond trading site, at www.msdw.com, lets you search for bonds and then buy from the resulting list by clicking on a Trade button. It has a complete list of treasuries in inventory now, and it is working to add other types of bonds. After filling in the order, you get a confirmation screen that details the total cost of the trade and the commission to be charged. Commissions are on a sliding scale that depends on the number of bonds traded, from $14.95 for up to 25 bonds to $49.95 for over 100 bonds. Morgan Stanley Dean Witter is developing a Fixed Income Center, including fixed income research features, historical data, archived web casts, and the ability to subscribe to research updates and forecasts.

Sites aimed at institutional investors

There are sites that are aimed at institutional investors and broker/dealers, too, such as TradingEdge (www.tradingedge.com), home of BondLink, and TradeWeb (www.tradeweb.com). These services are not available to the individual investor, however. BondLink is an interesting site, though it's packed with graphics that would probably drive an investor to distraction on a dial-up line to the Internet. TradeWeb's site is reminiscent of stock trading programs such as Interactive Broker's offering for day traders, with constantly updated lists of bonds on the market.

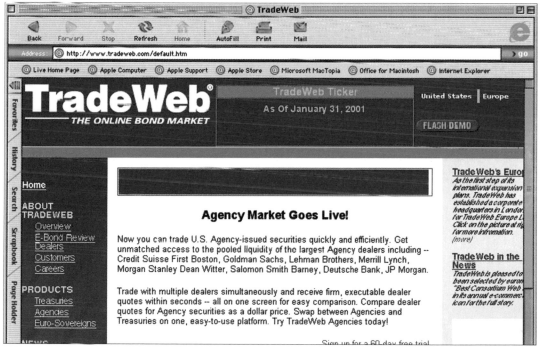

TRADEWEB

Frequent traders and data junkies

IF YOU TRADE FREQUENTLY, *you may find the browser-based brokers a bit on the slow side for your taste. There's an alternative: Direct connect brokers. These brokers give their customers a direct link to the broker's trading desk, usually via downloadable software or a CD.*

Unless you have a fast connection to the Internet, running one of these direct connect brokers is probably not a great idea. There's a lot of data pumped over the wire, and if the data is only trickling down to your computer rather than flowing freely, it's almost not worth it.

These services are not for the infrequent trader, nor are they for the faint of heart. They're also not for Macintosh users; all run on Windows 95/98/NT/2000 only. It'll take some time setting them up to your specifications, and in some cases you will need technical help from the gurus at the broker's office to help get you going. It's not as easy as typing in a web address and pointing and clicking, but if you want to stay connected to the market throughout the trading day, the tools are much more effective than those at most browser-based brokers.

These applications also are geared toward technically inclined investors and are not suitable for fundamental investors. They all offer after-hours trading and access to ECNs, so you can avoid market makers and payments for order flow. The trading screens show you real-time quotes, and in some cases you can watch your order being executed.

CyBerCorp

Acquired in spring 2000 by Charles Schwab, CyBerCorp (www.cybercorp. com), is the most heavily promoted of these applications. CyBerX has an interface that resembles a video game, and most of the pieces of the program are accessible from the main screen.

The main screen doubles as the trading screen, so you don't have to

CYBERCORP

move anywhere in the program to type in a ticker symbol and execute your order. Also accessible from the main screen are account status reports and one of the better portfolio analysis reports, showing unrealized gains and losses. CyBerTrader, CyBerX's burlier sibling, is available for frequent investors who want more information, dynamically updated, displayed on the screen at all times.

MyDiscountBroker

InvestorView, a direct connection program, and a browser-based system are offered at MyDiscountBroker (www.mydiscountbroker.com). InvestorView's order entry process is clear and simple. As soon as you type in a ticker symbol and hit the Tab key to begin entering an order, the screen displays the name of the security you've requested along with a real-time quote. After you complete the order entry screen and hit the Continue button, you're taken to a confirmation screen that shows you your order and lets you correct any possible mistakes. Market orders are executed within seconds when the exchange is open, and a trade execution screen pops up quickly. Your account status is updated immediately as well. Busy traders can search transactions based on various selection criteria, such as date, ticker symbol, and type of trade, to see how they're doing. Portfolio reports, which are updated with real-time quotes, display unrealized gains and losses for open positions. A mouse click on a Refresh button brings in new real-time quotes as necessary. Commissions are relatively low at $12 per transaction (up to 5,000 shares). You can use the same account for both the browser-based system and InvestorView, so you can trade even when you're away from your regular computer.

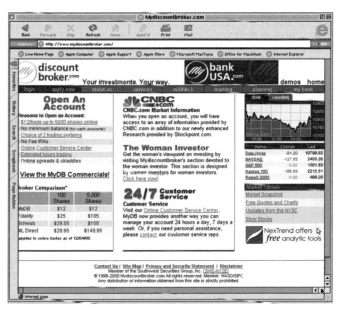

MYDISCOUNTBROKER

MyTrack

Provided by Track Data, myTrack (www.mytrack.com), has a one-click trading function that takes you quickly to a trading screen, where you can buy and sell stocks, options, and futures. There's a wealth of charting functionality provided by AIQ, a software publisher who develops expert systems for stock trading, and you can follow mutual funds (though you can't trade them here). You can also follow foreign exchanges.

MYTRACK

It's one of the easier applications to use of the group, though there's so much here that it will probably take you weeks to find all the bells and whistles. It has a contest going that helps new users get comfortable with the software before they start to use their own money, and you can chat live with someone in tech support if you have a problem. Additional data feeds are available at different levels based on whether you're a silver, gold, or platinum member.

One advantage to using direct access brokers is the price improvement technology they've developed. The software finds the best price available at the time you place your trade, scanning the available exchanges to help squeeze out another fraction of a point in your favor.

Onsite Trading

At www.onsitetrading.com, the software comes in two pieces: The trading application, RediPlus, and the charting and quotes application, AT Financial. They're both big downloads followed by extensive tinkering with network specifications as you configure your computer to talk to theirs. The online manual is a big help – actually, a must – for

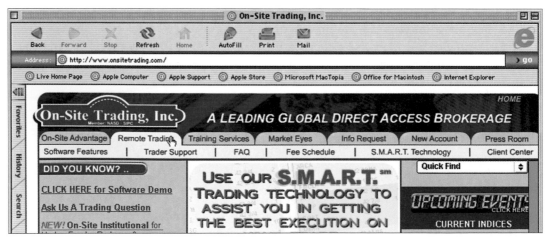

ONSITE TRADING

the new user. RediPlus puts a menu bar on the left side of your screen, giving push-button access to the order entry application as well as to quote and index monitors, charting, and tickers. You can also open up a window that lets you keep track of day highs and lows. A real-time quote pops into the trading screen as soon as you type in a ticker symbol. You can specify Limit or Better on the buy side when placing an order.

Sutton Online

At Sutton Online (www.suttononline.com) you get access to three different types of accounts: A browser-based account, a direct access account with real-time quote feeds, and a direct access account with Level II quotes. The Level II direct-access program, Sonic 2000, starts out as a blank gray screen that you can fill with windows depending on what you want to see. The Account window shows the current positions and updates unrealized gains and losses on a tick-by-tick basis, while the Orders window displays all open orders. You can open up as many Trading screens, which include the Level II quote display, as you can jam on the screen.

The Market Watch screen lets you set up a list of ticker symbols that are updated with each trade. The Trading screens, connected to the Level II quote display, offer up-to-the-second information on a stock's price. You can

SUTTON ONLINE

direct your order to SelectNet, SOES, Instinet, Archipelago, or ISLAND, or pick Any and the Sutton software tries to find the best price. Beginners should set their defaults to Confirm Orders, otherwise a click on the Buy or Sell button will instantly send an order to the market. Commissions drop based on the number of trades per month; once you're up to 20, you get the Level II software for free (otherwise it's $100 a month). You can use the Sonic software with what GCM calls "Level 1½" quotes, which still gives you real-time quotes and position updates.

TradeCast

TradeCast (www.tradecast.com) publishes Revolution, which includes premium research at no additional cost, such as S&P MarketScope, Stock Reports, and Mutual Fund Reports, as well as Instant Analyst (from buysellorhold.com), which gives a snapshot of real-time technical indicators and fundamentals for a particular ticker. The screen is similar to CyBerCorp's CyBerX, but it displays more information at startup. This

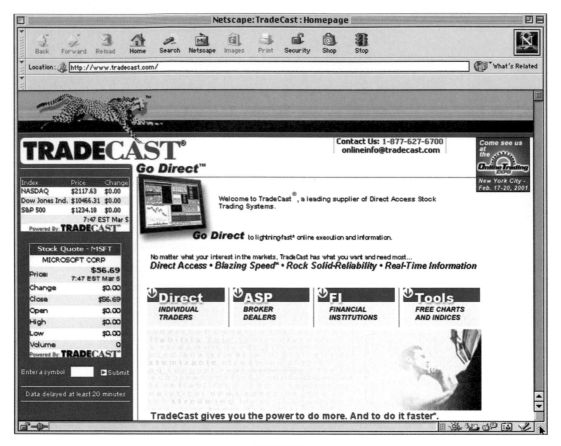

TRADECAST

program sets up easily and is simple enough to use that the online manual won't be your constant companion. It's got a good blend of direct access plus research tools. The trading screen is accessible from the real-time quote display. Clicking on the Advanced button brings up a screen that displays each trade as it hits the floor. Level I quotes are included; Level II quotes will set you back $60 per month. TradeCast was purchased by Ameritrade in early 2001.

Watley Ultimate Trader FREE

When you open an account with at least $10,000, Watley Ultimate Trader FREE (www.abwatley.com) offers free Level II quotes. It provides several profit and loss reports and up-to-date buying power and portfolio calculations as well. You can design and load multiple screens with Ultimate Trader FREE, so you can customize how you view different equities or industries if you'd like. Unlike some of the other brokers, Watley lets you view your account information on its web site as well as via its direct link software.

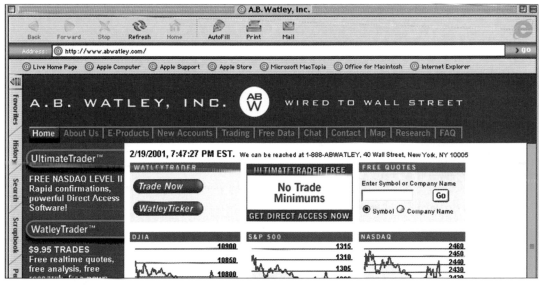

A.B. WATLEY

A simple summary

✔ If you trade outside the stock and mutual fund mainstream, you can find brokers who offer the specialized services you'll need.

✔ Brokers such as NetStock ShareBuilder, BUYandHOLD, Folio*fn*, and UNX.com let you buy stocks in set dollar amounts rather than by share lots.

✔ If you're an options trader, look for a broker that supports the strategies you want to implement.

✔ Though many mainstream online brokers automate bond trading, there are several that offer greater inventory or specific types of bonds.

✔ Frequent investors and day traders should look to the direct-access brokers, who offer software that links directly to Level II quotes and the trading floor.

Chapter 12

Understanding Costs

THE ADS YOU SEE about online trading focus on the commissions charged for trading stocks. That's not all you'll be charged for, however, and some of the fees that you have to pay might surprise you. Though it's true that trading online is almost always cheaper than talking to a real live broker, you should be prepared for other charges that can affect you.

In this chapter...

✓ *Basic costs*

✓ *Extra costs*

✓ *Hidden costs*

✓ *Getting price breaks from your broker*

WORKING OUT FEES IN ADVANCE WILL PREVENT UNWELCOME SURPRISES

Basic costs

THE LOW-COST ONLINE BROKERS *use cheap commissions to entice you to open accounts with them. Some even offer transactions free of commission charges, depending on your account balance and how often you trade.*

> To find your best deal, think about the equities you're most likely to trade and estimate how often you'll be trading.

If you'll be trading dozens of times per month, the broker's commission will be more important to you than it will be to an investor who trades just a few times per month. If you want to trade options more often than stocks, take a good look at the charges for options trading and make sure you understand them.

Stock trading commissions: The tip of the iceberg

Ever since stock brokerages were introduced, investors have had to pay to conduct transactions. The allure of online brokerages is that you can save a lot of money on commissions. Right now the range for commissions is from $0 to about $30, but there are a few "gotchas" to watch out for when you're looking over a broker's fee schedule.

Market order commissions are generally cheaper than limit orders. When you place a market order, you agree to take the next block of stock that's available. When you place a limit order, you control the price that you'll pay (if you're buying) or accept (if you're selling). Most brokers charge a premium for limit orders, but some do not. If you think your usual transaction will be limit orders, be sure to compare those commissions rather than market order commissions.

Some brokers charge a flat rate for trading up to a certain number of shares, usually 1,000, though some go as high as 5,000. If you trade a larger block, you might be subject to a per-share charge of one to two cents.

If you use one of the electronic communication networks (ECNs), such as Island or Archipelago, to place your trades, you'll pay a per-share fee of one-half to three cents on top of the brokerage commission.

You could qualify for lower commissions if you trade frequently. E*Trade, for instance, drops its charges from $14.95 to $9.95 for a market order if you trade 30 or more times per quarter.

If for some reason you can't get to a computer to place a trade, many brokers let you use a Touch-Tone trading service, or you can call to speak to a live broker. Check out the additional charges for these services. Touch-Tone trading usually has the same fee as online trading but can carry additional fees of $2–$20 per transaction, depending on the broker. Talking to a live broker can add $5–$50 to your transaction, unless there's a technical problem with the web site.

■ **Bear in mind** *that you need to factor in the cost of your phone calls when assessing the overall cost of a transaction. Talking to a real live broker may add considerably to the bill.*

Are you planning to trade stocks that are listed on non-United States exchanges? If so, there's usually a surcharge on the transaction, either a flat fee or a per-share charge.

Mutual funds: No load, no transaction fee

Mutual funds are available from the majority of online brokers, but their charges for placing a trade vary. Check through the broker's list of no transaction fee mutual funds.

Trivia...

The average per-share transaction commission charged by the top ten online brokers dropped from nearly $53 in 1996 to $15.50 by the end of 1999.

You pay in a variety of ways for mutual funds – the fee the brokerage might charge you to buy or sell shares in a fund are just part of the picture. Sometimes the funds themselves charge a fee, which is called a load, when you purchase or sell. If the fund has a front-end load, then you pay when you make your initial purchase. A back-end load is assessed when you sell. Many funds are advertised as no-load funds, but these funds are allowed to charge a fee, called a 12b-1 fee, for marketing, advertising, and other expenses. Regulations require these fees to be less than 0.25 percent of the fund's total assets if the fund is going to advertise itself as a no-load fund. The phrase pure no-load fund applies to those that don't charge 12b-1 fees at all.

No transaction fee funds are those that the broker supplies without charging commissions. It's possible that these funds carry loads, though, so check the prospectuses carefully. The fees charged by brokers for buying or selling funds that aren't on the no transaction fee list vary from $10 to $35.

Depending on the funds, when you exchange one for another, you might be charged a single transaction fee, two fees (one for the fund you're selling and one for the fund you're buying), or no fee at all. Check in advance to avoid a surprise when you swap that sluggish mutual fund for one that you hope will be a winner.

Options trading fees: Comparing apples with apples

Figuring out the commissions you'll pay for options transactions can be a real adventure. The formulas some brokers use to charge commissions on options trades can be incredibly difficult to follow. Though some assess a flat fee, most charge a base fee, say $20, plus a fee per option contract of $0.50 to $2. Others charge a higher commission on options contracts with higher premiums.

I recently looked at 25 online brokers that allowed options transactions and found an incredible range of fees – much wider than those charged for stock transactions. For instance, for ten contracts at a $5 premium, the fees ranged from $19.50 (at Interactive Brokers) to $67 (at Siebertnet). Most brokers charged $30–$45 for this transaction. For 20 contracts, the range was $39 (again at Interactive Brokers) to $95 (at TD Waterhouse), with the average running at $55–$70.

Not all online brokers publish their options commissions on their web sites. If you want to trade options online, you should take the opportunity to call the broker's customer support line for a clear explanation of the fees.

Buying bonds?

Here's another area with a wide range of fees. Isn't it interesting that the brokers seldom advertise their commissions for trading equities other than stocks? I think that's because their fee schedules vary so much and can be relatively difficult to figure out. As with options, bond commission schedules are complicated for most brokers. And, like options, many brokers don't publish their rates on their web sites, so you have to call to get the current information.

Some brokers sell bonds to their customers out of their own inventory and don't charge a commission. They do, however, take a piece of the profit by selling you the bond at a slight premium, which is not disclosed to you.

Several brokers, such as Charles Schwab, charge lower fees on bond transactions to customers with high account balances. If your account size is over $100,000, you should ask about a break on bond commissions.

Extra costs

EVERY ONCE IN A WHILE, you might ask your broker to perform a service that will result in a fee being charged. Let's take a look at some of the other things you might do that you'll end up paying for, which you'll find listed under Non-Trading Fees when you study an online broker's web site.

Account setup and maintenance fees

Fortunately, account setup fees are pretty rare these days, though five years ago quite a few brokers charged a small amount, between $25 and $100, just to deal with the paperwork it took to open an account.

■ **Read the small print** *to check whether you incur additional fees when you use a credit or debit card to pay.*

Inactive accounts are charged maintenance fees with some brokers. For instance, if you're not trading a couple of times a year, Fidelity will charge you $15 per quarter unless you have more than $30,000 in your account.

Your IRA account may be subject to an annual maintenance fee. Most online brokers waive the fee if you have more than $10,000 in the account, but you still might be charged $25–$100 per year. The excuse for this fee is the additional paperwork brought on by government regulations.

If your account includes a credit or debit card, you may be charged an annual fee for its use. High account balance holders often get this fee waived, but it's worth asking about before you accept the card.

Margin rates: When you borrow from your broker

As discussed in Chapter 9, you can borrow money on margin so that you can own more assets than your current cash balance would allow. One reason it's difficult to compare the costs of trading on margin is the wide range of fees used. Generally, the broker charges a premium over a base interest rate, but the base interest rate changes frequently and is defined differently from one broker to another. Some use the broker call rate as their base, and others use the prime rate. Dig through the broker's web site, or make a phone call to customer service, and make sure you understand the interest rate schedule as well as the timing of the charges.

Here's one broker's margin rate policy. At the time this policy was in effect, the broker call rate (as published daily in the *Wall Street Journal*) was 8.25 percent.

Margin balance	Interest rate
Up to $50,000	Broker call rate plus 0.25 percent (8.5 percent)
From $50,000 up to $100,000	Broker call rate (8.25 percent)
From $100,000 up to $500,000	Broker call rate minus 0.25 percent (8.0 percent)
$500,000 and over	Broker call rate minus 0.5 percent (7.75 percent)

You have to figure out how much you think you'll borrow on margin in a typical month, and then do the math to see if it's worth it. Frankly, many brokers entice customers into the fold with low commissions because they know they'll make more money off the margin fees.

Some brokers average out the size of your margin account over the month and charge interest based on that average. Others calculate your margin balance daily and add up your interest charges as the month goes on. For instance, if your margin balance was zero at the beginning of the month, $2,000 on the 10th of the month, then took a jump to $8,000 on the 15th, you'd be subject to different interest calculations depending on the broker. A daily calculation is best for you, since you're paying for what you're actually borrowing.

Here's Datek's relatively clearly worded description of its margin policies: "All Datek Online accounts, with the exception of retirement accounts and custodian accounts, are eligible to trade on margin. Credit balances [excluding short sales credits] in your Datek Account earn interest, while money borrowed on margin is charged interest. A daily debit or credit balance is calculated based on the sum of all settlement date balances in all account types, less the mark-to-market value of all net short positions. Interest charges are calculated on the average net debit balance in your account based upon a sliding scale of percentage above and below the Broker Call Money Rate."

Getting paper statements and confirmations

When you first open your account, you'll be inundated with paper for a few weeks. You'll get a copy of the broker's agreement and all kinds of brochures enticing you to deposit more money or sign up for some other financial services. Many brokers let you opt to receive future communications online if you'd like. Trade confirmations and monthly statements can be sent online, which will save a few trees as well as the time it would take to mail the piece of paper to you.

Once you've opted for paperless statements, you might be subjected to fees if you request a paper statement. E*Trade, for instance, duns you $5 for a copy of your statement if you want one mailed to you. If you request a copy of a check that you wrote on the cash in your brokerage account, many brokers charge a fee of $10–$20.

Stock certificates and other antiques

I can recall seeing a file folder filled with stock certificates at my grandmother's house when I was a kid. It was fun to take them all out and look at the drawings, then do the math and figure out how much all those pieces of paper were worth. Investors seldom get physical certificates that show how many stocks they own any more, opting instead to hold the stock at the brokerage. Given that you might buy a stock today and sell it before the end of the month, it doesn't make a lot of sense to physically file your certificates any more.

If you want your brokerage to issue you a certificate, you'll be charged a fee of $10–$30 per stock. The reason most often given for wanting a stock certificate is that the purchaser plans to give it as a gift. That's an expensive piece of paper!

Can brokers charge to send me a check?

Can they? Yes, they can. When I first checked on the fees charged by brokerages that were sending investors their own money, I found that the majority of them were deducting $5–$15 per check sent out. It's much rarer now to be charged for this, since most brokerages allow you to write checks on your cash balances. Expect to pay a fee if you want your broker to cut a check to a third party on your behalf.

If you want your funds wired to another bank account or financial institution, you'll pay $10–$25 for the privilege, unless you're a preferred customer with a high account balance.

■ **Some brokers** *still charge for sending out checks. If you want to avoid this expense, find a brokerage that has dispensed with such fees.*

Closing an account or transferring assets to another broker

Take special care when transferring mutual funds from one broker to another. Though brokers are happy to open your account and accept the assets you want to deposit, they put up a hurdle or two when you want to move on. Expect to pay $10–$50 for each asset (such as a block of stock or your holdings in a mutual fund) that you transfer out of your brokerage account. If you close the entire account, the broker may charge you an additional fee, usually $15–$50.

When you close an account and transfer a mutual fund out, your new broker may not have that particular item or family of funds on its approved list. So you may wind up having to liquidate the old fund, and transfer the cash to the new broker. Be careful here; you'll have to pay taxes on the capital gain.

Hidden costs

WHEN YOU BUY A BLOCK OF STOCK, *it's hard to know exactly who the seller is. Your trade might be routed through a variety of channels, invisible to you, that would come as a surprise if you were able to track them. Sometimes these channels add to your costs and line the pockets of intermediaries with profits, while all you're aware of are the low commissions you've paid.*

There's a reason so many brokers offer such cheap commissions. They want your business so they can route your trade to a market maker, and get a kickback in the process. Here's how it works.

A potential biggie

When selling shares of stock, be aware and prepared for the *payment for order flow*.

There are three players in this game: The individual investor, the broker, and a company called a market maker. As you recall from Chapter 2, a market maker is a firm that specializes in trading stock in a particular publicly traded company or group of companies.

> ### DEFINITION
>
> *Let's say you want to sell 200 shares of QRS. When you place your order, your broker sends it to a market maker in QRS stock. The market maker then pays your broker a small fee for routing your block of QRS stock to them. This fee is income for your broker and is called* payment for order flow.

Usually the stocks are traded on the NASDAQ or OTC, but you'll find market makers in other exchanges as well.

The market maker buys your stock at its bid price, then turns around and sells it at its ask price. The difference can be ⅛ to ¼ of a point (or dollar), thereby giving the market maker a gross profit of $25 to $50 on your order. You might be happy having paid just $7 or $15 in commissions, but in fact you've given away another $25–$50.

Can you avoid playing the order flow game? The only way is to find a broker who does not accept payment for order flow. When you open an account, and on an annual basis after that, your broker has to divulge whether or not they accept payment for order flow. Brokers also have to disclose on their trade confirmations whether they make money from order flow and give their customers the opportunity to get more information on their particular transactions. Using order flow as a method of making money is actually on the decline now, though it hasn't disappeared. But it's not just online and discount brokers that participate in payment for order flow. Plenty of full-service brokers have accepted payment for order flow while they're charging their customers large commissions. Proponents of payment for order flow say it makes the markets more orderly, since trades are routed through specialists.

When your broker is a market maker

The market maker quotes a bid, or the price it'll pay to buy the stock, and quotes an ask, or the price it'll accept when selling the stock. Market makers hope to make profits on the spread, which is the difference between the bid and the ask. As mentioned above, your broker can make a penny or so per share by routing your order to a particular market maker.

But what happens when your broker is also the market maker? In that case, you might be buying the stock at the current market price directly from your broker's inventory. On your confirmation notice, you'll see a line that reads, "We make a market in this equity," or some similar wording, when your broker is a market maker. Though this situation can be annoying, especially since you also pay your broker a commission to make the trade, it's pretty difficult to avoid. Many brokers maintain an inventory of shares of stock in the most active equities.

Trivia...

When I enter a transaction, I keep an eye on the Island ECN book at www.isld.com to see what the current best price is for a stock. You can print the screen out to have a record of the pricing during the time you placed your order, then compare it to the price you actually got.

Getting price breaks from your broker

THERE ARE PLENTY OF WAYS TO GET *special treatment from your broker, but they all involve either big bucks or executing a large number of transactions.*

Preferred customer status: Having a big account

It's good to be the King, as Mel Brooks often says. In the world of investments, a larger account gets you additional perks and you often get lower commissions. For instance, a Signature Platinum customer at Schwab, with over $1,000,000 on account, can get the online brokerage rates even when placing a trade with a live broker. In addition, some small fees such as wire transfers and statement copies can be waived for those with large accounts.

Many brokers offer breaks to clients with over $100,000 in their account, though some give you the goodies at $25,000. The more the merrier, though, so as your assets grow, look for a broker who will give you extra services and lower fees for the privilege of handling your account.

Preferred trading status: Making lots of trades

Another way to get treated royally is to make a lot of transactions. Quite a few brokers, including E*Trade, Fidelity, Schwab, and Wall Street Electronica, either lower their commissions for active traders or offer a quarterly rebate. Many of the direct access brokers offer free real-time streaming quotes to frequent traders. At Schwab, for instance, those who make 48 or more trades per year (that's just four per month) are also given access to their Signature Platinum services, just like clients with over $1,000,000 in their accounts.

When you have a huge block of stock to trade

Trading online is incredibly convenient, but if you're trying to buy or sell a large block of stock – say 2,000 shares or more – you'd be better off contacting your broker directly to find out if special services are available for you. Muriel Siebert's Siebertnet encourages customers trading large blocks to let a broker make the transaction personally. The company will negotiate commissions on a trade-by-trade basis.

A large block of stock might be chopped up into smaller pieces when trading online, and you can get prices that can vary depending on how the market is moving. Unless you specify All or None when placing the trade, your transaction might be charged additional commissions as each piece of it is bought or sold.

By letting your broker deal with the block personally, you can negotiate a single commission for the entire transaction, and possibly get a better price as well. It's worth asking for before you hit the market with a big block of stock. Similarly, if you're buying a large number of bonds, say $50,000–$100,000 of a particular issue, your broker should give you a break on the commissions.

My rule of thumb is that it never hurts to ask for a break when you think you can get one!

A simple summary

✔ Costs vary widely from broker to broker. Be sure to check out the fees that will be charged for the services you'll use most often.

✔ Besides the obvious charges – commissions for trading stocks, mutual funds, options, bonds, and other equities – brokers collect fees for account maintenance, issuing checks, and reprinting statements.

✔ Some brokers collect payment for order flow, which nets them a small fee per share from a market maker in the stock you're trading. You'll never see this fee but it can make what looks like a cheap commission much more expensive.

✔ If possible, build your account up to the point where you're treated as a preferred or elite customer. You'll avoid maintenance fees, and be given additional perks such as lowered commissions and premium research.

Chapter 13

Putting Brokers to the Test

Now that you have an idea of what online brokers have to offer and a sense of your own financial profile, choose three or four brokers to check out in depth. Narrowing your choices down to one is worth the time you'll invest in researching whether a broker works for you. Wading through the reports, trading screens, and research offerings is an important part of choosing a broker.

In this chapter...

✓ The online demo

✓ When the demo doesn't tell all

✓ Big broker versus the little guy

✓ Your broker scorecard

ONLINE DEMOS ALLOW YOU TO CHECK OUT A PROSPECTIVE BROKER BEFORE SIGNING UP

The online demo

A LARGE MAJORITY OF ONLINE BROKERS give you some idea, even if it's just by displaying snapshots of the site's screens, of what you'll get once you sign up as a customer. Several offer an interactive demo, usually with data that's fairly old or with restrictions on the stock you can pretend to trade. The interactive demos are preferable because they give you a feel for navigating around the site. You can wander around like Goldilocks in search of the perfect experience: Is this one too much, too little, or just right?

Customizing your first look

A recent, and welcome, trend is the possibility of customizing the broker's screens so that they fit your investing needs better. Some brokers, mostly those in our one-stop shopping list in Chapter 10, let you choose what you'll look at when you first sign on – your portfolio, market news, and tidbits on hot stocks are among the possibilities. Find out whether you can tweak the screen to your specifications.

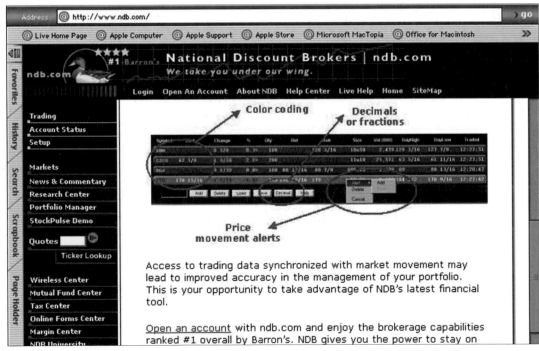

■ **Easy-to-navigate sites** *that offer features including real-time balance updates and clear, well-organized trading screens are essential to a good trading experience.*

Real-time quotes are one feature that many brokers dole out depending on how often you buy or sell stocks. While you're browsing the demo, find out whether you get real-time quotes free of charge, or whether you build up a "bank" of quotes whenever you make a trade.

How often do you think you'll be trading? The typical reaction people have to establishing an online brokerage account, according to a study published by Fidelity Investments, is to trade like mad, at least in comparison to pre-online brokerage behavior. Some brokers extend additional perks to customers who trade frequently. Check those out and see if they're enough to sway your decision.

What can you trade with this broker?

We haven't yet found an online broker that doesn't let you buy and sell United States-based listed stocks, but maybe you're interested in trading other types of equities. Does this broker let you trade mutual funds, options, and bonds online? How many mutual funds does it supply, and how many of those are no-load funds and free of transaction fees? If you're interested in *selling stocks short*, make sure the broker has that capability – not all of them do.

Checking out the online demo is also the time to find out whether you can telephone a broker or place a trade using a Touch-Tone phone. Many online brokers have offline offices – where is the nearest one to your home and your place of work? Alternatives to trading online can come in handy when you're away from your computer.

> **DEFINITION**
>
> *When you sell a stock short, you borrow shares from your broker (or another investor) and sell them, then buy them back later. You're betting that the price of the shares will drop, and that you will turn a profit by selling high and buying back low.*

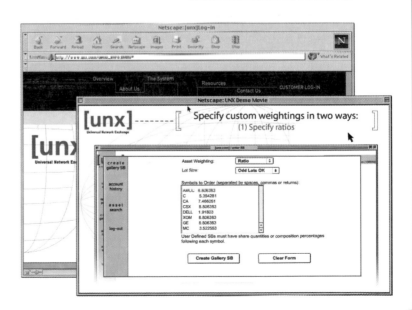

■ **Interactive demos** *are available at many sites. At UNX you can also apply for a demonstration account in order to practice your skills.*

The trading experience

Having a good trading experience is an area of investing online that is important to me, and one that I check out carefully when writing my reviews. I like to see a well-organized trading screen that offers a current real-time quote, provides drop-down boxes to help avoid data entry errors, and error checking procedures that can prevent an expensive mistake. Do you get a verification screen that shows you the full name of the equity you're buying, just to make sure you haven't made a typo with the ticker symbol? Confirmation reports that either pop up or are easy to find, along with portfolio, position, and account balance updates in real time, are also important.

Check out all the order entry screens you think you'll be using: Stocks, mutual funds, options, bonds. Do the screens clearly guide you through the transaction, or do they confuse you? You don't want to make a mistake, but you also want to be able to place an order quickly if the market is moving fast.

The amenity waltz

Be sure to look carefully at the reports the broker offers. How many different ways can you view your portfolio? Naturally, there should be an easy way to see your current holdings and current buying power. Beyond that, find out whether there's a report that shows your unrealized profits and losses and your portfolio performance over time. Can you set up a test portfolio and set price alerts on the stocks you want to follow?

Does this broker give you some help preparing your tax returns? You should look for a way to list your round-trip trades (purchase and sale of the same stock) to see if they match the tax lots for you so that your tax return is easier to prepare.

Now check out what kind of research you can do with this broker. Is there a stock screener and mutual fund selector? What kind of information can you get about a company you're researching – quotes, charts, news, analyst ratings, insider trading, income projections, and fundamental data are helpful things to have.

Some brokers give you proprietary research that's available only to their customers. Others send you out across the Internet to do it yourself. Check the broker's research offerings to see if it gives you information in a way that makes sense to you and is easy to access.

How to open an account

Most brokers require that you send them money or transfer assets from another broker to open an account. What is the minimum amount you need to open an account? What

If you have *Internet Explorer, check out which version you are using and that it supports 128-bit encryption.*

is the procedure for transferring some stocks or mutual funds from another account? If you're opening an IRA, what are the annual fees? Will those fees be waived if you have a specified amount in your account?

Check through the site to see if you can open an account online. You'll still have to print out a few forms and mail them in because your signature is required on some legal documents, but it's easier if you can get the bulk of the application process completed online. Find out how soon you can place a trade once you've filled out the forms and made your initial deposit.

While filling out forms to open an account, make sure your browser's Secure signal is on! Microsoft Internet Explorer users see a little padlock on the bottom bar of the browser screen, while Netscape users see a key.

As long as I'm discussing security, make sure you're comfortable with the way the broker handles your personal information. There have yet to be any reports of hackers removing assets from online brokerage accounts, so the brokerages are doing a great job so far.

You'll do yourself a favor by making sure you have the most secure version of your browser with 128-bit encryption. With your browser open, click on Help and then About to see which version you have.

In Internet Explorer, you'll see the version number, and on the next line a notation for "Cipher Strength." If that doesn't say 128-bit, click on the Update Information link for help with upgrading. In Netscape, scroll down to the description of your version's encryption software. If it doesn't say, "This version supports high-grade (128-bit) security," then go to www.netscape.com and download the most recent version.

When the demo doesn't tell all

THERE ARE A FEW THINGS that are difficult to figure out from a demo no matter how well it's put together. I highly recommend that you come up with a question, whether it's about a particular fee or the availability of a report, and call the broker's customer service line. How quickly is the phone answered? Do you end up in voice-mail hell, or does a human talk to you right away? Are you treated courteously?

A recent innovation for online brokers is immediate assistance using a chat feature. Check that out – just open the chat window and ask a quick question and see whether the reply is useful to you. I like this feature quite a bit now that I've gotten used to it – I keep my phone line free, and the response is usually rapid. Find out whether the person you're chatting with is a registered broker. He or she can often answer more technical questions about the process of placing a trade than a customer service representative.

■ **Do a little detective work:** *Ring a broker's customer service line with a query to find out how long it takes for your question to be answered and how much help you receive.*

Big broker versus the little guy

THANKS TO THE UBIQUITOUS *advertisements about online brokers, many of us are conditioned to think that the bigger brokers are automatically better, safer, and offer more features. You may find, as you explore what the brokers have to offer, that this isn't necessarily the case. I'm troubled by the reports of technical problems suffered by some of the larger brokers. They often have many more customers than they can handle during a busy market. Some of the larger brokers have the capacity to have only 5–10 percent of their customers online simultaneously.*

■ **The smaller the brokerage,** *the greater the chance of a more personal service. You could even get to know the member of the customer service team who is responsible for your account.*

Be sure when you're checking out brokers to include at least one of the smaller brokers in your search. A question you might consider asking brokers is, "What percentage of your customers can be online simultaneously?" Then ask what they'll do for you if you can't log on because their servers are bogged down.

The disadvantage of the smaller brokers is that they might not have an office close by that you can visit in person, or their customer service department might be slow to make your deposits available or to answer your questions. One positive aspect about a small customer service department, though, is that you might get to know the person who takes care of your account. So ask yourself whether you're more comfortable dealing with David or Goliath before you open an account.

Your broker scorecard

ONCE YOU'VE NARROWED YOUR LIST *of potential brokers down to two or three, use the following table as you go through the demos to note what you notice about the site's offerings. If one of these questions is important to you, and the demo doesn't tell you whether a broker offers the service or not, give the broker a call!*

You need to fill in only the blanks for the items that concern you. For instance, if you don't plan to trade options, you can skip over those questions. Be sure to take some notes on the final section, My Personal Reactions to the Site. Sometimes it's just your gut feeling about how the site will work for you that will make the difference between an online broker you avoid – and one that you'll use often.

Don't hire a broker blindly or by relying on the television ads or advice from a friend. As the old saying goes, "Your mileage may vary." Avoid frustration by taking a first-hand look at the broker's site before you deposit your cash or other assets.

ONLINE BROKER DEMO REVIEW

	Broker 1	Broker 2	Broker 3
Name of broker			
Web site address			

Part 1: What can I trade online? (tick for yes)	Broker 1	Broker 2	Broker 3
Stocks: Long			
Stocks: Short			
Mutual funds			
Number of funds available			
Number of no-load funds			
Number of no-transaction fee funds			
Funds currently in my portfolio?			
Options			
Complex option strategies			
Bonds: Corporate			
Bonds: US treasuries			
Bonds: Municipal			
Certificates of deposit			
Interest rate paid on money market funds (taxable or tax-free?)			
Part 2: Reports			
Portfolio holdings			
Portfolio performance (including cost basis)			
Tax reports (capital gains)			
Unrealized gains and losses			
Real-time buying power			
Real-time margin balance			
Transaction history: How long?			
Other reports I like:			

Part 3: Investment analysis	Broker 1	Broker 2	Broker 3
Ticker symbol lookup (find and test it)			
Stock screener available?			
Mutual fund screener available?			
Bond screener available?			
Options chain research			
Real-time quotes			
Stock charting			
How many years of stock history?			
Fundamental data			
Technical analysis			
Access to Government/SEC reports and filings			
Research reports on specific companies			
Analyst ratings (buy/sell/hold)			
Part 4: The trading screens			
Is the trading process understandable?			
Is a real-time quote available before the trade is placed?			
When I place a sell order, can I pick from my current list of holdings?			
Does the confirmation screen tell me the total cost including commission?			
How am I notified that my trade has executed? (onsite report, email?)			
Part 5: Fees			
Commission on market order			
Commission on limit order			
Mutual fund transaction			
Bond transaction fee			
Options fees			
Margin rate for $10,000 balance			
Margin rate for $25,000 balance			
Margin rate for $50,000 balance			

	Broker 1	Broker 2	Broker 3
Account maintenance fee (annual/quarterly?)			
Minimum balance to avoid maintenance fees			
Part 6: Opening and funding an account			
What is the minimum to open an account?			
Can I open an account online?			
Can I transfer money into my account online?			
How long will it take before I can place a trade?			
Part 7: My personal reactions to the site			
Is it easy to find my way around?			
Can I find customer service and help online?			
Are the instructions understandable?			

Other notes:

A simple summary

✔ Take a long look around a broker's site before you sign on the dotted line.

✔ Be sure you can trade the equities you want to trade with this broker, and that you have enough assets to open an account.

✔ Check out the trading screens carefully, assuring yourself that you're comfortable with them and that you understand the confirmation reports.

✔ Place a call to customer service to find out how responsive they are to your queries.

✔ Does size matter? Find out whether the broker can handle having a large percentage of their customers online simultaneously.

Chapter 14

What Could Possibly Go Wrong?

THE MARKET IS MOVING LIKE MAD. You log on to the Internet, open your bookmark file, and click on your online broker's listing. There's a delay. Then you wait a little longer. Check your email. Go back to the broker's site. And wait. And wait. Then pound the keys and cuss. In the meantime, the market is running away from you, and you're certain the delay just cost you some money. What can you do to prepare for the inevitable problems?

In this chapter...

✓ What are the pitfalls?

✓ Fail-safes and backups

✓ Avoiding online scams

COMPUTERS SOMETIMES CRASH, SO ENSURE YOU HAVE A STANDBY MEANS OF ACCESSING YOUR ACCOUNT

What are the pitfalls?

DEAR READER, IF YOU THINK *you're the only one who encounters trouble placing a trade, rest assured you're not alone. Not long ago, I was trying to execute a trade with a full-service broker. First, his line was busy for a couple of hours. His assistant wouldn't take my order because it involved exercising stock options. I had to fax them a document, but the fax line was tied up. It took me over a day of trying to get through before my order was processed.*

■ **Even the most dedicated** *online investor will encounter delays and problems with markets from time to time. You will need reserves of patience.*

I won't complain too loudly, though; the stock went up $7 per share while I listened to busy signals.

What's the point? Assume delays and slowdowns are inevitable during market frenzies, no matter what the mode of trading or type of broker you're working with. Frankly, while waiting on hold and listening to the fax machine's busy signals, I was wishing this full-service broker had an online option.

Mistakes you might make:
A typo will hurt you

When you're entering an order at a broker's site, you're prompted for the ticker symbol or *CUSIP*.

What if your fingers suffer a momentary disconnect from your intentions, and you enter the wrong symbol or code? If you don't read the confirmation screen carefully, you'll end up placing an order for something other than the equity you wanted to buy or sell. You could end up with a mutual fund you don't want, or you might inadvertently sell a stock short that you don't own. This can be an expensive mistake!

> **DEFINITION**
>
> CUSIP, *which stands for Committee on Uniform Securities Identification Procedures, is a number that identifies a particular stock or bond. The CUSIP numbers, issued by the aforementioned Committee, are used in the United States and Canada. Overseas equities have an International Securities Identification Number (ISIN), which is issued by each country's National Numbering Agency.*

Other possible errors are mistyped limit order prices or messing up the number of units of an equity you want to trade. I like the order entry forms developed by many online brokers that let you click on an item in your portfolio and automatically fill out an order to sell it, or to buy more. When you're entering an order, check and double-check all the details to make sure that you'll get exactly what you want when you press the Confirm My Order button.

Security issues

The possibility of a "hacker attack" is one that keeps some potential online investors offline. What if a hacker got into your account? Could your account information and password be stolen by a misanthropic teenager and used for nefarious purposes?

The most common way an outsider gets into an investor's account is when the investor leaves the broker's web page displayed on a computer shared by several people. If you leave a browser window open that you've been using to view your account, someone else might be able to get into your account by hitting the Back button. Most brokers have "time-outs" imposed on their web sites, which means you have to re-enter your account number and password every 15 minutes or so in order to keep the page open.

Be sure to close the browser window when you're done viewing your online brokerage account! This prevents the next person using the computer from paging back and seeing your financial information.

As yet, there haven't been any reports of a hacker getting into a broker's customer base or of money being stolen or equities being misdirected. Online brokerages are built with security in mind. Who's to say someone impersonating you, who knows your social security number, couldn't call the broker's toll-free number and execute a trade using your name? It can happen offline as well as online if you don't protect your account identity carefully.

Wild days on the trading floor

You want to be able to get into your brokerage account when the market goes crazy, if you decide to trade with the masses. Some of the big names in the online brokerage world can't handle more than 5 to 10 percent of their customers at once, which can make it difficult for you to access your online assets. One question I ask when reviewing online brokers for *Barron's* is, "What percentage of your customers can log on simultaneously?" I want to hear a number that's 30 percent or higher – 100 percent is the ideal answer.

The best insurance policy against missing big market moves is to have more than one online brokerage account. Many of my Barron's readers tell me they have multiple accounts already; most have two accounts and a few have three. One reader had five, which strikes me as an administrative nightmare. And a large percentage of readers who trade online also have traditional brokerage accounts.

I consider multiple methods of placing trades an essential element for a top-tier brokerage. Trading by Touch-Tone phone is frequently available as an option. But when the crunch comes, you want to reach a live person by telephone or by just walking into a local office. The latter also is an important consideration when you're opening an account. If you can cut down the delay before you can start trading, you'll probably do better – and get fewer ulcers.

When your broker's site crashes

There have been reports of hackers trying to disrupt online brokers' sites by engaging in a technique called denial of service attacks. This is a relatively crude way of bringing a site down, and involves organized cooperation by a group of hackers. What they do is barrage a company with email and requests to go

■ **It's best to retain** *a number of optional ways of placing trades. In the event of a computer crash you will want to talk to the broker direct, or use a Touch-Tone phone to trade.*

to the site's home page, so the saboteurs take up all the company's computers' attention, making it impossible for real customers to get through. It is the equivalent of making customers wait at the bank by getting a bunch of people off the street to clog the line waiting to see a teller. These attacks have received a lot of publicity, but they don't compromise the security anywhere.

Several online brokers suffer crashes while trying to update their computers and software so they can handle the increasing traffic. This is akin to changing a tire while traveling at the speed limit on the freeway, so the resulting outages shouldn't be such a surprise. Nevertheless, there are a lot of angry customers trying to access their accounts when this happens. The brokers respond to these crises by allowing their customers to trade with live brokers without charging additional fees. As the computers used by online brokers get more powerful and the systems mature, we'll see fewer of those outages that have plagued the industry since its early days.

Fail-safes and backups

HERE'S SOMETHING TO CONSIDER: *Set up duplicate methods of getting online, as well as have more than one computer handy. Computers crash from time to time, phone lines get chewed through by squirrels on occasion, and cable systems overload and prevent you from getting online.*

Live by the Scout motto "be prepared," and make sure you can access your brokerage account whenever you need to, by whatever means.

Department of redundancy department

Think about what could happen if your computer's hard disk got erased, and if you lost track of your account information and holdings. Scary idea, isn't it? It's a good idea to make frequent backups of your data onto a floppy disk if you're using a personal finance program. I've already emphasized the importance of having hardcopy records of your transactions.

Sometimes, an inability to connect to a broker's web site is the customer's problem, though. Your modem might go on the blink, or your Internet service provider can crash. A virus or a disk error can make necessary program files disappear. Protect yourself by making backups of your important files.

You can create a backup disk for yourself on the Internet. Xdrive (www.xdrive.com), FreeDrive (www.freedrive.com), and NetDrive (www.netdrive.com) give you a big chunk of free space where you can store files, photos, and documents. If you're using Windows 98 or 2000, you can make the drive look like part of your own system. You can "drag and drop" entire folders onto the virtual drive.

The need for multiple ISPs, brokers, computers

One worthwhile precaution is to have a backup Internet service provider (ISP) for those times when your main connection goes haywire. That goes for those of you with DSL, cable modems, fiber-optic connections, and ISDN. Have you ever turned on the TV, ready for the big game, only to be greeted by a screen full of snow? The same thing will happen to your cable modem during outages. And, almost inevitably, it will happen when the market's moving.

The solution? Keep a cache of all those CD-ROMs that America Online, Prodigy, Earthlink, CompuServe *et al.* send you offering a month's free Internet access. (Don't forget to cancel before the month is up.) Or sign up for an ISP that provides a limited number of hours for perhaps $9.95 a month, or take advantage of the free ISPs now proliferating. Most of them make you put up with an annoying ad banner, though.

Based on the number of computers stretched to (and often beyond) their limits during my online brokerage testing process, it wouldn't be such a bad idea to have more than one personal computer available, too, if you're really serious about online trading. Given that you can get a competent, if unexceptional, PC for under $500, it's not such expensive insurance if you're actively managing a significant portfolio. Those cheap computers probably won't help you run your market-modeling program efficiently, but at least they can get you onto the World Wide Web.

INTERNET

www.netzero.com

www.worldspy.com

NetZero and WorldSpy are two of the free ISPs you can use as a backup in case your ISP crashes. Unlike NetZero, WorldSpy doesn't make you view constant advertising while using its services.

If you're using a PC slower than a Pentium 200, with less RAM than 64 megabytes, and a hard disc with less than 2 gigabytes, it's time for you to upgrade; use the older computer as your backup. A quality (at least 17-inch) monitor costs less than a visit to an ophthalmologist. And do I have to tell you to back up your hard disc to protect yourself against the inevitable crashes? Free sites to store your data are burgeoning online now.

And as I mentioned above, it's a good idea to have more than one brokerage account.

Is it safe to trade online? Based on the nearly $1 trillion worth of assets currently being traded online, the public seems to believe it is. Online trading isn't just for techno-savvy thrill-seekers any more, though remember to take it steady if you're new to the game.

■ **It can take** *just one key stroke to seriously spoil your day. Ensure that you back up your important files regularly in case the unintentional actually happens.*

Avoiding online scams

CONSUMER WATCHDOG GROUPS *have recognized the power of the Internet: There are numerous online scams that target investors, and the watchdog groups are working to keep you from falling for them.*

Don't jump at the investing "opportunities" that drop into your email box or that you read about in discussion groups.

Trivia...

Securities frauds have existed as long as there have been equities to trade. The British Parliament first passed a law banning stock trading fraud in 1697, and there have been plenty of examples since then. One trait in common over the years is the use of technology to carry out greedy plans. Some historians blame the use of telegraph machines and radios, which sped up speculation in stocks, for the crash of 1929. Schemes seen in the 19th and 20th centuries include railroad scams, Ponzi (pyramid) schemes, penny stock fraud, phony oil and gas limited partnerships, and insider trading.

The types of investment fraud seen online mirror the frauds perpetrated over the phone or through the mail. Remember that fraudsters can use a variety of Internet tools, including bulletin boards, online newsletters, spam, or chat (including Internet Relay Chat or Web Page Chat), to spread false information. They also can build a glitzy, sophisticated web page, or lure you in with what appears to be a legitimate investing newsletter. All of these tools cost very little money, so consider all offers with skepticism. Investment frauds usually fall into the following categories.

Pump and dump

Pump and dump scams happen in online message boards. Someone posts a message urging readers to buy a stock quickly or sell a stock immediately before the price crashes. The writers usually claim to have inside information or some kind of data analysis methodology that's always right. In reality, they are insiders or even paid promoters, who want to reap investment gains by encouraging others to either pump the price up or dump their shares so the price goes down. This technique is usually used on small companies with stocks that aren't traded often, and with share prices of $5 or less, because it's easier to manipulate the price when there's not much information available about the company.

Penny stock fraud

Part of many pump and dump scams, penny stock fraud comes in many different forms. Penny stocks are extremely low-priced stocks, usually under $1 per share, and the companies that issue them are so small that they're not required to file SEC reports detailing their performance. These companies' stocks are typically called Over the Counter Bulletin Board (OTCBB) stocks. Some investors find them appealing because they can buy quite a few more shares if the price is $0.75 per share than if it were $75 per share. A move of a fraction of a point in an extremely cheap stock can net the investor a big gain. What's more likely, however, is that the company itself is on the brink of bankruptcy, and soon the 10,000 shares that you bought for under $1 each will be worth closer to $0. The SEC and the NASD have implemented new rules that require all OTCBB companies to file financial reports, so this style of fraud should be dying out.

Pyramid schemes

These deals start out with a line such as, "Make Big Money From Your Home Computer!" and "Turn $10 into $10,000 By Next Week!" Be instantly wary of come-ons with exclamation points in them. What's really going on here is the well-known pyramid scheme in which participants make money by recruiting others into the program. Those high up in the pyramid will probably get a fairly high rate of return, but the whole thing falls apart rapidly. If your rate of return is dependent on your ability to bring additional investors into the fold, you're being lured into a pyramid scheme.

> Trivia...
>
> *Pyramids are sometimes called Ponzi schemes after Charles Ponzi, who originated a very successful – at least for the initial investors – scheme involving international postal reply coupons back in 1920. Initial investors received 50 percent return on their money within 90 days, and talked up the opportunity to their friends, but the whole thing fell apart in a matter of months.*

Can risk-free investments be real?

Risk-free investment opportunities sound too good to be true. Guess what? They are. You'll probably get emails enticing you to participate in some exotic investments such as eel farms. There's no such thing as a risk-free investment, though – these are just scams. Watch out for proposals that promise you incredible profits and guaranteed returns. Make liberal use of the Delete key or a spam-blocking program, and avoid falling for these schemes.

Off-shore frauds

Off-shore frauds also are making their way into the world of investment scams. The Internet has removed the old obstacles – conflicting time zones, different currencies, high cost of telephone calls – that used to make offshore scammers shy away from preying on US residents. Be very careful when considering an investment opportunity that comes from another country, because it's difficult for law enforcement agencies to cross borders and prosecute foreign fraudsters. Watch out for promoters who want you to send money to an offshore post office box.

Bogus offerings

Those are highly touted offerings that just don't exist. You may be pressured to put up some money quickly, before the deal slips away. Initial public offerings in companies that exist only on a huckster's web site are the usual method used to separate bona fide investors from their money. You can avoid falling into one of these traps by assuring yourself that the company in which you plan to invest really exists. Contact the company's investor relations department, usually listed on a company's web site, and ask a lot of questions.

Prime bank securities

These securities are a subset of bogus offerings. They sound great, with promises of "credit guarantees" and "high-yield investment programs." The promoters claim that the debt obligations they're selling are guaranteed by a consortium of the world's top 100 banks. Unfortunately, this consortium doesn't exist, and neither do the securities the promoters are selling. Watch out for phrases such as "standby letters of credit" and "revolving credit guarantees." They're a sure sign that you're dealing with a fraudulent promoter.

Affinity frauds

This term describes investments that are marketed to a group of individuals with some socioeconomic trait in common, such as church membership, ethnic origin, or alma mater. The frauds themselves take one of the forms described above, but the person in charge of the scheme is a member of the affinity group – sometimes a trusted member.

Affinity frauds are fairly old-fashioned, but the Internet makes it much easier for a huckster to track down and focus in on a specific group. Watch out for promoters who won't take no for an answer, or who tell you how much money others in your group are making from this scheme.

INTERNET

www.investopedia.com/university/articles/100900.asp

www.sec.gov/consumer/cyberfr.htm

These two sites, Investopedia and the Securities and Exchange Commission site, contain details of numerous investor frauds and scams. Investopedia's article entitled "Protecting Yourself from the Swindlers" is a list of some of the most amazing frauds of the last 20 years, while the SEC's Cyberfraud list will make you aware of the methods hucksters use.

What if you get scammed?

If you find out you've become the victim of an online securities fraud, you have several avenues to explore. Send an email to the SEC's online complaint center at enforcement@sec.gov for a start. Through the North American Securities Administrators Association site above, you can find links to state regulators. The National Association of Securities Dealers (www.nasdr.com) handles complaints about online brokers. You might also check into the National Fraud Information Center (www.fraud.org) and the Federal Bureau of Investigation (www.fbi.gov) and look up your local contacts.

Don't be too embarrassed to report a suspected fraud. Unless you speak up you won't get your money back, and the fraudsters will still be out there preying on others.

■ **Do your homework:** *Get hold of as much relevant information as possible about companies in which you're interested, before you make your investment decisions.*

Protect yourself

You can save yourself a lot of grief by being careful. Here's a short list of dos and don'ts that you should take to heart:

1. Don't fall for high-pressure sales tactics. Take your time and investigate every potential investment thoroughly.

2. If you're being pressured to cash in a bond or a CD to invest in something with considerably more risk, remember that the promoter probably doesn't have your financial wellbeing in mind.

3. Phrases such as "Here's your opportunity to be one of the first to invest in the next Microsoft or Cisco," should inspire you to run – not walk – away.

4. Do your homework. Don't invest in something you don't understand. Check up on the firm you're being enticed to invest in, and take a look at the promoter's credentials. The Better Business Bureau (www.bbb.org) is one place to start.

A simple summary

✔ Better safe than sorry. Double-check the orders you enter online to make sure you haven't made a typo.

✔ Investigate alternate ways of contacting your broker, just in case something goes wrong with its web site or your computer.

✔ Back up your data at regular intervals and store it in a safe place. Make sure all disks are clearly labeled.

✔ Develop a finely tuned "baloney filter" and save yourself the grief of falling for an online investment scam.

PART FOUR

FELLOW INVESTORS CAN POOL THEIR KNOWLEDGE

WEB TOOLKIT FOR INVESTORS

RESOURCES FOR ONLINE INVESTORS go far beyond charts, quotes, and brokerages. If you're more comfortable learning along with a group of like-minded investors, the discussion of *community investing* will help guide you to fellow travelers. I'll show you how you can delve deeper into  *technical analysis* using your computer, and which web sites and programs will best serve your needs.

There's more to money management than investing: Banking online is growing to the point where your only contact with your bank's offline presence may be when you use the ATM to withdraw some cash. Come along and learn how you can find the *best rates* for your savings and for loans.

Chapter 15

Community Investing

TALKING ABOUT INVESTMENT OPPORTUNITIES online has been a staple of bulletin boards and chat rooms ever since they were invented. Investing communities abound on the Web, and you can do more than just participate – you can start your own. The concept of community has grown beyond mere discussion, though: Now you can help managers choose the components of a mutual fund, or you can put your money where your mouth is and become a manager yourself.

In this chapter...

✓ Message boards and chat zones

✓ Start your own investing community

✓ Community mutual funds

✓ Spreading and collecting rumors

COMMUNITY INVESTING ENABLES INDIVIDUALS TO SHARE DIVERSE EXPERIENCES

Message boards and chat zones

INVESTMENT COMMUNITIES PROVIDE *a way for individuals to tell each other about the companies they're watching. Dozens of financial sites have discussion areas where individual investors can talk amongst themselves. Individuals are marketing their own financial newsletters based on the performance of the stocks they discuss on message boards.*

Most of these communities have grown to the point where you can do a lot more than just talk. There's research, market commentary, graphs, and news as well. You can track your portfolio and play stock-picking games. Whether you post on the boards or not, you can often pick up interesting tidbits about a company or an investing strategy.

Watch out for scammers, who often frequent message boards. Be sure to confirm the rumors you hear in a community before making an investment decision!

The downside of the message boards, besides scammers and constant advertising, involves the type of language many of the posters use. Some people hide behind an anonymous "handle" and spout obscenities or attack other board members just because nobody's there to wash out their modem with soap. Fortunately, most of the boards include commands that will enable you to block out the individuals whose messages you don't want to see.

Will an investing community fit into your online toolkit? If you manage to find a place you can call "home," you'll end up not only with tips from far-flung correspondents, but also new friends to visit when you're on the road. I've belonged to two active online communities for about 15 years now, and I thoroughly enjoy the camaraderie and friendships I've formed.

Become a Fool

The Motley Fool (www.fool.com) is one of the oldest investing communities online. Tom and David Gardner, brothers based in Virginia, named their community after the court jester who could tell the King what was really going on without being sent to the chopping block. Outside of the discussion boards, this site is packed with information

ONLINE DISCUSSION

There are two ways to participate in discussions online – real-time chat and bulletin board postings. If you take part in real-time chats, you have to be online simultaneously with the other members of the discussion. Some chats are somewhat formal and have a guest speaker and a moderator who controls the pace of questions being asked. Others are more of a free-for-all in which anyone in the chat room can jump into the discussion at any time. All the sites listed in this section have both scheduled formal chats as well as impromptu discussions. Check to see if there's a chat topic that interests you.

Bulletin board postings are done at your own pace. One member might post a question at 10 a.m., then other members would post their replies over the course of a few days. Some boards have posts several years old that you can read, while others present only the most recent messages. You can search for the topics that interest you – trying to read every message on a board can be overwhelming!

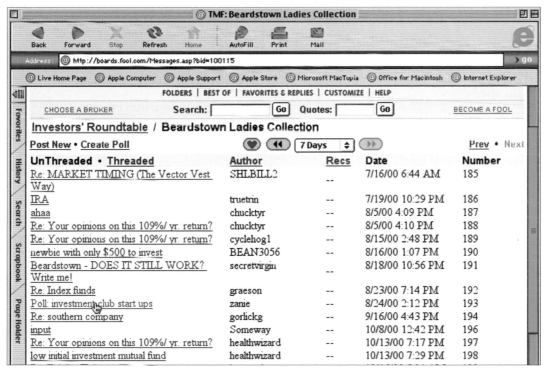

DISCUSSION BOARD AT MOTLEY FOOL

about investing that's written for those people just starting out, as well as for people who want to keep learning new techniques. The bulk of the material works for investors who focus on fundamentals.

You can check out discussions about individual companies in Stocks A to Z, or talk up industries in Industry and Market Analysis. There's plenty to talk about besides investing; the Fool encourages community building by letting its members talk about their pets, kids, and hobbies in the Fools of a Feather area.

Become a Prophet

ProphetTalk, part of the ProphetFinance site (www.prophetfinance.com), can be found by clicking on the Community button. The technology that drives this bulletin board system is among the best I've ever seen. You can find a particular company by typing in its ticker symbol, but you can also use the navigation bar on the left side of the screen to find the most active discussions by topic. You can also check out who's talking about the stocks that are most active. If you find a message writer you particularly like, you can find all of his or her messages – or easily block the writers (and ad posters) you decide you don't want to see again.

Other features to explore at ProphetFinance include its SnapCharts, which are easy to customize, and the SectorSurfer, which lets you analyze industries in a hierarchical

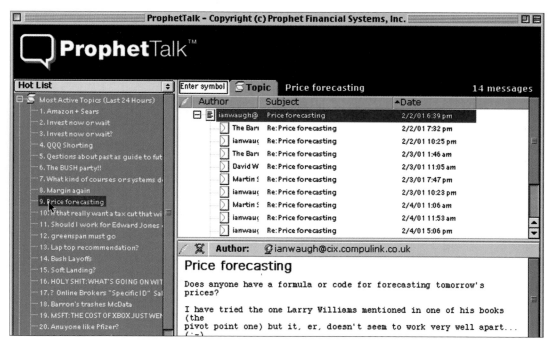

PROPHETTALK

structure. For instance, you can click on the financial sector, then drill down and pick a category, such as Insurance, then a subcategory, such as Health Insurance.

When you click on Health Insurance, you're shown a group of companies in that particular sector, with statistics displayed in a table so you can compare their performances.

Tech talk

Silicon Investor (www.siliconinvestor.com) is another site where tech-savvy investors hang out. You can "mark" a particular subject or author and have new marked messages show up in a special in-box the next time you visit. If you check into a discussion about a particular stock, you'll see a current quote and a 30-day price chart displayed along with the messages from other members – a nice touch. While you're reading your messages, you can also browse SEC filings or find out whether a company has a dividend reinvestment program.

This is a great place to ask questions about a particular technical analysis technique (see Chapter 16) and find out how others are applying their investment strategies. A higher percentage of Silicon Investor members use their real names compared to other online discussion boards, which seems to keep the conversations civil. A premium membership ($9.95 per month) nets you additional search tools, the ability to exchange private messages with other premium members, and discounts on products and services.

Clear community

ClearStation (www.clearstation.com) has a web site that is definitely worth visiting just to learn about its three-point approach to investing, which encompasses fundamental analysis, technical analysis, and discussions with other investors Community members can share their list of recommended stocks, and the site aggregates all the recommendations so you can get an idea of which investments are currently popular.

ClearStation's Tag and Bag area is a great place to go when you're just looking for investing ideas. There are numerous lists of stocks organized by selection methodology, whether fundamental or technical. For instance, you can check out the stocks that have had a "Record Price Breakout" during the day, and peruse the Education area to find out exactly what that means.

INTERNET

www.quicken.com/ boards

www.quote.com/ quotecom/community

www.ragingbull.com

Quicken.com message boards, Quote.com community, and Raging Bull are other great spots for investors to talk amongst themselves. Quicken.com covers a range of topics that include investing as well as personal finance issues. Quote.com and Raging Bull have boards that focus on individual companies along with industries and investing strategies.

Start your own investing community

INVESTING CLUBS *have been around for decades. Like-minded groups get together and choose investments with their pooled resources of energy and money. It's a way for people who don't have a huge pile of cash on hand to get into the market and learn more about the investments that fit their interests.*

When investing clubs first began, they were usually made up of people who lived or worked near one another. The Beardstown Ladies is an investing club that was made famous by their book, *Common Sense Guide to Investing*. Thanks to the Internet, though, geography is no longer a defining element for an investing club. You can get involved in a group that connects online.

Join the club

The grandfather of investing clubs is the National Association of Investors Corporation (NAIC), which was formed in 1951. Check out their web site at www.better-investing.org, and see how the group's focus is on long-term sensible investing, specifically the discipline of investing regularly in quality growth stocks. The group started out as a collection of four investing clubs, and though they have much to offer in the way of investor education to the individual, they encourage club participation.

You can set up a group and join as an offline club, or participate in NAIC's Computer Group, which helps its members choose and use computerized investment analysis tools. Its club accounting program is a worthwhile tool for the treasurer of an investing club.

The NAIC's annual convention, CompuFest (usually held in late June or early July), is held in a resort area, so you can combine your investment education with a family vacation.

Collective wisdom

WeVest.com (www.wevest.com) lets individuals form groups and put together recommendations based on the collective wisdom of the members. Once you're a member of the WeVest community, you can look around for an existing group to join or bring a group of friends in and form your own. The resources at WeVest.com are aimed

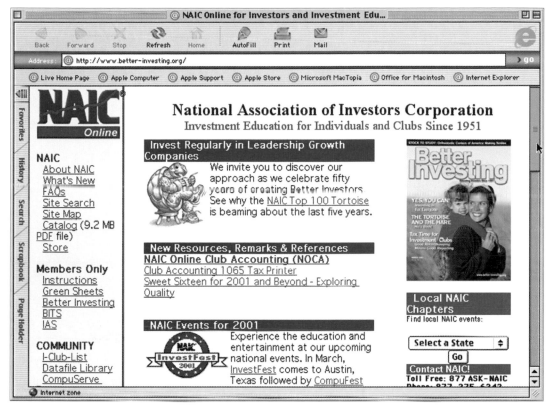

NATIONAL ASSOCIATION OF INVESTORS CORPORATION

at group collaboration, and your group can develop its own mutual fund on the site. Maybe we should start a "KISS Guide" group and see if we can win the competition!

At WeVest, your group can use the private forums, portfolio tools, and the collaborative portfolio engine, which helps the group generate a group intelligence portfolio, or GRIP. There's an ongoing competition, and winners can earn trips, money, and other prizes. Portfolios are assigned an InvesRating, which indicates the percentile ranking of both individual and group portfolios. It's a fun way to see how your investments stack up.

Investorama clubs

Investorama (www.investorama.com) members can form or join investing clubs. There are over 250 active clubs on the site now, which can be found by accessing http://www.investorama.com/groups/categories/2. You can easily start your own club, or use the Investorama site to set up a virtual meeting place for your offline group. Groups can be open to everyone, or the leader can set up a password for accessing group files.

Community mutual funds

COLLABORATION HAS BECOME the latest buzzword for setting up a mutual fund. This concept takes stock-picking games to another level, setting up funds based on picks made by consistent winners. These new mutual funds, which are currently very small in terms of total assets, have evolved from discussions in online investment communities and portfolio game sites.

What's going on here? These communities appear to have sprung up out of a distrust of professional analysts and mutual fund managers, who have a mediocre record when it comes to beating the market averages.

STOCK JUNGLE

A recent development in investment community is sites where the top stock pickers turn into advisers to mutual fund managers. The optimistic philosophy espoused at MetaMarkets (www.metamarkets.com), Stock Jungle (www.stockjungle.com), and Marketocracy (www.marketocracy.com) is that individual investors, having been empowered by the wealth of data available online, are often better judges of investment potential than the professionals on Wall Street. The web site members act as advisers to the fund managers. Though all of these funds promote themselves as site-member advised, in fact there are professionals who decide which recommendations to follow.

It's a jungle out there

Stock Jungle's Community Intelligence fund (symbol SJCIX) is currently the darling of the collaborative mutual fund world. It's called a naked fund because its holdings are published daily, so everyone knows which stocks are in the basket. At its one-year birthday, with approximately $4 million in assets, mutual fund analysis site Morningstar.com calculated a 23.2 percent annual return, well above the NASDAQ or S&P 500's performance. A *no-load fund,* SJCIX's expense ratio should be lower than the professionally run funds, and was reported as 1 percent in its annual report dated March 31, 2000.

DEFINITION

Mutual funds are supported by the investors in a variety of ways. A no-load fund charges no fees up front when you buy in or when you sell or trade it.

The stocks that go into the Community Intelligence fund come from the recommendations made by Stock Jungle's members, but they're not implemented blindly. Two managers review the hundreds of recommendations made, but just a handful of these recommendations actually get implemented. Top stock pickers among the Stock Jungle community are rewarded with a $50 prize every day. Tech stocks, typically popular among online investors, make up over 60 percent of the fund. Morningstar offers this cautionary note: "Strong returns aside, investors should tread carefully due to this fund's gimmicky nature." Compared to Stock Jungle's two professionally managed funds, Pure Play Internet and Market Leaders, the community is doing much better than the pros.

MetaMarkets

MetaMarkets.com's Open fund (OPENX), established in August 1999, took off like a shot, with its NAV more than doubling in the first 5 months. It has faltered since then, though, along with the rest of the tech market. It charges 1.45 percent in fees. Morningstar reports over 60 percent of this fund in tech stocks also.

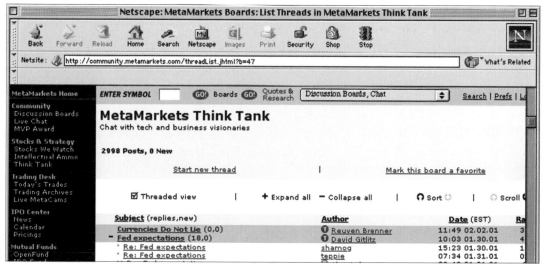

METAMARKETS

Beat the crowd

Marketocracy is running a competition now to determine who will be put in charge of its mutual funds. You get $1 million in virtual money and the opportunity to develop your own fund. The site tracks your net asset value and performance, so you can stack your picks against those of professional mutual fund managers as well as other Marketocracy members. You can add your voice to the Medical Specialist fund (MSFQX); President Ken Kam is looking for a few members to hire as fund advisers based on their picks and performance.

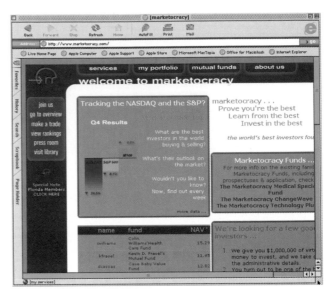

MARKETOCRACY

Spreading and collecting rumors

RUMORS, BY THEIR NATURE, are unverified stories that often have basis in fact. When it comes to your investments, it can help to know what rumors are being spread about the companies you've bought into.

The Internet has made it possible to find out instantly who's saying what about whom. Whether or not you believe the rumors and whispers, knowing what's being said is a good self-defense strategy.

When there's a takeover in the works, often the rumor sites pick up the scent before the news hits the public wires, though what you hear might not be totally correct. But they'll give you an idea that there are changes in the air. Unlike most other sites discussed in this book, the following areas require a subscription fee, ranging from $10–$50 per month. You'll have to decide whether having a jump on verifiable news is worth it to you. When you join a rumor site, you're also given access to its discussion board, which lets you be a rumormonger too. The usual caveats regarding checking up on items you read on message boards apply here.

Fly on the wall

The Fly on the Wall (www.theflyonthewall) is one of my favorite news and rumor sites with its Super Fly feature. Super Fly finds the companies that have multiple stories posted and brings them all together on the site's opening page, so you can immediately see which stocks are buzzing. Stocks rated as Flying High are those that have generated the most recent news; if any of those companies are in your portfolio, it's worth checking out what's being said. Type a ticker in the box at the top of the page to search the news for the past 90 days, pull up historical and intra-day charts, and, for NASDAQ stocks, check how they're trading on the Island ECN.

The Fly will alert you to company meetings, analyst recommendations, conference calls, pre-opening news, and highlights from business publications. Set up an email news alert system by putting together your watch list; whenever an item pops up from your list, you'll get an email. You can also have the alerts pop up on your screen so you can have the Super Fly watching out for you while you're elsewhere on the Internet. This site works best when the market is open, given its connections to live news and NASDAQ. There is a $9.95 per month fee for access to Super Fly.

Digest of whispers

Wall Street Whispers (www.wallstwhispers.com) publishes a daily newsletter that's distributed around 11 p.m. Eastern time, so you can set up trades when the market opens the next morning, if you're so inclined. The reports are sent via email or fax, or you can log onto the web site and take a look. A subscription costs $29.95 per month, but you're not pestered with ads. The publishers pull together information from investment analysts, advisers, and newsletter writers and make buy and sell recommendations based on the variety of data gathered. This site gives you an investor's digest of evaluations of stocks, options, upcoming IPOs, and mutual funds. There are guest commentaries as well as items culled from investment bankers and merger experts.

You can't sign up for a trial membership at Wall Street Whispers, but there's a sample issue you can peruse to see if the information available here will help you with investment decisions.

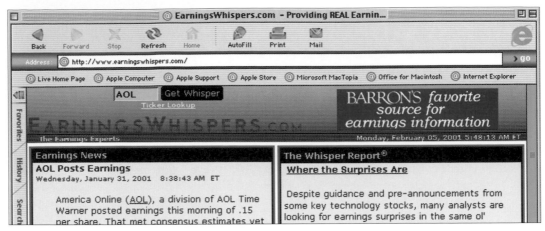

EARNINGSWHISPERS

Whisper about earnings

EarningsWhispers (www.earningswhispers.com) provides educated guesses on a company's upcoming earnings statements, pulling information from analysts as well as numerous other sources. The site is free, so it's worth bookmarking and checking from time to time. Sometimes an insider tips it off, and it'll use that information to revise the estimates provided by First Call, which publishes earnings figures for publicly traded companies and other analysts.

Stock price moves are often triggered by changes in earnings estimates, so keeping an eye on the direction of a potential change can give you a jump on other investors. The Warnings page collects information on companies that report earnings shifts. You can subscribe to the daily email newsletter, Whisper Report, when you sign up for a free membership on the site.

Opinion summaries

StockSelector.com (www.stockselector.com) isn't a rumor site per se, but it has a section devoted to swirling rumors. The Analyst Comments page brings together changes in opinions about stocks, and includes some commentary explaining why a particular shift is significant. This site also contains quite a few other tools for the investor, such as the Company Comparison, which lets you take a critical look at two companies side by side. Once you've set up a comparison, you can email the page to yourself or to a friend.

StockSelector has ties to EarningsWhispers — you can sign up for the latter's reports as a membership benefit if you'd like. Registration is free, so the price is right.

Buzzing about rumors

StockRumors.com (www.stockrumors.com) is dedicated to the premise that rumors and significant changes in trading volume precede a stock's price shifts. There are three different pricing plans that give you access to the web site, email reports, or fax reports, depending on how much you'd like to pay (starting at $9.95 per month). You can access the Buzz and Bits report for free, which collects one-liner news updates about mergers, earnings reports, management changes, and other items. For an additional charge of $95 per month, you can have rumors sent to your wireless device.

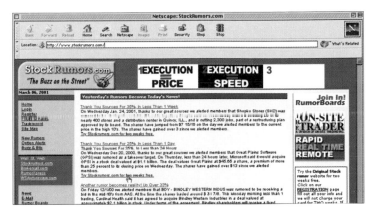

STOCKRUMORS

StockRumors is published by the same group that creates the rumor site BrokerCall.com, which (for an additional fee) brings you up-to-date analyst reports. BrokerCall covers the big players (Merrill Lynch, Goldman Sachs, etc.) as well as some of the smaller players (Thomas Weissel Partners, KBW, etc.).

A simple summary

✓ Leverage the knowledge of other investors by participating in bulletin boards and chats.

✓ Join with friends and other like-minded investors by setting up an online investment club.

✓ Take the idea of stock-picking games to the next level by checking out mutual funds

created by fellow investors. It could be worth it – some of them are even outperforming the pros!

✓ Sign into sites that collect rumors and earnings changes to stay half a step ahead of other investors. These sites are especially helpful to the frequent trader.

Chapter 16

Technical Analysis

T HE MAIN REASON to use technical analysis to help time your trades is to remove emotion from the process. Too often, investors are caught up in owning a particular stock just because they like the company or because it's a media darling. Technicians trade on the numbers and do so with all the emotional involvement Mr. Spock gives to plotting a course through the universe. Technical indicators measure market upswings and downturns in specific ways, and the analyst decides whether a particular signal means "buy" or "sell."

In this chapter...

✓ Basic concepts

✓ Software to help you get started

✓ Advanced tools for numbers junkies

✓ Learning more about trading systems

BY USING STOCK PRICE CHARTS AND OTHER TOOLS, ANALYSTS ARE ABLE TO IDENTIFY TRENDS

Basic concepts

TECHNICAL ANALYSIS REVOLVES AROUND the idea that the correct price for a stock is reflected in its current value. That price takes into account all the fundamental measures (such as earnings, price/equity ratios, insider moves, and all the news that fits), so the true technical analyst doesn't bother with that information. A technician uses patterns and trends in the stock price to predict the future. Some technical analysts pride themselves on knowing practically nothing about a company beyond patterns on a price/volume chart.

The name of the game in technical analysis is trends. The first order of business when analyzing a stock is to decide whether it has a tendency to trend, to form a definite upward or downward pattern over time, or not. If it doesn't, it's not of interest to the technician. If a stock has a history of forming clear trends, a technical analyst can see what made it tick in the past, and figure out where it will go in the future.

Technicians study charts, adding some calculations and ratios to the pictures. Each method designed has the ultimate objective of determining whether it's time to buy or sell a particular security. Indicators give the analyst a measure of the strength of the market as well as the direction it's trending. I use technical analysis to help time trades in stocks that I've selected using fundamental and sector analysis first.

Trivia...

Charles Dow is considered the father of technical analysis as many of the basic ideas were developed by him in the early 1900s. The Dow Jones Industrial Average was created out of Dow's theories of market analysis.

If you decide to become a pure technician, commit yourself to a period of studying and testing before you lay your money on the line.

Starting with charting

The main tool used by technical analysts is a stock price chart. As the old saying goes, "A picture is worth a thousand words." The most basic chart is a line chart, showing the price of a stock over time. Eyeballing a line

■ **A line chart** *is the most basic type of chart, showing at a glance the highs and lows experienced by a particular item over time.*

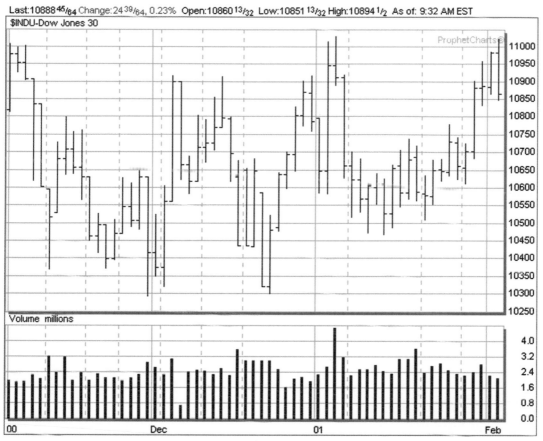

Last:10888 45/64 Change:24 39/64, 0.23% Open:10860 13/32 Low:10851 13/32 High:10894 1/2 As of: 9:32 AM EST

$INDU-Dow Jones 30

ProphetCharts

Volume millions

■ **A High/Low/Close chart** *is more complex than a line chart. The upper part shows price highs and lows in the form of vertical bars. The lower section uses a different scale and reveals trading volume.*

chart is a quick and simple way of determining whether there's a trend in the stock's price. Technical analysts take it much further than that, though.

The most popular type of chart is the High/Low/Close chart. High/Low/Close charts show the price range for the period you're examining, usually daily data over 3 to 24 months. A bar represents the price range, with cross-marks that represent the opening and closing prices for that day. The top of the bar shows the highest price at which the stock traded during the day, and the bottom shows the lowest. This type of chart is also called a bar chart, and it's by far the most popular tool used by technical analysts. The trading volume is usually displayed under the price bars in the form of a smaller bar with a different scale. You can get an immediate feel for the timing of large price changes as well as changes in the number of shares traded just by studying a chart for a minute or two.

Using bar charts, analysts determine the stock price's resistance and support levels. The price at which a stock trades illustrates an agreement between a buyer and a seller.

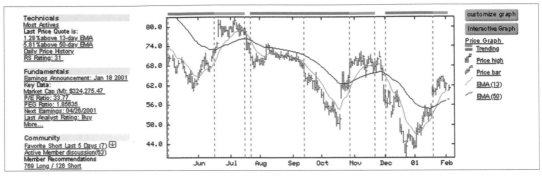

■ **Moving averages are extremely useful** *in helping to smooth out the jags in a stock, and therefore illustrate the underlying trend.*

Buyers are generally feeling favorable about the stock, and will push the stock price up. Sellers are feeling less positive, and will push the stock price down. As the stock price fluctuates, you can usually see a price point where the investors who own the stock decide it's high enough, so they sell enough shares that the price goes down. That peak price is called the resistance level, and there's a similar support level when buyers decide a price has dropped too low, so they jump in and bring it back up. Think of resistance level as the ceiling, and support level as the floor.

Technical analysts want to figure out resistance and support levels so they can time their purchases and sales, and so they can evaluate the meaning of a price breakout.

A breakout occurs when the stock price surges through the resistance level, or drops through the support level. Technicians often argue the meaning of these breakouts, and so they apply numerous other indicators to decide where the stock is going.

Making sense of price changes

One of the simpler technical indicators is the moving average. Add up the closing prices over a certain period, say five days, and create an average price, either by using simple averaging or an exponential moving

INTERNET

www.clearstation.com

ClearStation's graphing tools illustrate many of the basic concepts of technical analysis well. Trends are color-coded, and the standard charts displayed when you type in a ticker symbol show six different technical indicators. You can quickly shift to an interactive chart, which shows intra-day data for the last 10 trading days, and add your chosen indicators to the chart. The interactive chart is easy to customize, so you can analyze up to 10 years' data. The explanations of technical analysis techniques are illustrated with real-life charts. Be sure to bookmark this site as you learn about technical analysis.

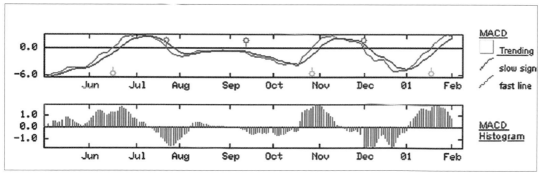

■ **MACD lines and histograms** *compare short-term and long-term moving averages to produce buy and sell signals at crossover points.*

average (EMA), which gives greater weight to the most recent figures. The EMA is considered a more powerful measure, because it emphasizes the current trend.

Technical investors usually use a short-term moving average of 5–12 periods, and a longer term moving average of 20-50 periods, so they can compare the current price changes to the longer term averages. In addition, technicians will compare short-term moving averages to the longer term averages, creating a graph called the Moving Average Convergence/Divergence (MACD).

When a short-term moving average is heading upward and crosses over the line generated by the long-term moving average, technical analysts consider this a "bullish" signal and will consider the stock a candidate for purchase. The upward trend is considered over when the long-term and short-term averages cross again.

Now that intra-day stock prices are fairly easy to come by, frequent traders apply moving average techniques to every tick of a stock price. Rather than calculating a moving average that runs over several days, they average the last five to 30 trades and graph the MACD to figure out the price to set on a limit order.

Thousands of techniques

As you delve deeper into technical analysis, you'll find that there are hundreds of indicators in use, and thousands of ways to use them. What intrigues investors about technical analysis is the ability to develop a trading system based on their own hunches about the market, backed up by some algebra and charting. In essence, it's a combination of art and science – you are the artist, so you get to create as well as interpret the pictures.

OTHER TECHNICAL INDICATORS

Two other types of technical indicators, the Relative Strength Indicator (RSI) and stochastics, are relatively simple and have been used for decades. The RSI compares changes in the stock's price to a particular index (such as the Dow Jones Industrial Average or the NASDAQ Index) and determines whether the stock is doing better or worse than the average. When an RSI line is going up, that means the stock is outperforming the market. When it heads down, the stock is doing worse than the overall market.

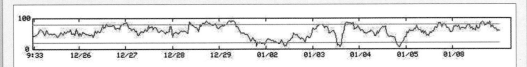

■ **RSI graphs** *are an invaluable help when you want to compare the movement of a particular stock's price to the wider market.*

Stochastics measure the stock's price moves against its own history. This indicator is often referred to as an oscillator because it refers to the movement in a stock price. Generally, technicians use stochastics to refine the trends indicated by the MACD, using the level of the indicator to decide whether a stock is overbought, thus ripe for a drop in price, or oversold, thus ready to swing back up again. A stochastic measure comes in between 0 and 100, and a value of 2 to 30 means the stock is oversold. When the measure hits 70 to 80, the stock is overbought.

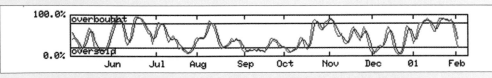

■ **Technical analysts** *watch for a bullish or bearish ACD crossover, then check the stochastics to see whether the stock is simultaneously overbought or oversold.*

What is the most important data point on a price chart? It's the most recent price. When you start studying charts, read them from right to left, starting with the current price. Then look at the patterns that led up to the present.

Picking the appropriate length of time to study is also part of the technician's art. Day traders should invest in real-time data and look at charts that can be updated by the minute. If you're a short-term investor, 3 months of data is about right. For those of you who buy a stock and hold onto it for the long run, 3 to 10 years of data is appropriate.

The techniques for my style of investing that I've developed over time have four stages. First, I identify an industry or a group of stocks I want to study further, based on fundamental criteria. I further winnow the group down by looking at their long-term technical performances, then delve into the chosen stocks using shorter and shorter time frames. Finally, I choose the price I'll set for my order by studying the last 3 days of trading data. I regularly review the technicals on everything in my portfolio to decide when it's time to sell.

Software to help you get started

I KNOW THIS MUCH IS TRUE: You can't set up a good technical analysis system without using a computer. Sure, the pioneers used slide rules, and pencil and paper, but the market was smaller then, and real-time data wasn't available. The computer helps you cut through the clutter and stay on top of the necessary analysis. You can also specify particular conditions, such as a bullish MACD crossover, and sort through the stocks that meet your criteria. That's tough to do by hand.

Your computerized assistant

Just a decade ago, the pickings for technical analysts were slim and expensive. They were also incredibly inconvenient, requiring the purchase of data as you used it, with high monthly fees for updates. You had to buy the software, which came to you on diskettes or CD-ROM, and take the time to install it on your computer.

Thanks to the Internet, software publishers not only provide quick data updates, but changes to the programs can be distributed instantly. Program setup has been simplified greatly, and you can download it from the publisher's web site. As a result, technical analysis is becoming more popular simply because it's easier to access and the price has dropped.

The price you pay for technical analysis programs and their accompanying data depends mostly on the timing of data updates. Expect to pay $50 and upward per month for streaming real-time data. The more features a program offers, the more you'll pay.

Programs that work well for technical analysts include Window on Wall Street, MetaStock, and IQ Chart. If you're seriously considering performing real-time technical analysis, you should also seriously consider having high-speed access to the Internet as well as a fast computer.

■ **High-speed access** *to the Internet, and a computer that is capable of downloading information quickly, are necessary tools for investors who wish to perform real-time technical analysis.*

CANDLESTICK CHARTING

Candlestick charting is a technique originally developed in Japan to analyze the rice market. It's a variation on the High/Low/Close chart. The range of prices for the period is drawn as a line, with a box, or body, that represents the opening and closing prices. If the price went up during the day, the body is white, but if it dropped, the body is colored black. The patterns that emerge are studied carefully to discover the underlying trend.

CANDLESTICK CHART

Window on Wall Street (www.windowonwallstreet.com) has 40 technical indicators and expert commentary built in that tells you which indicator works best in a certain situation. The online tutorials are well-written introductions to technical analysis concepts. The program and associated data are $80 per month, plus $10 for real-time Level II data. Because of the way Window on Wall Street delivers data, it's one of the few packages that works well for users who have slower dial-up access to the Internet. Window on Wall Street is great for beginners, but has techniques that will keep an intermediate or advanced user happy as well.

The MetaStock family of products, published by Equis (www.equis.com), includes MetaStock for Windows (approximately $400), which works on end-of-day data, and MetaStock Professional (approximately $1,500), which works with real-time data. Both programs allow analysis of stock data utilizing different charting styles as well as over 200 indicators. You can create your own custom indicators with the Indicator Builder function. These are very powerful programs, more suitable for intermediate or advanced technical analysts.

IQ Chart, published by IQC Corp, is a winning package that combines the data-gathering possibilities of the Web with a downloadable program that crunches numbers, scans through extensive databases for stocks that fit your criteria, and creates charts that you can analyze with technical indicator overlays. A feature unique to this program is what's dubbed the candlestick scan, which allows you to search for a specific pattern. IQ Chart isn't as flexible as Window on Wall Street or MetaStock, but the stock scanner is a terrific feature. There are two versions: One that uses delayed data (approximately $25 per month) and one that accesses real-time data ($35–$50 per month). You can download a 2-week free trial at its web site, www.iqchart.com.

Web sites that cater to the newly minted techie

As you get started in your quest for technical analysis techniques, the two sites ClearStation and ProphetCharts should be on your Bookmark list.

Technical Analysis from A to Z, a book written by Steven B. Achelis, is available online in the Free Stuff section of software publisher Equis' web site, at www.equis.com/free/taaz/index.html. All of the concepts are clearly illustrated with charts, and you can open up the MetaStock interactive graph program and try it out yourself when you're ready.

IQ Chart has an Education Center at www.iqchart.com/education/ that has a good explanation of candlesticks and chart patterns. When you're ready for some more

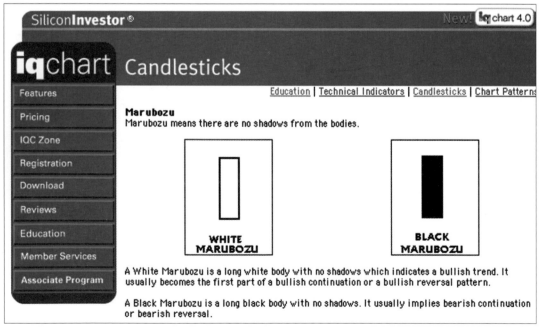

IQ CHART

advanced concepts, check out the Hard Right Edge (www.hardrightedge.com), a site that's geared for day traders as well as technical analysts. Its beginning course in technical analysis is The Trader's Wheel at www.hardrightedge.com/wheel/beginners.htm. Other tutorials you can read on this site are more advanced; peruse them once you're comfortable with the basic concepts.

SectorUpdates.com provides a comprehensive list of technical analysis links if you'd like to delve even deeper into the subject. Click on over to www.updates.com/charting.asp.

Advanced tools for numbers junkies

ONCE YOU'RE FAMILIAR WITH TECHNICAL CONCEPTS, you can develop a trading system and test it to see how it works using historical data. Trading systems were initially developed for commodity markets, such as agricultural products and currencies. The techniques developed were picked up by stock traders over time, and now you can find programs and web sites that use technical analysis techniques to determine when it's time to buy or sell an equity.

A typical trading system analyzes stock prices and volumes, then alerts the user to buy or sell when the conditions have been met. An example of a simple trading system is to buy 100 shares of the stock being studied as soon as there are three upticks in a row, or three trades with the price going up without any price drops. Trading systems actually in use are not nearly that simple, though, which is why it helps to have a computer do the number crunching.

An important part of implementing a trading system is back testing. To measure how well a trading system works, you run it using historical data to see whether you would have made or lost money with it — and how much your gains or losses would have been. Test two or three systems against one another to refine your trading signals.

Programs for developing a trading system

TradeStation (www.tradestation.com) has technical analysis techniques galore, as well as strategy development and testing. The program seems to be endlessly customizable, and allows you to create your own view of the market that includes Level II quotes, time and sales tables, fundamental as well as technical analysis techniques, all accessing their 30-year historical database. My favorite part of the program is developing and testing trading strategies, which now work on tick-by-tick real-time data. The program links to an online broker, so you can set up a hands-off trading strategy if you're brave. The program will run you about $300 per month.

Nirvana Systems publishes OmniTrader (www.nirv.com/omnitrader), which comes with over 100 trading systems that you can test and use immediately. You can also use the program to develop your own system while learning how to build and test a trading system by analyzing the built-in formulae. My favorite feature of OmniTrader is the ability to rank the built-in trading systems on a set of stocks, which illustrates the adage that one size (or trading system) does not fit all. You can also tell the program whether you're planning a short-term or long-term investment, and it will choose a method depending on your choice. The software is approximately $400 to $1,000, depending on whether you want real-time or delayed data.

INTERNET

www.daytrading.about.
com/money/daytrading/
library/weekly/topicsub
_tradesys.htm

About.com's Day Trading subject area includes the article, "How to Develop a Trading System." It's a step-by-step look at how the author came up with his original idea, tested it, and how you can use the system to make money on the stock market.

Look out for programs that offer buy and sell signals but don't tell you what the trading system is that's behind them. There's no way you can back test a trading system if you don't know what it is.

Learning more about trading systems

MOST OF THE INFORMATION FOR TRADING SYSTEMS *and technical analysts is geared toward short-term investors and day traders. If your investment horizon is longer, don't be put off by the near-term outlook espoused. There are some techniques that are applicable to longer term investors, and as you learn about market patterns and shifts, you'll find ways to apply them to your own situation.*

Check out The Big Easy Investor (www.bigeasyinvestor.com), which is a free program that explains the basic technical analysis indicators, and lets you develop an entry-level trading system. It runs only under Windows, however, and can take some time to update if you're following more than 100 stocks simultaneously. This program will whet your appetite and let you see whether you want to develop your own trading system.

A simple summary

✔ Technical analysts study stock prices and volumes to determine patterns in the market, and to forecast future prices.

✔ Start with the basics of technical analysis – line charts and moving averages – and then move on to relative strength and stochastics.

✔ Check out ClearStation and ProphetFinance on the Web.

as you learn how technical analysis works, then delve deeper into the subject with programs such as Window on Wall Street, IQ Chart, and MetaStock.

✔ Develop a trading system and then test it using historical data to see if your technical forecasts will help you grow your portfolio.

Chapter 17

Banking Online

ONLINE BANKING has been available in some form since the early 1980s. I write about ten paper checks a year on three different bank accounts. I pay the rest of my bills, from both my business and personal checking accounts, online. I transfer money from my checking accounts into my brokerage accounts over the Web. Online banking has attracted more accounts than online brokerages, with an estimated 27 million adults performing some of their banking chores online as of mid-2000. That outpaces significantly the 11 million or so online brokerage accounts that had been opened by that same date.

In this chapter...

✓ Choosing an online bank

✓ Taking out a loan online

✓ Finding the best rates

NO STAMPS, NO CHECK PRINTING FEES, AND NO CHARGES: BANKING ONLINE IS QUICK AND CONVENIENT

Choosing an online bank

BANKING ONLINE IS A NATURAL EXTENSION to having an online brokerage account. This revolution in managing household finances online has been quieter than the move to online stock trading. One reason is that most of us haven't had to change banks to go online. All we have to do is get a password from our existing bank, so it's an easy shift; similar to the way Fidelity and Schwab moved their customer base online to grab the majority of the online brokerage market share. You may already have an online banking account without knowing it.

> ## Trivia...
> *Online transfers will save you quite a few trips to the bank! I have my daughters' savings accounts linked to my checking account, and I give them their allowances from our home computer.*

Online banking encompasses more than just paying bills, though. You might need a loan, or want to move some of your cash into a higher rate account or CD. Figuring out which bank is best for you can take some doing though – Quicken.com currently lists 1,604 banks on its "Find a Bank" page (www.quicken.com/banking_and_credit/findbank/), ranging from 1st Choice Bank to Zions Bank. The odds are high that your bank is on this list. Check it out and find out which services you can access without switching banks.

Bricks or clicks; why not both?

Banks are partnering with other financial institutions, especially brokerages, to bring their customers a one-stop online destination. E*Trade's services include the E*Trade Bank, and Merrill Lynch has its own bank built into its site as well. Traditional "bricks and mortar" banks, such as Citibank and Wells Fargo, have a huge online presence, while "clicks only" banks, such as directbanking.com (a subsidiary of Salem Five Cents Bank), are establishing a physical presence.

There's a blurring of what used to be strongly defined lines as banks offer brokerage services and brokers offer mortgages. And all of these financial supermarkets are online, so you can fill out the application forms with your keyboard.

Online-only banks try to compete for your business by offering higher interest rates for deposits and lower rates for loans.

Directbanking.com, for instance, has no minimum balance requirement for its no-fee checking accounts. In general, due to lower overhead, online-only banks have lower fees for their services, and pay higher interest rates for your deposits.

Checking and bill paying

Online bill paying is a remarkable convenience, and one I've relied on for most of the last decade. If you can access your checking account over the Internet and have signed up for bill-paying services (which are usually free, or less than $5 per month), you can pay your bills wherever you access the Web. If you have multiple accounts with one bank, for example a checking account and a money market account, be sure you have all of them set up so you can transfer money between them online.

Quicken.com is the online companion to Intuit's popular financial management software by the same name, but you don't have to use the software to get a lot out of the site. You can pay your bills from the site just by linking to your existing bank account. The "MyAccounts" feature lets you link all your bank relationships on one page – credit cards, loans, checking, and savings accounts – so you can look at the whole lot at a glance, even if you're banking with several different institutions.

Most online brokers have "Webified" their cash management accounts, allowing customers to pay bills and transfer funds without killing off any trees. Fidelity Investments (www.fidelity.com) has added electronic bill receiving to their services, which will cut down on the volume of "snail mail" you receive.

■ **If you subscribe to online bill-paying services,** *you can organize transactions and transfer money between accounts whenever it suits you.*

■ **All online banks** *offer toll-free telephone support to help you run your finances. Some let you chat online with a representative.*

With electronic bill receiving, you direct your bills to a mailing address managed by the bank. They scan your bills, letting you view and pay them online. The bills are saved in electronic storage for a certain period of time — 6 months in the case of Fidelity Investments. This is a convenient service for the frequent traveler or for those with disheveled offices.

Though online banking is certainly convenient, one ongoing criticism I've had of the sites over the years is their somewhat disconnected feel. With few exceptions, it's difficult to get a big picture overview of your entire relationship with a financial institution. Citibank uses its Yodlee-powered account consolidator, myciti.com, to bring all the pieces of a customer's financial life onto one page, but most online banks treat your various accounts the same way they treat you on paper: Checking on one page, savings on another, loans on yet another. Putting it all together requires either a third-party program, such as a personal finance program, or an online consolidator, such as Yodlee.

Moving money around online

It's easy to transfer money from one account to another within the same bank. Moving funds from Bank A to Broker X (and vice versa) can be a little trickier to set up. Once it's set up, though, the fund transfers are a snap. For example, online brokerage BuyandHold (www.buyandhold.com) has its own "B&H BankLink" feature built in. When you set the link up, you have to specify your account's ABA Routing Number, which is a nine-digit number that can be found on your checks. You also have to type in your account number.

The art of withdrawing cash from an online bank account has not, however, been perfected. We can't hit a button and get a pile of $20 bills from our color printers yet! If your online bank doesn't have a physical presence, you'll usually get an automatic teller card that offers rebates for using the machines at your local bank.

All online banks offer online help, answers to frequently asked questions, and toll-free telephone support. Some let you chat online with a representative. Depositing a paper check can be problematical, but Mail Boxes Etc. is giving Juniper Financial and National Interbank a drop-off point for customers and will deliver the deposits free of charge.

If for some reason your bank doesn't yet offer online bill paying, and you don't want to switch institutions, check out PayMyBills (www.paymybills.com). Setting up the service can take some time, since you have to change the mailing address on your bills so that they go directly to PayMyBills instead of to you. Once you're up and rolling, paying bills is as easy as logging on and making a few mouse clicks – assuming you have the funds available.

Taking out a loan online

MUCH TO YOUR SURPRISE, *your apartment is being converted to a condominium. Now what? Can you afford to continue living there as an owner rather than a renter? There's a quick way to find out: Log onto an online mortgage site, plug in a few financial details, and find out over your post-work glass of wine whether you'll qualify for a loan – and how much it will cost.*

The number of online lenders is growing quickly, and there are many advantages to obtaining your loan over the Internet, including convenience and lower rates. Many online lenders offer lower rates than are available offline as they build their portfolios.

In reality, though, online loans only start over the Internet. They're completed and funded with a great deal of personal contact, just as if you'd negotiated the loan with a

■ **Looking for a loan** *to buy a new car? As the number of online lenders grow, you could find it easier and cheaper to obtain your loan over the Internet.*

local bank. Most borrowers use an online service to search for a lender, but they fill out the application – and get funded – offline. The usual method of business at mortgage sites is that you apply online, and then are referred to a traditional lender. The lender then contacts the lead (that's you) and the process usually continues from that point via telephone, fax, and paper.

Mortgages

Mortgage lenders have proliferated like rabbits online. It's almost impossible to visit a financial web site without being offered a loan. The great advantage to searching online for a loan is that when you contact a lender, whether on the phone or in person, you have an idea of what the best rates are already, and you can ask him or her to match or beat what you found on the Internet. You'll also find that it will take some personal contact to nail down the details of your loan, especially if your situation warrants creative financing.

Shopping online for a mortgage, even if you don't end up completing the process with the electronically enabled lender, is a good way to learn about the range of rates and loans available. You can even find out quickly whether or not your credit is good enough to qualify you for the loan you want.

Several sites, such as QuickenLoan.com, allow you to obtain pre-approval for a loan, so you can go home-shopping with its letter in hand, which can speed up the purchase process.

SPEEDY PAPERLESS MORTGAGES

Some problems stand in the way of completing the mortgage process online, such as the need to verify the identity of the borrower and notarize signatures.

In a pilot program during fall 2000, eOriginal, a Baltimore-based company providing secure, paperless, and legally enforceable e-commerce transactions, completed an entire mortgage process online. The buyer electronically executed the pilot promissory note and mortgage at a title company's Florida office, and authentication of the signatures was accomplished with specialized software. According to eOriginal, the company's technology cuts the mortgage closing process from an average of 45 days to less than 3 hours. Technology itself is making it possible to complete the mortgage loan process online.

■ **Learn about** *the range of house loans and rates available by shopping online for a mortgage and making sure you get the best deal.*

Getting a mortgage online won't work for you if you don't have an absolutely spotless credit record, however. Your loan process could grind to a halt if the lender has trouble finding an appropriate loan for you, so it's best to search offline if you think you might have problems. A seasoned local loan officer or mortgage broker is a better resource for you if your credit record has a blemish or two.

Don't get blindly attached to obtaining your mortgage online. Shop around, contacting some local offline vendors, and compare rates and service.

Home equity

Once you've lived in your house a few years, you'll build up some equity that you can use either to upgrade your home or for other purposes. Lenders are enthusiastic about loaning money to people with high equity balances and low debt other than a first mortgage. A *home equity line of credit (HELOC)* can offer a lot of flexibility for making large purchases.

Numerous online banks offer competitive rates and terms for HELOCs, especially for borrowers with good credit records. DeepGreen Bank (www.deepgreenbank.com) offers a Quick Cash option for borrowers who are applying for a HELOC. While it's going over your loan application, you can get up to $15,000 wired to your checking account in a few hours, and you'll be told during the application process whether you're eligible. What's the catch at DeepGreen? All your business will be conducted with them over the Internet – no paper statements. You should print out the reports the bank presents on-screen for your records, though.

DEFINITION

A home equity line of credit (HELOC), which is a variation of a home equity loan, allows a homeowner to, in essence, write checks on an account that is linked to a percentage of the equity held in the house. For instance, if you bought your house for $100,000 and it's worth $300,000 now, and you want to borrow against the $200,000 equity you hold without taking out a standard loan, you could get a HELOC and use what you need for some extraordinary expenses, such as remodeling or college. The interest rate is usually variable, fluctuating with the prime rate, and you can access the equity for a certain period of time, called the draw period. A HELOC is best used for a series of expenses rather than a single specific expense.

Finding the best rates

BANKERS WHO WANT YOU TO DEPOSIT MONEY typically advertise the compounded interest rate or annual percentage yield you'll earn if you leave your money with them for an entire year. The compounded rate is a fraction of a point higher than the uncompounded rate they actually pay, assuming you don't make any withdrawals. But when you're shopping for a loan, the advertised rates are the straight percentage, without compounding, which is a slightly lower rate than what you actually pay. Kind of a tricky scheme, isn't it? Just keep it in mind when you're shopping around.

CDs and savings accounts

Looking for a CD or a place to stash some cash? Imoneynet.com (www.imoneynet.com) ranks banks, from highest interest paid down to lowest, for nine different types of CDs. It also has a good loan search table. Another great place to seek out the best rates available for your deposits is Bankrate.com, which not only lists the interest you can earn, but also assigns a star rating to each bank. Using standards set by the Federal Deposit Insurance Corporation (FDIC), Bankrate evaluates the financial condition of various institutions, and assigns from zero to five stars depending on their performance. Most banks fall in the three to four star range, but you want to make sure the bank that's storing your cash for you is performing at the three star level or above.

Credit cards and loans

Credit Card Menu (www.creditcardmenu.com) has dozens of credit cards to choose from, depending on your financial situation. Set up a profile, indicating the annual fee and interest rates you're willing to pay, and the site finds a card for you. You can apply online, and get an approval (or rejection) within a few minutes.

When it comes to loans, several online banks will fund you quickly, and often by interacting with you only online. If you're loan shopping and don't need an instant answer,

INTERNET

www.gomez.com

www.bankrate.com

Bank comparisons help you shop around for the best deal if you're looking for a place to borrow – or to save. Gomez.com ranks 30 online banks, basing the points awarded on ease of use, customer confidence, on-site resources, relationship services, and overall cost. The rankings are re-weighted based on four different customer types too: Internet transactor, saver, borrower, and one-stop shopper. Bankrate.com surveys thousands of financial institutions nationally and compiles tables that show the best (and worst) rates for various types of loans as well as deposits.

Lending Tree (www.lendingtree.com) lets you explore various forms of financing and fill out the appropriate application online. Then it shops your application among a group of lenders, who compete for your business and contact you with their offers. The explanations of how loans work are excellent, and its collection of calculators help you compare offerings with differing arrangements of points and interest rates.

Before you go loan shopping, know what's in your credit report. You can request a copy of your report from Equifax (www.equifax.com), who will give you online access to your report for 30 days. Potential lenders want to know if you've handled other loans responsibly in the past, and the approximate amount of debt you're currently holding. Close any unused credit card accounts before you go loan shopping – the limit on each card is counted as potential debt.

Make sure you don't allow too many potential lenders to check your credit report. Each request to look at your report (except your own, of course) is logged. Some lenders look askance at reports filled with requests, and might turn you down just because you're shopping around.

A simple summary

✓ Online banking has more customers than online brokerages.

✓ You can use your checking account to pay bills online, saving yourself some time, as well as avoiding check printing charges and standing in line to buy stamps.

✓ The advantages to obtaining your loan online include greater convenience, lower rates, and better choice in lender.

✓ Shop for the best online bank or find the lowest loan rates by using bank comparison web sites.

PART FIVE

DAY TRADING DEMANDS A COOL HEAD AT ALL TIMES

DAY TRADING

SOME INVESTORS MOVE BEYOND THE REALM of managing their finances online and go into the world of day trading. This section is intended to give you a glimpse of what it takes to be a successful day trader, and the level of *commitment* you'll need to devote to the process. Frankly, this section  is more of a *warning* than an enticement: Day trading is a difficult and stressful way to earn a living.

Is this high-speed freeway your road to financial freedom? Find out in this overview of day trading tools, techniques, and strategies, whether day trading is something you want to pursue further.

Chapter 18

Investing Versus Day Trading

CONVENTIONAL WISDOM dictates that investing and day trading are two completely separate animals. Day traders hold equities only while the sun is up, and they can make a hundred trades in a day, buying and selling as the stock price changes by a fraction of a point. An investor chooses companies in which to invest, and holds the stock for a longer period of time. Which is right for you?

In this chapter...

✓ **What are the differences?**

✓ **Can you handle the pressure?**

✓ **Accounting for taxes**

263

DAY TRADING IS HIGHLY STRESSFUL, SO BE SURE YOU CAN COPE BEFORE JUMPING ON THE BANDWAGON

What are the differences?

DAY TRADING IS AN EXERCISE *in high-risk, volatile price playing. Day traders follow the price movements of one or several stocks, hoping that their prices will rise and fall quickly so they can turn a quick profit. A committed professional may make as many as 100 trades in a day, or as few as one or two. It all depends on the trader's strategy.*

The true day trader has cash on hand only as the sun sets on the stock market. Nothing long, nothing short, just cash – hopefully more at the end of the day than at the beginning.

Day trading versus long-term investing

The length of time an equity is held is typically quoted as the difference between day trading and long-term investing. Investors are thought of as buy-and-hold strategists, carefully choosing a stock based on its fundamentals and on the company's prospects for the future. Investors want to participate in a company's growth, whereas day traders try to take advantage of the changes in the company's stock over very short periods.

Day trading takes specialized tools, such as technical analysis charts, discipline, intensity, focus, and quick reflexes, which we'll look at in more detail in Chapters 19 and 20. It's not as simple as sitting at a computer, watching price changes, and buying and selling at the click of a mouse. You may have to switch through multiple order books, manipulate advanced software, and try to separate fact from fiction from the information you see on your screen.

Buy-and-hold investors have their day jobs, during which they might spend a little time taking a look at their investments. Day traders don't have time for a regular job – trading is their job.

Day trading versus frequent trading

As more investors go online and have access to the tools that were once available only to mutual fund managers or high-priced investment advisors, the pace of their trading usually picks up. Those who engaged in buy-and-hold strategies, mainly because it was a lot of trouble to locate a live broker and make a trade, often start turning their investments over more rapidly, reacting to changing market conditions. One phenomenon noticed in a study published by a major broker is that an investor's trading frequency typically triples in the first 6 months after going online, turning a buy-and-hold investor into a frequent trader, making 15 to 20 transactions per month rather than just one or two.

■ **If you choose to be** *a day trader, you will need to be psychologically prepared for downturns in the market as well as ups. For small investors, the markets are a gamble.*

Day trading goes a level beyond frequent trading, though. Day traders try to take advantage of imperfections in the price of a stock, buying when it looks low and then selling it when the rest of the market catches up and pushes the price up even higher. Day traders also make frequent use of their margin balances, which adds significantly to their risk.

Is it just gambling?

I've been known to say that day traders use the capital markets like gamblers use a casino. Day trading is a tough game for small investors to win. If you let yourself get too emotionally engaged, you'll have a hard time dealing with market downturns. There are psychologists who work with day traders the same way a coach might work with athletes, pumping up the confidence of the "players" and helping them to avoid emotional mistakes.

The simple truth is that just like gamblers in a casino, most day traders lose money. If you decide to be a day trader, the odds are stacked against you, and there are other traders, with much more experience, who are looking for weakness – possibly yours – to exploit. Not every high school basketball star can cut it in the NBA

Trivia...

Listen to dedicated day traders talk about their techniques and strategies at TraderInterviews.com. You'll need RealPlayer, a free audio program available at www.real.com, to listen in.

either. Successful day traders, who can handle the stress and strain of split-second judgments, are a different breed from buy-and-hold investors.

Can you have it both ways?

It sounds as though day trading and investing are mutually exclusive activities, but that's not necessarily so. A true day trader, who executes many trades daily, typically considers the money made at that endeavor his or her regular income. The same day trader might have a retirement account that's invested using buy-and-hold strategies.

Many day traders have strategies that let them hang onto a security if they see it riding a wave of increasing prices. At the same time, long-term investors can make short-term plays if they think it will help their portfolios grow. Thanks to the plethora of tools available online, both types of investors have access to information that helps them make informed decisions concerning the length of time they should hold their investments. So it's not as cut and dried as it might appear at first glance.

Can you handle the pressure?

BEYOND THE COMPUTERIZED TOOLS *available, successful day traders also have a mindset that supports their job. Day trading has been presented as easy, glamorous, and exciting by some of my fellow members of the financial media, but think about this point: If it's so easy, why aren't all day traders rich? Day trading is a remarkably risky venture, so if you can't handle the heat, stay out of the fire.*

Becoming a day trader is, in essence, a career change. If you're currently a salaried employee, think long and hard about whether you have what it takes to be a self-employed entrepreneur before you take the leap.

Day trading can be an exciting profession, but it's not a stable one. If you're the sort of person who gets depressed due to a setback or overly exuberant due to small successes, you're going to burn out as a day trader in short order.

Stop considering a life as a day trader unless you really like the idea. Some people feel relaxed when they're under pressure, whereas others reach for antacids. It's not a job for the timid. Can you imagine feeling restless on the weekends, anxious for Monday to

■ **Being a day trader** *can be highly stressful. Be honest with yourself when assessing if you have the right attitude to deal with the risks involved.*

come, because the market will be open again? If you can't, then this isn't the life for you. However, if your eyes sparkle with anticipation at that thought, then keep reading.

Being objective vs. being emotional

The tools to be discussed in Chapter 19 are all aimed at finding and exploiting small swings in the price of a stock. Successful day traders divorce their emotions from the process of timing their trades and are also aggressive about selling short as well as buying long.

INTERNET

daytrading.about.com/
money/daytrading/
library/weekly/
bl_becomeatrader.htm

Check out Robert J. Rak's series of articles on day trading at About.com.

The stocks I hold, especially those in my retirement-oriented portfolio, are in companies with which I feel intimately involved. I read their news reports, study their charts, and analyze what's going on when analysts publish upgrades and downgrades. I wouldn't be able to put any of those stocks on a day trading schedule, simply because I've become emotionally, as well as financially, involved with the companies.

Day traders can't get that attached – they have to be ready to cut and run when the price drops, or they have to consider a downturn as a buying opportunity rather than the end of the world.

Though day trading is not a new endeavor, psychologists have found a relatively new syndrome to treat: Obsessive online trading. The Center for Online Addiction (www.netaddiction.com) lists eight signs that are indicative of this obsession. If you've lost control of your life, lied to loved ones, or stolen money to support your online trading habit, you're probably an addict. Keep your trading under control.

WHAT DO YOU KNOW?

Robert J. Rak, author of the *Day Trading Guide* at About.com, strongly advises potential day traders to assess their knowledge of trading and markets before getting into the business. Here are some questions you should be able to answer with confidence prior to starting up a day-trading business:

- What is a bid? An ask?
- What is a bid size? An ask size?
- What is the tape?
- What is Level II?
- What is a market maker?
- What is a specialist?
- What is a block trade?
- What is a gap open?
- What is a tick?
- What is a market order?
- What is a limit order?
- What is a stop order?

Accounting for taxes

WHEN IT COMES TO TRADING, *online or otherwise, winning isn't everything, or even the only thing. Taxes are a big thing, too, because whether you win or lose, you still have to account for it to the IRS. Before you leap into the wild and wooly world of day trading, be sure you understand the tax consequences and are up for the challenge of proving what you've done to the IRS.*

A very informal and completely unscientific survey (of four of my friends who are income tax preparation experts) turned up the startling finding that day traders seldom turn a profit. Among these four tax preparers (one lawyer, three accountants), there were 36 day traders represented. Of those, only 8 showed a gain. That, however, doesn't necessarily mean these online investors really wound up in the red. It actually could reflect their tax and investing savvy if they booked their losing trades and let their winning ones run.

■ **Make sure you** *keep good records of all your trading activities. You'll need to justify all the accounting figures to the IRS on an annual basis, whether you've gained or lost.*

Tax accounting for day traders has to be part of your toolkit from Day One. Otherwise you'll spend days poring over thousands of trade confirmation notices trying to make sense of your gains and losses when tax time rolls around.

Taxing times for day traders: The basics

The IRS rewards those who hold stocks for more than 12 months by limiting the tax rate on capital gains to 20 percent. Your gains on stocks held for less than 12 months are taxed at your usual marginal tax rate, which could go as high as 39.6 percent. A relatively new tax law, passed in 1997, allows traders to write off all of their losses in the year they happened; this replaces a law that restricted write-offs to just $3,000. The higher your tax rate, the more you gain by holding stocks longer.

Reducing your tax bill is more a function of planning ahead than filling out forms. Before you get started, be sure you understand how frequent trading will affect you personally. If you plan to make day trading your day job, you will be making a series of short-term trades and will have to account for the gains as well as for your expenses. It might be worth your while to consider incorporating your day trading business, if you're serious about trading full-time. One main reason is that a day trader's return can look extremely fishy to the IRS's computers – you might have exchanged $10 million worth of stock in a year but be reporting an income of under $100,000. If you incorporate, all your trading activity stays under the corporate umbrella, so you report just a salary on your personal tax return.

Use a personal finance program, such as Intuit's Quicken or Microsoft Money, to track your office expenses, or step up to a business accounting package such as Intuit's QuickBooks or Peachtree Accounting if you want to create more formal business reports.

Wash sale rules

A factor that affects the high-velocity trader is the IRS rule on wash sales. The wash sale rule says, in essence, that you cannot deduct a loss on the sale of a security if you buy that same security back within a 30-day period. Most day traders

---

INTERNET

www.green company.com

www.daytradertax.com

For the glorious, gory details on these rules and how they apply to traders, check out the Trader Tax Solution Package offered by GreenCompany.com and the tax preparation services offered by DayTraderTax.com. They're not cheap, but they can help you determine which category of trading activity you qualify for as far as the IRS is concerned. They also handle the problem of managing hundreds (thousands?) of trades better than the packages that are geared for long-term investors. And, if you get lucky, the expense is deductible on your return.

will buy and sell the same security multiple times in the same day, taking some losses as well as achieving some gains. It's easy to see that the wash sale rule can present accounting problems as well as record-keeping nightmares for the active trader.

How can you avoid subjecting yourself to the wash sale rule? You can take advantage of IRS loopholes that allow day traders to classify themselves in different ways. If you qualify for one or more of these classifications, you're exempt from the wash sale rule. Have you given up your day job to become a full-time trader? You can be classified as a Trader in Securities as far as the IRS is concerned, which allows

■ **The tax rules** *are complex and must be taken seriously. Reducing your tax bill is often just a question of planning ahead.*

you to write off items like office expenses, seminars, supplies, and educational materials on your Schedule C. Read on.

Self-employed day traders

The active trader, who is mostly a short-term speculator, can choose to be classified in one of three categories: Investors, Traders in Securities, and Mark-to-Market Traders. A Trader in Securities is an IRS term used to describe an individual who is actively engaged in trading stocks, commonly referred to as a day trader. This individual trades on a full- or near full-time basis, essentially carrying on a trade or business. If you can achieve TIS status, the restrictive tax laws on deducting trading expenses are greatly relaxed, thereby enabling you to reduce your tax bill.

If you achieve Trader in Securities status, you then become eligible for Mark-to-Market accounting treatment. *Mark-to-Market* accounting provides the Trader in Securities with even more relaxed tax accounting rules.

You have to inform the IRS by April 15 that you plan to use TIS and/or Mark-to-Market status for the current year in order to write off your losses. If you don't, you're restricted to $3,000 in losses for the year and will have to carry over any additional losses into the next tax year. As I mentioned above, planning ahead is important.

■ **Rather than send in** *every single trade confirmation slip with your tax return, you can keep hold of this mound of paperwork – but be prepared to make it available to the IRS at their request.*

Preparing your tax return

Tax software does a good job of sorting out long- and short-term gains for the typical individual investor for whom trading is an avocation but not a vocation. For the devoted day trader, things get more complicated. Starting now, if you haven't done so already, match your purchases and sales for the IRS's benefit so you can do some tax planning.

The tax return of a day trader can be a mighty complicated document if every single trade is listed; one ruling says you can get around this as long as the figures on all your 1099s add up to what you list on your tax returns. You should still include a monthly summary or perhaps a summary by holding, and tell the IRS they can request the 22-inch stack of confirmation slips you've been hoarding if they really have to see it.

It doesn't matter whether you gained or lost, Uncle Sam will still need to know about those trades. If you've bought shares of a particular stock at different times, you'll need to match each purchase with its subsequent sale. This matchup is called tax-lot accounting. Day traders might purchase several blocks of stock in a single day, then sell all but one by the close of trading. The ability to do tax-lot trading with your online broker is important; you want to be the one who decides which stack of (virtual) stock certificates you're selling rather than leave it up to an automated system to pick last-in-first-out or first-in-first-out on your behalf.

Win, lose, or draw, you still have to track those trades and inform Uncle Sam of their consequences. Tax software does a good job for the typical individual investor, but things get more complex for the day trader.

Minimizing taxes may be one reason why more and more buy-and-hold investors are forsaking mutual funds and opting to buy stocks on their own. They get all the gains – and losses – from their trading, and they take them when they want to. Not so with mutual funds. For example, suppose you buy a hot fund whose performance owes to past savvy buys of, say, Internet stocks, at prices that are a small fraction of their current quotes. And say the fund's manager thinks their current price reflects not irrational exuberance but outright insanity, so he takes his profits. If you're a holder of that fund when those capital gains are distributed, you're socked with the tax bill – even if you didn't participate in the run-up. No wonder folks would rather buy their own on AOL.

The only surefire way to avoid paying taxes is to have no income. I don't know about you, but I'm not willing to go quite that far.

A simple summary

✓ Day trading differs significantly from buy-and-hold investing in terms of pace, pressure, and time commitment.

✓ Assess your own personality honestly, and decide whether you can handle the pressure.

✓ Make sure you've got the tools in hand to deal with the tax consequences of day trading before you get started.

✓ Keep good records of all transactions so that your tax position can be assessed fairly.

Chapter 19

Techniques and Strategies

D AY TRADING IS AS OLD as the stock market, though the Internet has made it much more accessible. To some, it's a game. To others, it's war. Your success as a day trader will depend on how well you understand the tools of the trade, and your ability to develop a winning strategy.

In this chapter...

✓ Charting techniques

✓ Keeping an eye on the market makers

✓ Developing a strategy

YOU NEED TECHNIQUES AND A STRATEGY TO BE ABLE TO CONSISTENTLY BUY LOW AND SELL HIGH

Charting techniques

DAY TRADING IS BEST ACCOMPLISHED *in a market that has plenty of price movements. A flat market, where prices aren't going up or down very much, doesn't typically provide many opportunities to get in and get out quickly with a profit. If the overall market seems to be flat, there still may be plenty of opportunities within more narrow areas of the market, such as a particular sector (for example, high tech or financial services) or a particular group, such as small cap stocks (which are stocks of relatively small companies).*

Identifying areas of the market that are trending up or down is a key part of a day trader's toolbox. The techniques discussed in Chapter 16 are of utmost importance to the day trader. Let's go into some more detail on how a few technical analysis techniques help sort through the universe of potential trades.

Two key components of a day trader's toolkit are Level II quotes, which display the current bid and ask prices as well as the number of shares available, and time of sales data, which show what really happened in the market. Day traders and institutional investors who think of the stock market as a war zone often place bogus orders that will show up on Level II screens and manipulate other traders into thinking a lot of stock at a particular price is up for grabs. So Level II screens display the direction the market might go, but the time of sales data shows what actually happened. It's the difference between theory and reality.

Stochastic oscillators

To the rescue are stochastic oscillator charts. As discussed in Chapter 16, stochastics measure the stock's price moves against its own history. It's a rather complex formula, comparing the current price against the highest high and lowest low measured over a specified number of periods, so it's best to have a program that can make the calculation for you based on real-time tick-by-tick data.

As you may recall, a stochastic ranges between 0 and 100. A value of 20–30 means the stock is oversold and the price will swing higher in the near future. When the measure hits 70–80, the stock is overbought and the price is about to drop.

To make things a little more complicated, stochastics are usually displayed as two lines. The main line is called %K and is solid. The second line is a moving average of %K, and is called %D. Using a computer as your assistant, you can specify how many periods should be used to construct %D.

USING STOCHASTIC CHARTS

There are many ways to use stochastics, so I'll summarize one effective method here. You need to have two charts open simultaneously. The top chart shows 1-minute or 5-minute price bars, and the lower one displays the stochastics. Set up the stochastic chart so that it displays the current value of the stochastic oscillator, which is usually referred to as %D, and a moving average of the stochastic oscillator, which is referred to as %Dslow. Watch the %D chart, and when it moves below 20, keep an eye on the %Dslow line. When the %Dslow line crosses over the %D line, so that both lines are heading in an upward direction, that's a buy signal. Conversely, when %D rises above 80, a sell signal is generated when %Dslow crosses over its line and both lines head lower.

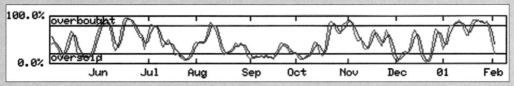

■ **The trigger to action occurs** *when both stochastic measures cross the "oversold" line on the way up – that's a signal to buy.*

Moving averages

Moving average charts help you figure out the price you should specify when you're buying or selling a stock. In your charting program, set up bars that represent the price in 1- to 3-minute intervals. On the same chart, add two moving averages: One based on a short range, such as 3–7 periods, and one based on a longer range, such as 12–20 periods. Now you can see the overall trend in a stock's price as well as the range in which it's trading. The trading range has upper and lower boundaries. The upper boundary is called the resistance level, or the price at which there are more sellers than buyers because the stock turns down at that level. The lower boundary is the support level, at which there are more buyers than sellers as the stock price heads back up. The two moving average lines might run horizontally for a stretch, which means the buyers and sellers are even for that period.

Making profitable trades depends on getting in early when the price is about to head up, and getting out as soon as it looks like the price is turning down.

THE MOMENT TO BUY

Based on movement the day before in the stock shown below, a trader might have decided to buy into this stock near the open, around 18. You can see the sell signal where the price drops below the green and blue bars (15-minute and 3-minute moving averages respectively) right at 12 o'clock, when the price was 18½. A buy signal is generated at 2.15 p.m., when the bars cross again at 18⅜ with a price breakout. This stock continued to climb through the rest of the trading day, so the day trader would sell it off just before the close, at 18¹⁵⁄₁₆.

■ **The careful study** *of a stock price's fluctuations is extremely important when you're looking to determine entry and exit points.*

Breakouts, which occur when the price bar breaks through the resistance level, are considered prime buying opportunities. They often signal a significant upswing in a stock's price. A breakdown, which happens when the price drops below the support level, indicates the start of a dropping trend, and is a signal to sell out, or sell short.

The example opposite, showing one way to use moving averages to decide when to trade as well as the price to specify, is simplistic and blessed by the advantage of 20/20 hindsight. Day traders typically work out much more complicated buy and sell signals, often a combination of stochastics and moving averages. Stochastics, typically assessed on a 1-minute or 3-minute basis, are used to decide whether to get in or out of a stock when the price has hit extremes. Moving averages help determine price trends.

> ## Trivia...
> The term relative strength is somewhat misleading because the RSI actually compares the stock's price to its own history. A better term might be internal strength.

Assessing momentum

Momentum is measured not only on a stock's price, but also on the number of shares traded at that price. The relative strength index, or RSI, is one way of measuring a stock's momentum. The number calculated varies between 0 and 100, and is based on upward and downward price changes over a specified period.

Students of the RSI use it to decide when a stock's price is about to swing. If a stock's price is trending upward, but the RSI is falling, that could mean the price of the stock is about to take a turn for the worse. Day traders often use the RSI to determine support and resistance levels, in addition to moving averages.

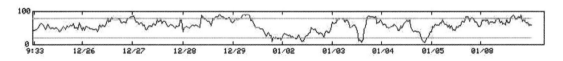

■ **RSI charts** *are a helpful method of gauging a stock's momentum, based on upward and downward price changes over a predetermined period.*

Day traders also have to keep an eye on the news regarding the stocks they follow. There's a stocktrading strategy called momentum strategy, not related to the RSI or other technical concepts, which works on predicting swings in the stock price. A key component of this strategy is the cockroach theory, which asserts bad news tends to be released in bunches. Therefore, just as cockroaches travel in large groups, investors will bail out on a hint of bad news, assuming that one piece of bad news will soon be followed by another.

Keeping an eye on the market makers

MARKET MAKERS CAN SELL SECURITIES *to their own customers out of their inventory, or they can buy or sell a large block of stock on behalf of a customer. Typically, they try to make money on the spread – the difference between the bid (buy) price and the ask (sell) price. This spread can be a tiny fraction of a point or up to half a point. On the large blocks of shares that market makers trade, they can make a lot of money.*

Day traders have to keep an eye on the market makers because these firms are allowed to adjust their bid and ask prices whenever they want, due to the risk they're taking by committing to trade a certain stock. Market makers must register for each stock in which they will make a market, but there's no limit on the number of firms that can be registered for an individual security. Some highly traded stocks, such as Microsoft (MSFT) and Intel (INTC), can have 60 market makers registered. On average, a NASDAQ-listed stock has 11 market makers.

> *You and I will seldom execute trades of a size that will influence the entire market, so we have to be aware of those who do in order to be successful at day trading.*

DEFINITION

Market makers *are securities firms who have fulfilled a number of rules and regulations set out by the National Association of Securities Dealers, and then commit to buy and sell the NASDAQ stocks in which they make markets. The regulations with which a market maker must comply include an agreement to publicly report the price and volume of each transaction within 90 seconds, and a guarantee that each order will be executed at the best price available.*

Reading the Level II display

A market maker's bid and ask will appear on Level II displays, so you can study its behavior over time. Once you've defined your personal "basket" of stocks that you'll trade, start studying the major market makers because they will strongly affect your profits.

Level II screens are split into two sides. On the left, you'll see the buyers, or those bidding on a stock. On the right, you'll see the sellers, or those asking for a particular price for a stock. The display shows the abbreviation for the market maker, the bid or ask price, the size of the block of stock up for grabs, and the time of the quote.

KEY MARKET MAKERS

This chart lists the most active market makers overall and their abbreviations, which are displayed on Level II screens. Bring up the Island book (www.isld.com) on your computer now, enter the symbol for Intel or Microsoft, and see how many you can spot.

Market maker	Level II abbreviation
Goldman Sachs	GSCO
Morgan Stanley	MSCO
Herzog	HRZG
Knight Trimark	NITE
Montgomery Securities	MONT
Meyers & Schwartz	MASH
Hambrecht & Quist	HMQT
Robertson Stephens	RSSF

The block size is shown in hundreds, so a 1 in the size column means 100 shares, while a 25 means 2,500 shares. The market makers are stacked up, from best to worst quote, on each side. You'll see the market maker offering the highest bid price on top of the buy side, and the market maker with the lowest ask price on top of the sell side.

The market makers are grouped by the price they're bidding or asking. If two market makers are set at the same price, the one with the larger block is displayed on top. By looking at the number of shares being offered or asked for at a particular price, you can see the depth of the demand for a stock. One caveat: Market makers often mask the size of the block of stock they're trying to buy or sell, so unless you have access to Level III quotes, you don't have the complete picture.

■ **It's important to** *study the markets carefully before acting. Many day traders follow the activities of a few key market makers and use their actions as a pointer for buying and selling.*

The ax

With up to 60 market makers in a particular stock, which one should you use as your key? Day traders try to identify the ax market maker, the one who is both stabilizing the market and influencing changes in the price. Most experienced day traders follow Goldman Sachs (GSCO) and Morgan Stanley (MSCO) closely, and try to buy when they're buying, and sell when they're selling. As you study the markets, you may discover a market maker who suddenly widens the spread between bid and ask, which is an indication of where that market maker thinks the stock is going in the next few minutes.

For example, let's say you're watching GSCO's activity with Company XYZ stock. According to longtime GSCO watchers, they typically maintain a ¼ point spread on a stock, so that they might bid 20 for a block, and ask 20¼. When that spread widens, the direction indicates where GSCO thinks the market is going. Should the bid drop to 19¾, it looks like GSCO thinks the price is heading down. Experienced day traders become aware of the market makers who try to "fake out" the market by entering phony orders which they pull as soon as the market reacts, as well as the ones who play it straight. As you're developing your system, be sure to study the market makers and figure out which ones are worth using as your ax.

Program trading

The big institutional investors, such as mutual funds, and the market makers don't sit there with their fingers on the "buy" and "sell" buttons all day. They've developed computerized trading programs that measure the state of the market continually and automatically trigger purchases and sales. The New York Stock Exchange defines program trading as the simultaneous buying and selling of at least 15 different stocks totaling $1 million or more in value. Most institutional investors have program trades that are much larger than that. These program trades act like the tide in the stock market, pushing prices up or down, depending on the formulas used.

Programmed trades are typically based on the difference between futures prices and a particular stock index. The S&P 500 is usually used as the index that triggers these programs.

Since program traders usually use the S&P 500 as the index, they estimate a difference between the current, or cash value, of the S&P 500 index, and the futures of that same index. The difference is called the fair value, which measures the benefit of owning cash versus owning futures. Each program trader establishes its internal fair value and also decides what the premium will be that triggers buy orders and sell orders.

So these premiums are really estimates, but they drive the program trading. It's tough to tell from the outside what the actual triggers might be for a particular institution, but once their program is launched, you can watch it in action. Day traders use a 3-minute stochastic chart of both the S&P 500 and the S&P 500 Futures to observe this. When the futures charts show a sudden move, either up or down, you can tell that a program has been triggered. Now your challenge is locating the individual stocks that are in play, which is a subject often discussed on community web sites that cater to short-term traders.

INTERNET

www.3dstockcharts .com

Check out 3DStockCharts.com for a view of the price book for a particular stock. This interesting site summarizes the activity on a group of the larger ECNs in graphical format. The larger blocks of stock are represented with bars, with each ECN represented by a different color. The price of the largest block of stock currently available is displayed at the bottom of the graph.

Developing a strategy

THE ESSENCE OF ANY TRADING STRATEGY *is to maximize the number of times you buy low and sell high. Sounds simple, doesn't it? There are numerous styles of day trading, and over time, you'll find the one that's most comfortable for you. Experienced day traders move with the markets, adapting their strategies as the waves of momentum shift.*

Two of the more popular schools of thought are scalping and swing trading. Scalpers look for that fraction of a point, and are willing to hold stocks for very short periods of time – as short as a minute. Scalpers pop in and out rapidly, and strive to take advantage of as many small movements in a stock price as they can. Swing traders usually hold the stock a little longer, but they also go into a trade with an exit strategy already defined – the amount of profit desired, as well as when to sell the stock if the price drops. A swing trader might even hold a stock for a few days, which is behavior you won't often find in a scalper. A swing trader will decide in advance how much of a loss is acceptable, and will sell out of a position if the market declines.

You may start out a day trading career thinking you're a scalper, and then find out that it's not the best way of life for your particular personality. Keep a diary as you get started, and make a note of what you do when you're making a winning trade versus a losing trade. Is there a pattern of good habits that keep you on the winning side? What happens before and after a losing trade? Study yourself as well as the markets.

Finding your "basket"

The stock market is huge. Thousands of equities are trading in dozens of markets all over the world. You need to find a few stocks to focus on because there's no way you will have the time to make sense of the entire market. Keep in mind as you're picking the stocks that you'll study that the most obvious issues are popular among day traders, and thus the competition is extremely stiff.

How can you choose the stocks to watch? At the beginning, narrow the potential list down to those that trade under $50 per share. You'll minimize your risk while you're learning. Sure, there have been some amazingly volatile stocks, the darlings of hundreds of day traders, that trade in the $150–$200 range. But you need a lot more money up front to start trading at that level than you do if you start out with lower priced equities.

The next key component of any stock in your basket is a lot of movement in the price. The average daily range should be four to eight times the usual spread between the bid and the ask. So if a stock's usual spread is ¼ point, look for a stock that has 1–2 points per day in price movement. Another key component is relatively high trading volume. You don't want a stock in your basket that has only a few buyers and sellers because it can be difficult to find an investor on the other side of the trade you want to make. A quick scan of the top 25 stocks traded on the NASDAQ, ranked in order of the number of shares that change hands daily, will give you some good candidates for your basket.

Are you regularly on the losing side for one of the stocks in your basket? Don't keep it in your target group – throw that loser out and find a new stock. If you consistently lose money on a particular stock, there's obviously something going on in the market that's not being reflected in your trading system. Time to bail and start anew.

Timing is almost everything

The goal of every trading strategy is to make money: Buy low, sell high. Technical analysis techniques help the day trader figure out when to get in and at what price. Though some trading strategies allow market orders in which you buy or sell the next block of shares available, most dictate the use of limit orders. With a limit order, you set the price, and if there are the appropriate number of shares available at that price, your order should go through. I say should rather than will because market makers might have prices listed in the order books that are referred to as head fakes, intended to influence the direction of the market but without actually buying or selling at those prices.

Another key component of a profitable strategy is deciding how big a block you want to trade. If you usually trade 100 shares at a time, pretty soon commissions are going to eat up all your profits. Let's take a look at how much you can make on trades of different sizes.

Dealing with breaking news

There are, as with just about every investing-related topic, several schools of thought regarding how to react to news about a stock. Some traders watch CNBC just

INTERNET

www.b4utrade.com

B4Utrade, a subscription site that costs $25 per month, has a terrific stock screener that not only displays CNBC news stories in a small window, but also lets you find out which stocks are being discussed in the media. You can also select stocks that have been upgraded or downgraded, as well as those announcing spin-offs or mergers. This is a terrific site for the news junkie.

BLOCK SIZE DETERMINES YOUR PROFITS

Assume you picked a stock that's trending upward in price, and it continues along that path. Take a look at how much you'll make, depending on when you sell.

Block size	Profit at $\frac{1}{16}$	Profit at $\frac{1}{8}$	Profit at $\frac{1}{4}$	Profit at $\frac{3}{8}$	Profit at $\frac{1}{2}$
100	6.25	12.50	25.00	37.50	50.00
200	12.50	25.00	50.00	75.00	100.00
500	31.25	62.50	125.00	187.50	250.00
1,000	62.50	125.00	250.00	375.00	500.00
2,500	156.25	312.50	625.00	937.50	1250.00
5,000	312.50	625.00	1250.00	1875.00	2500.00
10,000	625.00	1250.00	2500.00	3750.00	5000.00

Now subtract your commissions paid on both sides of the trade from your profits. You can see that the smaller blocks don't leave you much cash to put in your "Win" column. Clearly you need to start out with quite a bit of cash just to get started as a day trader. The smaller the spread, the larger the block you'll have to trade in order to make a profit.

to avoid the stocks that are mentioned. The theory behind staying away from those companies is that the mere mention on television brings out the amateurs, so the market for the stock gets thrown into a tizzy. Others listen to the financial news and head straight for their online broker's site when one of their basket companies is mentioned. They figure they know the stock better than any of the amateurs and can take advantage of them.

Whatever you decide to do about the news, whether to avoid it or embrace it, you'll have to know what it is. Most online brokerages flag companies that have appeared in the news, so you can find out what's being said with a mouse click. Serious day traders have a television or two on in their offices, tuned in to CNBC and other financial shows.

■ **Television can provide** *good coverage of up-to-date financial news as it is breaking, and you will need to keep up if you intend to be a serious investor.*

A simple summary

✓ Identifying areas of the market that are trending up or down is a key part of a day trader's toolbox.

✓ Day traders have to study the behavior of market makers to predict where the market is going.

✓ You need to find a few stocks to focus on because there's no way you will have the time to make sense of the entire market – it's simply too extensive.

✓ Decide how big a block you want to trade when you develop your system. The bigger the block, the more you can make at a time (and, equally, the more you can lose).

Chapter 20

Specialized Tools of the Trade

D AY TRADERS NEED to stay closer to the markets than longer term investors. Every tick, every piece of news, and every shift in momentum that affects the day trader's target stocks must be observed in order to understand what moves the market. As a day trader, you also need to understand what happens to the orders you place in order to squeeze out an additional fraction – which could be the difference between profit and loss.

In this chapter...

✓ **A day in the life of a day trader**

✓ **Understanding order routing systems and ECNs**

YOUR PROFITABILITY DEPENDS UPON BEING EQUIPPED TO ANTICIPATE EVERY MOVE OF THE MARKET

A day in the life of a day trader

ARM YOURSELF WITH A POT OF *coffee and have some snacks on hand so you can recharge your batteries at your desk. A day trader's working hours start out before the official markets open, which for longer term investors begins at 9.30 a.m. eastern time. Thanks to ECNs such as Island, which open at 8.15 a.m., you'll have to be ready to roll rather early in the morning. For those of you who live on the West Coast of the United States or in Hawaii – I hope you love being up before sunrise. The end of the day comes when the after-hours markets close at 6 p.m. eastern time. Let's take a look at the typical rhythms of a trading day.*

■ **Make sure** *you have a ready supply of snacks and drinks to hand so that you can keep up your energy levels. You'll need them!*

Before the open

From 8.15 a.m. to 9.30 a.m., ECNs (electronic communication networks) such as Island, Redibook, Archipelago, and Instinet are open for business. This premarket session doesn't generate much volume, and you'll see wide spreads between the bid and ask price. Market makers cannot be "hit," or required to fill orders, before the open, but they can and do post bids and asks. Some of them post outrageous bids, a point or more higher than the previous day's close, in an effort to trick the amateurs into thinking a stock is about to *gap* up.

The premarket period generally tends to be a seller's market. If you notice a gap up, the chances are that it will disappear when the entire market opens at 9.30. Keep an eye on the S&P 500 Futures during the premarket; as mentioned in Chapter 19, you can pinpoint upward and downward movements in the market, using stochastics, by tracking how the futures are trading.

At the open

Ding! When the bell rings at 9.30 a.m., opening the NASDAQ, you've entered the scramble period as traders and market makers try to establish the trading ranges on their key stocks. Price swings tend to be exaggerated as the orders entered overnight and premarket hit the system. This period is very risky because the intra-day charts, showing each tick as trades execute, are still developing, and the patterns aren't immediately obvious.

Experienced day traders are ready at the open, and some are able to make their profit targets for the day in the first half-hour. There are three basic patterns that most stocks follow, though there are of course, exceptions.

1. **A strength open** is characterized by a large rush of buying, driving the price up. The stock hits a peak, and then the sellers charge in to take their profits. Many day traders avoid the strength open, because the stock tends to linger in the doldrums for the rest of the day.

2. **A gap and trap open** happens when there's a gap up or down in the S&P 500 Futures index, which induces traders to jump in and close the gap, reversing the trend. Day traders watch the stocks that open with a gap and trap, and assess when the reversal has taken place.

3. **A weak open** starts with a drop in the stock price, then a bounce when the price hits bottom. A day trader who correctly plays the bounce can pick up a profit.

A large majority of stocks establish their high and low prices for the day at the open. You can spot where the market makers are going, and if you've identified the correct ax, you can figure out its motive as well.

Market makers can reap profits only when the volume is high. You'll see them jiggle the bid and ask prices to generate more interest in a stock, and suck other traders in, when the volume slows down.

As the world turns

The period from 10 a.m. to 11.30 a.m., also called the postopen, is when the markets start to settle down from the opening frenzy. Trading ranges have been established, and the pattern for the day is easier to discern. During this period, you can examine the stocks you're following, and the market overall, to determine how strong the prices are, and how each sector is tracking.

New day traders should spend some time observing the open and making paper trades. The postopen period is considerably less risky as patterns are established, and it's a much safer time for the new day trader to get into the market.

■ **By late morning,** *markets will be starting to settle down and you may be able to take a moment to examine your stocks in the context of the overall market picture.*

As Alan Farley, author of "The Master Swing Trader" and founder of The Hard Right Edge (www.hardrightedge.com), says about the beginning of the trading day, "Avoid the open. They see you coming, sucker."

"The dead zone"

Lunch time! Between 11.30 a.m. and 2 p.m., volumes drop off and the momentum established in the first 2 hours begins to fade. Since volume is down, there aren't very many shares of stock on the table, and some traders might execute orders just to do something. Be wary of trying to stave off boredom by entering random orders. Market makers are often out there trying to trap day traders into dead ends. Don't let them take away your morning profits.

Before the close

Around 2 p.m., the markets perk up, and the momentum gets rolling once more. At 3 p.m., the fun begins again. This last hour of the market, from 3–4 p.m., is often characterized by a similar frenzy as you see at the open. The difference is that you can study intra-day history on all your stocks and determine a trend. The last 30 minutes of the market are typically volatile as traders wrap up their profits (or losses) on the day.

The last hour of the trading day inspired Alan Farley to say, "The trend is your friend in the last hour. As volume cranks up at 3 p.m., don't expect anyone to change the channel." In other words, if the stock is tracking up in the last hour when volume is high, it will continue up until the close. Traders are now establishing the patterns that will be carried forward when the market opens the next day.

One pattern day traders have noticed is that a stock that closes strongly, with an upward moving trend on high volume, tends to open lower the next day as market makers take some profits. If you're planning on holding onto a stock overnight (also called "taking the stock home"), then buy a smaller lot than your usual block. If you normally trade 1,000 share blocks, buy 500 to hold overnight. The odds are high that the price will drop first thing in the morning, but the upward trend established at the close could well continue through the rest of the following trading day.

After hours

A recent trend among online brokers is after-hours trading, which takes place from 4–6 p.m. Publicly traded companies often announce bad news at the close of market, so the after-hours session establishes a drop in the stock price that usually continues on through the following day's open. Market makers and ECNs are not required to participate in after-hours trading, so the volume is very low. Always use a limit order when trading outside of the usual market hours.

Day traders who hold stocks after the close of the regular market should keep a sharp eye on the after-hours market. They might be able to lock in a profit, avoiding the chaos of the following day's opening session.

For most experienced day traders, the most productive times to trade are at the open and during the last hour.

Understanding order routing systems and ECNs

WHEN YOU ENTER A NASDAQ order with most brokers, whether offline or online, a market maker typically ends up with your trade. You don't have control over how the order is executed or which system will handle it. As discussed in Chapter 12, market makers often shave a fraction of a point off your trade, and your broker might be making money by funneling your trade to a particular market maker. There are some gray areas in the regulations that govern the NASDAQ that allow market makers the leeway to shave points off your order. These gray areas, by the way, don't exist on NYSE-listed stocks, which is the reason order routing systems and ECNs exist only for the NASDAQ.

> ### Trivia...
> The SOES was first introduced in 1984 and was designed to execute small orders against the best bid and ask prices. Market makers were required to fill orders on SOES after the market crash of October 1987 in response to outcries from small investors who felt as though they were squeezed out by institutional investors. Day traders like to get their buy orders filled via SOES because the market makers are required to fill them.

An emerging trend in online brokerages, especially those that cater to day traders, is your ability as an investor to route your order yourself. You choose which order routing system or ECN to use for your trade. Brokers that cater to day traders offer benefits such as Level II screens, quotes, technical charting, time of sales screens, and also allow direct access to the market.

ECNs are electronic order books that automatically match up bids and asks as they come in. They eliminate the middle man by pairing buyers and sellers directly. Order routing systems allow investors to pick which market makers they want to work with. If you're going to make a living as a day trader, you have to have the most efficient way of getting your order to market. Let's take a look at the major order routing systems and ECNs.

Small order execution system (SOES)

The SOES was designed to give small investors fast order fills on blocks of up to 1,000 shares. Market makers cannot send orders to the SOES, but they have to fill them. SOES operates on a first come, first served basis – if two traders enter orders to buy 500 shares of XYZ Company at 22½, the one that entered the order first will get the first fill. If a market maker is offering shares of XYZ Company at the specified price, it has to fill the order within 17 seconds or change its quote. Some market makers hide the number of shares they are either offering or trying to buy by displaying a block size of 100 or 200 shares, but they may actually fill a larger order.

SOES has a few points in its favor, primarily fast fills and the absence of professionals. On the downside, you can't access an ECN, and SOES is open only during regular market hours. In a rapidly moving market, you might run into a traffic jam or be unable to fill your entire order. I've seen reports of strange fills on the SOES too – a trader enters an order for 1,000 shares and ends up getting 458 instead. That's an odd block size to deal with.

SelectNet

SelectNet, which is run by the NASDAQ, can be used by market makers and individual traders, and allows you to specify either a market maker or an ECN for your order. Unlike SOES, there's no limit on block size, so trades of over 1,000 shares can be sent here. Orders on SelectNet can be filled, at the discretion of the market maker, in 27 seconds. If the market maker doesn't fill the order in that time frame, it must change its posted quote. In the world of day trading, 27 seconds can seem like forever and can also give the market maker a chance to assess the supply and demand of a stock and change its quote.

On the plus side of the ledger, traders find it convenient to route through SelectNet to any ECN or market maker. In addition, SelectNet is open both pre-open and after hours. However, day traders generally dislike having a market maker fill an order on this system. The time lag allowed makes day traders feel as though the deck is stacked against them – a market maker wouldn't fill an order unless there was something going on behind the scenes that hurt the day trader. Other complaints about SelectNet include the logjams experienced at the open and close, especially on extremely high volume days when the market is fluctuating wildly.

Archipelago

Archipelago was developed by Townsend Analytics, a software company that has published real-time investor tools since the mid-1980s. It was one of the first four ECNs approved in 1997, and you can access it if you're a customer of a brokerage that has licensed Townsend's RealTick software. The abbreviation you'll see in order books for Archipelago-listed orders is ARCA, and if you're using RealTick, you'll see ARCHIP. ARCA will first try to execute your limit order against ARCHIP orders, and if one does not exist there, it will go out and search other ECNs for a fill. If it still can't find a match for your order, ARCHIP heads over to SelectNet and tries to fill it against one of the market makers. If, after all that, Archipelago can't find a way to fill your order, it will be displayed on the ARCA book.

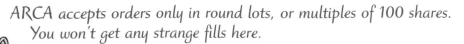

ARCA accepts orders only in round lots, or multiples of 100 shares.
You won't get any strange fills here.

ARCA gives you full access to all market makers and ECNs and can be used pre-market and after hours. It's easy to use, in that your order is "shopped around" on your behalf with no additional work on your part. That ease of use means that many new day traders are on the system, reacting (some might say overreacting) to every tiny shift in a stock price. Its ease of use also means some fills are very slow, as ARCA will check with every market maker on SelectNet and give them each 27 seconds to deal with the order. You might be waiting a long time for your fill. View the ARCA book at www.tradearca.com.

Island

On average, 10 percent of the NASDAQ volume goes through the Island book every day. That means most day traders prefer Island, and its speed and liquidity are the main reason. As a result, most day trading-oriented brokers give you access to the Island book from your computer, and if they don't, you can send the order to Island through SelectNet. Orders on Island typically fill in 3–10 seconds when there's a match on the other side.

If you enter a large block on Island, you may wind up with the trade being broken into smaller chunks of stock, and some of them might fill in odd ways.

I watched an order for 500 shares fill in three blocks once: 300 shares, then 147, and then the remaining 53. The order filled at three different prices as well, and generated three commissions, until I complained to the broker and got two of the commissions erased. You can view the Island book at www.isld.com.

refresh | island home | system stats | help

WIND

GET STOCK
WIND go

LAST MATCH		TODAY'S ACTIVITY	
Price	29.6875	Orders	708
Time	15:00:23	Volume	19,383

BUY ORDERS		SELL ORDERS	
SHARES	PRICE	SHARES	PRICE
100	29.2500	500	30.0625
60	29.0000	200	30.7500
33	28.0000	20	31.0000
475	28.0000	50	31.5000
200	27.0000	500	32.0000
30	26.8750	400	32.8750
50	26.5000	100	33.5000
100	26.0000	100	35.0000
100	26.0000	20	36.0000
250	26.0000	50	36.0000
100	25.0000	1,000	36.8750
100	25.0000	20	38.0000
100	21.0000	100	38.0000
20	20.0000	20	39.0000
150	19.8000	44	42.0000
(1 more)		(7 more)	

ISLAND

Instinet

Instinet, originally called the Institutional Networks Corporation when it was founded in 1969, had as its original mission the lowering of trading costs for institutional money managers. Its primary mission is to handle large blocks of stock, such as those traded by pension funds, mutual fund managers, market makers, and other large institutions. Individuals can't access Instinet directly. Instinet orders don't show up on Level II screens, because the orders are filled within the system. If you see INCA on a Level II screen, which indicates an Instinet order, that means it couldn't be filled by trading with other Instinet clients. Another interesting factoid about INCA orders that are displayed on a Level II screen is that the actual size of the block is probably being masked. An Instinet customer might be trying to buy up 10,000 shares of a stock, but you'll see 200 or 500 shares on your Level II display.

Some day traders take advantage of large block trades by keeping an Island book open in conjunction with an Instinet book. Let's say you keep seeing a block of 500 shares of XYZ on the INCA book with a bid of 25⅜. Over on ISLD, you see some XYZ with an ask price of 25⅛. You can buy up the shares offered on ISLD, and then sell them to the INCA bidder and pocket ¼ point.

Smart order routing

If you have a collection of trading-related buzzwords on file, as I do, smart order routing should be there. Direct access brokers that cater to day traders are offering technology that is designed automatically to send buy and sell orders to the trading venue with the best price at any moment. This technology scans the markets at the instant the order is entered, and locates the market maker or ECN who has the best price available. Smart order routing systems are also designed to provide price improvement, which means finding a lower price when you're buying, or a higher price when you're selling.

These systems are most likely to help the trader during the chaotic periods of the market – the opening half-hour and the hour before the close. During the "dead zone," a smart order routing system probably won't be of much help.

Smart order routing comes at a price, though; typically the brokers that offer smart order routing systems also charge monthly fees in addition to the commissions on each transaction.

Trivia...

Day trading firms are still active, and at last count (early 1999) have a total of approximately 5,000 customers. The demographics reflect a predominantly young and male customer base. They offer a desk and a computer with high-speed access to the markets. They also offer an informal support group composed of the customers of the firm, who usually spend the day together pounding on keyboards, executing multiple trades.

WEB SITES FOR DAY TRADERS

Day traders, since they're online all the time anyway, are the target market for a huge number of web sites, newsletters, books, online training courses, and stock information sites. Here are some you should add to your Favorites list, along with those mentioned throughout Chapters 18 and 19.

Site name	Web address	Key feature
The Rookie Day Trader	www.rookiedaytrader.com	Tips and tools for the beginning day trader.
The Hard Right Edge	www.hardrightedge.com	Alan Farley's *20 Golden Rules for Traders* is a must.
Daytraders Chat	www.daytraders.org	An Internet relay chat for day traders.
Pristine Day Trader	www.pristine.com	Education and tools for day traders.
TraderBot technical	www.traderbot.com	Execute searches on criteria. Flexible and free.

Online trading versus renting a desk

Numerous online brokers offer services that are of intense interest to the day trader. Refer to Chapter 11 for a description of several top brokers in this market.

Before the Internet allowed day traders to access the markets from the comfort of their own homes, quite a few day trading offices sprang up, mostly in metropolitan areas across the country. The trader rents a desk, complete with a computer and access to the markets, from the firm. Most trades are done in a margin account. Some day trading firms are organized as limited liability companies (LLCs), and they sell an interest in the firm to individuals who want to become day traders. The firms themselves are listed as broker-dealers under SEC regulations, but the individuals who buy an interest are

INTERNET

www.sapphirebay.com /trading/firms.htm

Sapphire Bay, a software publisher, offers this web site with a long list of specialty brokers for day traders as well as retail brokers suitable for day trading.

considered "associated persons" of the firm rather than customers. The day trading firm allows the "associated persons" to trade, using a portion of the firm's capital, which is tied to the person's interest in the firm.

Customers are often lured in by advertising that promises huge returns, whether the market goes up or down. One day trading firm that was censured by the Federal Trade Commission in May 2000 ran ads guaranteeing a return of up to 2,041 percent. The FTC settlements require the firms to prove any earnings claims or claims about profits, and also require any future advertisements to contain the disclosure "DAY TRADING involves high risks and YOU can LOSE a lot of money." As you can probably tell, I'm not a huge fan of these rent-a-desk firms, because they make money when you lose yours. I'd rather see you be an educated, self-directed day trader, controlling your own destiny – if that's the route you choose.

■ **Renting a desk** *is an option for the day trader who does not want to work from home, but don't forget that firms offering this service make money from your losses.*

A simple summary

✓ Know the rhythms of the trading day – your profitability will depend on it.

✓ The path your order takes from the time you enter it until it's executed can be short and sweet, or long and tortuous.

✓ Smart order routing systems are designed to automatically send buy and sell orders to the trading venue with the best price.

✓ Watch out for empty promises if you rent a desk from a day trading firm.

Investment web sites

THERE ARE MANY SITES on the Internet that deal with investing. The following list contains some of the most useful, including some international pages. Please note, however, that due to the fast-changing nature of the Net, some of those listed may be defunct by the time you read this. Happy surfing!

Search engines

www.altavista.com
Results organized by type: Web page, video, audio, etc.

www.askjeeves.com
Ask a question, get well-organized answers.

www.dogpile.com
Searches web sites and newsgroups, plus a joke of the day.

www.google.com
Easy, fast, simple interface.

www.lycos.com
Results are listed by popularity.

www.metacrawler.com
Sends your search to 12 engines at once.

www.nbci.com
Editors and users rate sites for usefulness.

www.northernlight.com
Organizes results into folders.

www.search.com
Start your search in a particular category.

www.yahoo.com
Locates web sites, news, and online events.

Financial directories

businessdirectory.dowjones.com
Has reviews from the *Wall Street Journal* with links to money-related sites.

www.money.looksmart.com
Click on Categories to get links to other sites.

quote.yahoo.com
News, links galore, and real-time quotes.

search.aol.com/cat.adp?id=68
Has thousands of links, arranged by category.

www.cyberinvest.com
Has a terrific collection of online investing guides.

www.financenter.com
Helps you create your own ranking of brokers and banks.

www.gomez.com
Has scorecards ranking banks, brokers, insurance providers, etc.

www.investorguide.com
Has articles, quotes, and news clips, as well as links.

www.moneyclub.com
Has links organized by channel. Includes investment club directory.

www.moneyweb.com
Includes links to education resources as well as the usual financial suspects

Discussion boards

go.compuserve.com/investors
Investors' forum.

go.compuserve.com/naic
National Assocation of Investors Corporation.

messages.yahoo.com
Yahoo! discussion boards. Look for the Investing chat areas.

www.clearstation.com
ClearStation features discussions with other investors as well as fundamental analysis and technical analysis.

www.fool.com
The Motley Fool is one of the oldest investing communities online.

www.investorama.com
Investorama members can form or join investing clubs.

www.prophetfinance.com/prophettalk
Find the message board by clicking on the Community button. The technology that drives this bulletin board system is among the best there is.

www.quicken.com/boards
Quicken.com message boards are organized by topic. Investors come here to talk amongst themselves. Investing as well as personal finance issues are discussed.

www.quote.com/quotecom/community
Quote.com Community is organized by company. This web site has boards that focus on individual companies along with industries and investing strategies.

www.ragingbull.com
Raging Bull is an investor discussion site. This web site has boards that focus on individual companies along with industries and investing strategies.

www.siliconinvestor.com
Silicon Investor focuses on discussions of high-tech investments and attracts tech-savvy investors.

www.smartmoney.com/intro/forums/
Smart Money Forums.

www.wevest.com
WeVest.com lets individuals form groups and put together recommendations based on the collective wisdom of the members.

Asset allocation help

Moneycentral.msn.com
Simple asset allocator based on expected returns.

www.AmericanCentury.com
Mainly aimed at the mutual fund investor.

www.armchairmillionaire.com
Offers asset allocation worksheets (go through the Five Steps to Financial Freedom).

www.fidelity.com
Different planners depending on your current savings strategy. Offers asset allocation worksheets (click on Planning and Retirement, then click on General Planning).

www.fs.ml.com
Offers asset allocation worksheets (for Merrill Lynch customers only).

www.investorama.com/calc/riskprofile.html
Offers asset allocation worksheets and education about life phases and investing goals.

www.quicken.com
Planner focused on investing for retirement.

www.strong-funds.com/strong/Planner98/asset.htm
Offers asset allocation worksheets.

Quotes and charts online

finance.yahoo.com
Provides free delayed and real-time quotes.

moneycentral.msn.com
Provides free access to delayed and real-time quotes.

rtq.Thomson.com
Provides free delayed and real-time quotes.

www.bigcharts.com
Provides free access to delayed quotes. Offers price history of up to 30 years on many stocks.

www.clearstation.com
ClearStation's graphing tools illustrate many of the basic concepts of technical analysis well. Trends are color-coded, and the standard charts displayed when you type in a ticker symbol show six different technical indicators. You can quickly shift to an interactive chart, which shows intra-day data for the last 10 trading days, and add your chosen indicators to the chart. The interactive chart is easy to customize, so you can analyze up to 10 years' data. The explanations of technical analysis techniques are illustrated with real-life charts. Be sure to bookmark this site as you learn about technical analysis.

www.esignal.com
Provides free access to delayed quotes, and charges a fee for real-time and streaming quotes.

www.freerealtime.com
Provides free access to delayed and real-time quotes.

www.pcquote.com
Provides free access to delayed quotes and charges a fee for real-time quotes.

www.prophetfinance.com
ProphetFinance offers online interactive charting, including data going back as far as 30 years and up-front information about market movers. You get free access to individual stock and index charting. Those who want to analyze futures and options can do so by subscribing to the Pro version for $24.95 per month. Once you register, Prophet even remembers your own personal favorite charts and stores them on an expandable menu bar,

a plus for those of us who strive to minimize typing. The quick access to the most active issues and gainers and losers is a great help when searching out new investment opportunities.

www.quicken.com
Provides free access to delayed quotes and charges a fee for real-time quotes.

www.quote.com
Provides free access to delayed quotes, limited free access to real-time quotes, and charges a fee for streaming quotes.

www.stocksqueeze.com
Charges a fee for real-time and streaming quotes.

International markets

investingcanada.miningco.com
The Mining Company provides analysis of Canadian companies.

www.bloomberg.com
Provides world market updates, equity indexes, and currency rates. Choose the country in which you're interested from the drop-down list on the home page.

www.canada-stockwatch.com
Canada Stockwatch has been tracking information about Canadian companies since 1984, and it has moved its publications from paper to pixel. The information it presents is gleaned from news releases and other documents released by the companies themselves, which is reformatted for presentation on the Web. You can also take a look at quotes from Canadian exchanges while you're there, along with price/volume charts and insider trading data for every public Canadian company.

www.cnnfn.com
Offers up timely, original news stories on Asian and European markets. Click on World Markets in the left-hand column to go to its international page, or just go straight to cnnfn.cnn.com/news/worldbiz/.

www.ft.com
The *Financial Times*, the peach-colored paper that covers international finance, has an online version that's

a must-visit for the international investor. With sections devoted to the United Kingdom, Europe, and Asia, the site brings you breaking news as well as quotes and analysis. It also compares international markets, so you can see how one exchange is performing compared to another.

www.wsj.com

If you have a lot of international stocks, the portfolio manager at *Wall Street Journal* Interactive, a subscription-based service that gives you the text of the *Journal* plus *Barron's* and other Dow Jones publications, can handle it for you. You can add a link to the *Journal's* powerful Briefing Book feature to your portfolio; customizing the columns shown on the report is easy.

Brokers online

www.abwatley.com

AB Watley WebTrader charges just $9.95 per transaction, for which you get access to a well-designed trading screen. Watley Ultimate Trader FREE offers free Level II quotes when you open an account with at least $10,000.

www.americanexpress.com/trade

Offers American Express Financial Advisors, whose mutual fund research is free to account holders, as are financial planning applications and an equity evaluator.

www.ameritrade.com

Ameritrade has a serviceable site that gets the job done at a reasonable price, charging an $8 commission on market orders.

www.bondagent.com

BT Alex Brown's BondAgent is a bond broker.

www.brownco.com

Brown and Company, with its $5 commission for market orders ($10 limit), is one of the cheapest brokers online.

www.buyandhold.com

This is an easy-to-use web site that lets you build a basket of stocks one by one.

www.csfbdirect.com

CSFB Direct, formerly DLJ Direct, is a one-stop online broker.

www.cybercorp.com

A direct-connect broker, CyBerX has an interface that resembles a video game, and most of the pieces of the program are accessible from the main screen. The main screen doubles as the trading screen, so you don't have to move anywhere in the program to type in a ticker symbol and execute your order.

www.datek.com

Datek is a broker that appeals to frequent traders due to its low commissions and streaming quote ticker. It has information-packed trading screens.

www.etrade.com

The original hands-off all-electronic online broker, E*Trade is a one-stop online broker. It has bond trading capabilities, including calculators that help you build ladders. It also has a fun stock-picking game.

www.fidelity.com

Offers online management of 529 Plans, which grow federal income tax deferred, as well as other investing services.

www.financialcafe.com

Financial Café has unlimited free market-order stock commissions and fixed-rate options commissions (up to ten contracts) for only $14.75. The site is cleanly laid out, with easy navigation by clicking on file folder tabs.

www.firstrade.com

FirsTrade posts its commissions at a low $6.95 per market order ($9.95 for limit orders). The site is basic and thus easy to navigate, but most services are aimed at experienced traders with access to outside research.

www.foliofn.com

Foliofn takes the basket idea several steps beyond any other site. Rather than pay an individual commission, customers pay $29.95 per month or $295.00 per year to maintain an account. Each account holder can have up to three "folios" of stocks (additional folios may be established for $9.95 per month or $95.00 per year), each of which can contain up to 50 stocks.

www.jboxford.com

JB Oxford, one of the first brokers to move into the online world, has stock and mutual fund screening tools as well as an IRA center, where you can learn about retirement planning and figure out what you'll need to sock away.

www.jpmorgan.com

JP Morgan Online is the online equivalent of the private banking services offered by Chase, Hambrecht & Quist, and JP Morgan Bank.

www.mlol.com

Merrill Lynch Online is a full-service broker.

www.mrstock.com

Mr. Stock is an online broker that focuses on options trading. You can also trade stocks here.

www.msdw.com

Morgan Stanley Dean Witter Online is a full-service broker.

www.msiebert.com

Muriel Siebert offers a combination of online and offline tools and services. There are stock and mutual fund screeners, unlimited real-time quotes, and after-hours trading.

www.munidirect.com

Muni Direct is a bond broker.

www.mydiscountbroker.com

Offers InvestorView, its direct connection program, as well as a browser-based system.

www.mytrack.com

MyTrack is a direct-connect broker with a one-click-trading function that takes you quickly to a trading screen, where you can buy and sell stocks, options, and futures. This site is for frequent traders.

www.ndb.com

National Discount Brokers is a one-stop online broker.

www.onsitetrading.com

A direct-connect broker, Onsite Trading has software that comes in two pieces: the trading application, RediPlus, and the charting and quotes application, AT Financial.

www.quickandreilly.com

Offers stock, mutual fund, option, and bond trading online, along with online bill paying. Suretrade's services were folded into Quick and Reilly's site in early 2001.

www.schwab.com

Charles Schwab is a one-stop online broker. It has bond trading capabilities, including calculators that help you build ladders.

www.scottrade.com

Scottrade provides just the basics for the equity and options trader.

www.sharebuilder.com

NetStock Investor is an easy-to-use web site that lets you build a basket of stocks based on dollar amounts rather than shares.

www.suttononline.com

This site provides access to three different types of accounts: A browser-based account, a direct access account with real-time quote feeds, and a direct access account with Level II quotes.

www.tradebonds.com

TradeBonds is a bond broker.

www.tradecast.com

TradeCast, a direct-connect broker, publishes Revolution, which includes premium research at no additional cost. This site is for frequent traders.

www.unx.com

Universal Network Exchange (UNX) is open only to investors brought in by their investment advisers. The trading system is designed to let you put together a customized mutual fund weighted in equal dollar amounts, by market capitalization of the companies you've chosen, or by some other user-selected criteria.

www.wallstreete.com

Wall Street Electronica is an online broker that offers personal assistance for valet and full-service customers. This is a good broker for options traders, as well as stock investors, with its policy on offering price improvements on limit orders.

www.wallstreetaccess.com

Wall Street Access aims itself at high-asset account holders, and says that its main benefit to investors is that it shops each trade to get the best possible price. Wall Street Access's average assets per account are among the highest in the industry, so it obviously appeals to investors who want a personal touch when placing trades.

www.wangvest.com

Wang Investments is a workable site for investors who like low commissions, don't need much hand holding, and are tracking the performance of their portfolios elsewhere.

www.tdwaterhouse.com

TD Waterhouse has a network of live brokers, giving you a flesh-and-blood alternative to web trading if you'd like. It offers a wide range of assets to trade as well as online banking services.

www.Webstreetsecurities.com

Web Street Securities is the broker for you if you like to look at a lot of data.

www.wingspan.com

Wingspan Investment Services, offered by Wingspan Bank, supplies great portfolio performance reports and tax accounting tools.

Broker information/ratings

www.barrons.com

Rates brokers on trade execution, ease of use, customer reports and access, range of services, research amenities, and costs.

www.gomez.com

Rates brokers on ease of use, customer confidence, on-site resources, relationship services, and overall cost.

www.keynote.com

Provides a weekly list of response times and order execution speed.

www.kiplinger.com/tools/brokerrank.html

Rates brokers on overall quality, fees, and services. Resort the list based on your own criteria.

www.money.com/brokers

Rates brokers on ease of use, customer service, system response, products and tools, cost. Reweight for your own personalized ranking.

www.sia.com

The Securities Industry Association (SIA) is a trade group that the majority of online brokers have joined. You can see what issues they're working on and read up on proposed laws that affect your investments at its informative web site.

www.smartmoney.com./brokers/

Profiles three investor styles (do-it-yourselfer, navigator, delegator).

www.sonic.net/donaldj/brokers.html

Rates brokers from least expensive to most expensive. Collects comments from web site visitors.

Day trading sites

daytrading.about.com/money/daytrading/library/weekly/bl_becomeatrader.htm

Check out Robert J. Rak's series of articles on day trading at About.com.

daytrading.about.com/money/daytrading/library/weekly/topicsub_tradesys.htm

About.com's Day Trading subject area includes the article, "How to Develop a Trading System." It's a step-by-step look at how the author came up with his original idea, tested it, and how you can use the system to make money on the stock market.

www.daytraders.org

An Internet relay chat for day traders

www.daytradertax.com

For tax rules and how they apply to traders, check out the Trader Tax Solution Package offered by DayTraderTax.com. This site can help you determine which category of trading activity you qualify for as far as the IRS is concerned.

www.greencompany.com
For tax rules and how they apply to traders, check out the Trader Tax Solution Package offered by GreenCompany.com. This site can help you determine which category of trading activity you qualify for as far as the IRS is concerned.

www.hardrightedge.com
Alan Farley's *20 Golden Rules for Traders* is a must-read for any day trader.

www.investorfactory.com
At The Investor Factory, you can take part in a 6-week long "simvesting" game, designed to test your day trading investment strategies, build your confidence, and enhance your investment knowledge.

www.pristine.com
Education and tools for day traders.

www.rookiedaytrader.com
Tips and tools for the beginning day trader.

www.sandbox.com/finalbell/pub-doc/home.html
Get a feel for what day trading involves by joining in the free competitions at The Sandbox. The competitions take place over a calendar quarter, so you can test several strategies and see what works for you.

www.sapphirebay.com/trading/firms.htm
Sapphire Bay, a software publisher, offers this web site with a long list of specialty brokers for day traders as well as retail brokers suitable for day trading.

www.traderbot.com
Execute searches on technical criteria. Flexible and free.

Other web sites

finance.yahoo.com
Yahoo! Finance offers real-time tick-by-tick charts free of charge.

library.thinkquest.org/10326/index.html
Describes itself as a site for high school students to learn about the stock market, but it's a good introduction for novice investors of any age. The market simulation is a great spot to test your knowledge.

moneycentral.msn.com/investor/charts/charting.asp
Microsoft's Money Central Investor provides daily and weekly charts that include symbols that clue you in to when a company has posted a dividend or earnings announcement.

moneycentral.msn.com/investor/finder/predefstocks.asp
Learn how to set up your own filter by first checking out the pre-defined filters.

moneycentral.msn.com/investor/finder/welcome.asp
Check out the stock-filtering program at MSN Money Central to find companies with particular characteristics, such as industry and market cap, to see the range of performance results. You can filter by price/earnings ratio or by earnings growth.

screen.morningstar.com/FundSelector.html
This site at Morningstar (www.morningstar.com) has a terrific mutual fund screening tool, which rates mutual funds by performance. By playing around with this tool, you'll learn all the ways a mutual fund can be evaluated, and maybe find a few that are worth your investment.

www.3dstockcharts.com
Check out 3DStockCharts.com for a visual view of the price book for a particular stock. This interesting site summarizes the activity on a group of the larger ECNs in graphical format. The larger blocks of stock are represented with bars, with each ECN represented by a different color. The price of the largest block of stock currently available is displayed at the bottom of the graph.

www.adsubtract.com
Keeps banners and pop-up advertisements from displaying on your computer.

www.alert-ipo.com
On this web site, you search through a database of upcoming IPOs and set up a list of up to 20 issues that you can easily track. The sort of information you can get before a company goes public includes its newly

established ticker symbol, the report the company had to file with the SEC about its current financial state and management team, proposed price per share, and the name of the underwriters.

www.amex.com
Learn more about the American Stock Exchange, and get valuable investor information.

www.annuity.com
Check out a range of annuities and annuity calculators at this site, which brings together quotes and information about annuities offered by insurance companies.

www.b4utrade.com
B4Utrade, a subscription site that costs $25 per month, has a terrific stock screener that not only displays CNBC news stories in a small window, but also lets you find out which stocks are being discussed in the media. You can also select stocks that have been upgraded or downgraded, as well as those announcing spin-offs or mergers. This is a terrific site for the news junkie.

www.bankrate.com
Bankrate.com surveys thousands of financial institutions nationally and compiles tables that show the best (and worst) rates for various types of loans as well as deposits.

www.bondagent.com
BondAgent is offering Bond University (click on Learning Center on the home page). The Bond Terminology Glossary is an A to Z list of words you'll hear bandied about as you explore investing in bonds further.

www.cboe.com
Most options trading in the United States takes place on the Chicago Board Options Exchange, or CBOE. The CBOE's web site includes an education section that explains how options work as a part of a strategy.

www.cnet.com, www.zdnet.com
These are great sites for comparing computer systems and components. They both let you search through reviews and find the best prices available online.

www.collegesavings.com
Offers online management of 529 Plans, which grow federal income tax deferred.

www.creditcardmenu.com
Credit Card Menu has dozens of credit cards to choose from, depending on your financial situation.

www.download.com
C|net's download.com is a great spot to visit every few weeks if you want to check out the latest utilities and web browser add-ons.

www.earningswhispers.com
Provides educated guesses on a company's upcoming earnings statements, pulling information from analysts as well as numerous other sources.

www.econedlink.org
An online guide to economics offered by the National Council on Economic Education.

www.equifax.com
Equifax gives you online access to your credit report for 30 days.

www.federalreserve.gov
Keep an eye on the Federal Reserve by logging onto its web site.

www.fiafii.org/tutorial/index.html
The Futures Industry Institute offers online tutorials that will teach you about the complexities of trading options.

www.fibv.com
The International Federation of Stock Exchanges maintains a web site with information about its member exchanges. A summary of each exchange's requirements, in Excel spreadsheet format, can be viewed at www.fibv.com/stats/infobour.xls. This site is fascinating reading for any investor who wants to learn about the international exchanges and how they compare to our (relatively) familiar US markets.

www.gomez.com
Gomez.com ranks 30 online banks, basing the points awarded on ease of use, customer confidence, on-site resources, relationship services, and overall cost. The rankings are reweighted based on four different customer types, too: Internet transactor, saver, borrower, and one-stop shopper.

www.grc.com

"Shields Up" is a program that tells you if anyone on the Internet can crawl into your computer.

www.investingonline.org

Offers resources you can use to educate yourself further about investing opportunities. You also get tools to avoid online fraud.

www.investopedia.com/university/options

Investopedia offers online tutorials that will teach you about the complexities of trading options. It also has a financial dictionary, articles about investing, and financial topics that are updated several times a week, plus a series of lessons focused on investing.

www.investorprotection.org

Offers resources you can use to educate yourself further about investing opportunities. You also get tools to avoid online fraud.

www.lendingtree.com

Lending Tree lets you explore various forms of financing and fill out the appropriate application online.

www.manticsoft.com

Reeally!, published by ManticSoft, is a tool that helps investors improve the overall performance of their portfolios in a unique way.

www.marketplayer.com

Offers a stock-picking game.

www.microsoft.com/money

Offers personal finance software. Demos are available.

www.mlol.com

Offers Merrill Lynch Direct, which gives clients free access to numerous high-quality research reports, including its weekly Focus 1 stock recommendations and in-depth analysis of various industries and corporations, as well as unlimited free real-time quotes. ML Direct's portfolio reports are chock full of helpful information, including intra-day balances, so you can see where you stand immediately after placing a trade.

www.nasaa.org

Offers resources you can use to educate yourself further about investing opportunities. You also get tools to avoid online fraud.

www.nasdaq.com

Learn more about NASDAQ, and get valuable investor information.

www.nasdr.com

You can file a complaint online at the web site of the National Association of Securities Dealers if your broker did something you think is illegal. The NASD Regulation site offers the NASD Notice to Members 99-11 (February 1999), which contains quite a bit of information on the topic of margin trading.

www.ndb.com (click on the NDB University icon in the border)

Has 24 clearly written lessons about everything from budgeting to investing to estate planning.

www.netcaptor.com

An add-on for Internet Explorer that lets you open a group of web sites simultaneously.

www.netzero.com

A free Internet service provider (ISP) you can use as a backup in case your ISP crashes.

www.nqli.com

StockVue, a free portfolio analysis package by NQL, Inc., lets you set up portfolios of unlimited size, with subcategories set according to your specifications.

www.nyse.com

Learn more about the New York Stock Exchange, and get valuable investor information.

www.orionfutures.com/fut101.html

Futures broker Orion Futures Group offers Futures 101, an online course in understanding futures and commodity trading.

www.paymybills.com

This is an online bill-paying service.

www.quicken.com

Offers personal finance software. Demos are available online.

www.quicken.com/shopping/debt

The Quicken.com Debt Reduction Planner will show you the best strategy for paying off your current debt and the amount of money that will be freed up when you reach your goal.

www.ritlabs.com

If you have numerous email accounts, this web site will check your email for you and let you know when you've received a new message.

www.sec.gov/consumer/jneton.htm

For information on margin in the context of online trading, there's the Securities and Exchange Commission's Tips for Online Investing, available on the SEC web site.

www.sec.gov/consumer/tradexec.htm

The Securities and Exchange Commission provides a guide to trade execution at their site. This is a must-read for online investors!

www.secure-me.net

Intensely probes your computer to find any security holes

www.symantec.com

Provides software that protects your computer.

www.theflyonthewall

The Fly on the Wall is a terrific news and rumor site.

www.validea.com

Who's doing the best job analyzing a particular sector? Validea ranks the analysts according to how well their recommendations have performed over the last 3 months. Click on Sources then choose a sector from the drop-down box and find out who's giving the best advice.

www.virtualstockexchange.com

Offers stock-picking games.

www.wallstreetcity.com

This site has easy access to fundamental and technical data to its portfolio analysis page. It also has a price projection page, showing you expected prices for the near term and intermediate term (1 week to 4 months in the future) for each of your holdings. The rankings page shows how your portfolio as a whole ranks according to 11 different characteristics, and the DCipher

My Portfolio button on that table creates an essay that describes your performance.

www.wallstwhispers.com

Wall Street Whispers publishes a daily newsletter that's distributed around 11 p.m. eastern time, so you can set up trades when the market opens the next morning.

www.windowonwallstreet.com

Window on Wall Street (WoW) is a subscription service that brings together a huge historical data set plus technical analysis and interactive charting, along with streaming quotes and portfolio analysis.

www.worldspy.com

A free Internet service provider (ISP) you can use as a backup in case your ISP crashes. WorldSpy doesn't make you view constant advertising while using its services.

www.zonelabs.com

Provides software that protects your computer.

Glossary

Asset allocation To have a strategy for spreading your investments around different sectors of the market and across different types of investments. There are plenty of worksheets that help you figure out what your asset allocation model should be based on your goals, your expected rate of return, and your point in life.

Bear An investor who believes the market is on the way down.

Broker call rate The broker call rate is published daily in the *Wall Street Journal* and is usually less than the prime rate of interest as set by the Federal Reserve. It's the rate of interest banks charge brokers.

Bull An investor who believes the stock market will rise in value.

Candlestick charting This is a technique originally developed in Japan to analyze the rice market. It's a variation on the High/Low/Close chart. The range of prices for the period is drawn as a line, with a box, or body, that represents the opening and closing prices. If the price went up during the day, the body is white, but if it dropped, the body is colored black. The patterns that emerge are studied carefully to discover the underlying trend.

Complex option strategies Complex option strategies include spreads, which are the purchase of a call or put and the sale of another of the same type on the same instrument; straddles, which involve the simultaneous purchase or sale of a put and a call at the same strike price; and strangles, in which the investor makes a simultaneous purchase or sale of a put and call, but with different strike prices. *See also* Simple option strategies.

CUSIP CUSIP, which stands for Committee on Uniform Securities Identification Procedures, is a number that identifies a particular stock or bond. The CUSIP numbers, issued by the aforementioned Committee, are used in the United States and Canada. Overseas equities have an International Securities Identification Number (ISIN), which is issued by each country's National Numbering Agency.

Gap A gap occurs when the bid or ask for a stock is outside the range of the prior trading range. Let's say WXYZ was trading between 15 and 15¼ during a five-minute period, then suddenly there's a bid at 15⅜. This is a gap up because it's higher than the prior range. A gap down occurs when the price drops below the bottom of the prior range. Day traders look for these gaps to see which way the market is heading.

Home equity line of credit (HELOC) A home equity line of credit (HELOC), which is a variation of a home equity loan, allows a homeowner to, in essence, write checks on an account that is linked to a percentage of the equity held in the house. For instance, if you bought your house for $100,000 and it's worth $300,000 now, and you want to borrow against the $200,000 equity you hold without taking out a standard loan, you could get a HELOC and use what you need for some extraordinary expenses such as remodeling or college fees. The interest rate is usually variable, fluctuating with the prime rate, and you can access the equity for a certain period of time, called the draw period. A HELOC is best used for a series of expenses rather than a single specific expense.

Margin account Trading on margin means you're borrowing money from your broker to buy stocks. Though the rate of interest offered is usually lower than, say, a loan for a vacation home, you'll still have the expense of interest payments that will offset your investment gains.

Market makers Market makers are securities firms that have fulfilled a number of rules and regulations set out by the National Association of Securities Dealers, and then commit to buy and sell the NASDAQ stocks in which they make markets. The regulations with which a market maker must comply include an agreement to publicly report the price and volume of each transaction within 90 seconds, and a guarantee that each order will be executed at the best price available.

Mark-to-Market The Mark-to-Market Trader status is a bit more complicated than Trader in Securities, but it has its advantages – if you can justify to the IRS that you're trying to make a profit. Simply stated (and I assure you it's more complicated than this), you're allowed to claim income and losses as though you'd liquidated all your positions on New Year's Eve, even though you may still hold some open positions. You're also allowed to avoid the wash sale rule (which prevents you from repurchasing a security for 30 days after you've taken a loss for tax purposes). So leaping in and out of the same issue is okay if you can prove to the IRS that you're a full-time trader.

Moving average A moving average is a useful tool for showing general price trends over a period of time, smoothing out the highs and lows. You can calculate a moving average for a particular period of time, say 15 days, by adding up closing prices for the previous 15 days and then dividing by 15. If you do that for a long series, say a couple of years' worth of data, you can get a picture of price trends. An exponential moving average gives additional weight to the more recent data. Many web sites let you choose the number of days to include in a moving average calculation.

No-load fund Mutual funds are supported by the investors in a variety of ways. A no-load fund charges no fees up front when you buy in or when you sell or trade it.

Online investing Online investing should be easy to define, but it has a couple of guises. One, of course, is trades that are placed by an investor using a computer. Many brokers count trades placed using a Touch-Tone phone as online trading as well.

Payment for order flow Let's say you want to sell 200 shares of Company XYZ. When you place your order, your broker sends it to a market maker in XYZ stock. The market maker then pays your broker a small fee for routing your block of XYZ stock to them. This fee is income for your broker and is called payment for order flow.

Portfolio Your portfolio is a list of the stocks, mutual funds, options, and other investments that you own at a particular point in time. You'll want to track the date you purchased the investment, the number of shares, how much you paid for it, and the commission you paid the broker.

Price improvement When brokers say they'll give you price improvement, they mean they'll work to get you either a lower price for the buy side or a higher price for the sell side when you place an order with them.

Proxy All voting by proxy means is that you indicate your vote on a paper ballot and mail the ballot in or dial the toll-free number to place your vote.

Quotes Quotes tell you the price someone in the market just paid for a particular stock. On some stock exchanges, for instance on the New York Stock Exchange (NYSE), you're given a single price that shows the amount paid per share during the most recent transaction. Other exchanges, such as the NASDAQ, display two prices for each quote: The bid, or the price a potential buyer is willing to pay, and the ask, which is the price a potential seller wants to receive.

Retail trades Retail trades are those conducted by individuals. The other main type of trades is called institutional trades; these are conducted by large portfolio managers such as mutual fund and pension fund managers.

Sector analysis Sector analysis is a way of analyzing companies by industry group. For instance, all the automobile manufacturers are grouped together, and their statistics are reviewed as a whole. You study the characteristics of a group of companies, then decide whether you'll invest in one of the members of that group.

Selling stocks short When you sell a stock short, you borrow shares from your broker (or another investor) and sell them, then buy them back later. You're betting that the price of the shares will drop, and that you will turn a profit by selling high and buying back low.

Simple option strategies Simple option strategies are puts and calls. When you buy a put, you're saying you believe the stock price will drop by a certain date (the expiration date). When you buy a call, you're saying you believe the stock price will rise by a certain date. If you don't have a long or short position in the stock itself, then you're trading in naked puts and calls. *See also* Complex option strategies.

Wireless A wireless device lets you access financial information, email, and some web sites without having a physical line connecting you to a phone or network. It uses two-way radio technology rather than telephone lines for hooking you up to your online resources.

Index